GILLIAN ANDERSON
AND
JENNIFER NADEL

A Manifesto for
Women Everywhere

9 PRINCIPLES FOR A
MORE MEANINGFUL LIFE

Thorsons

The information provided in this book is for educational purposes only. It is not intended to be a substitute for professional advice, diagnosis or treatment that can be provided by your own medical or mental health provider. Neither the authors nor the publisher are providing health care, medical or mental health services, or attempting to diagnose, treat, prevent or cure in any manner any physical, mental or emotional issue, disease or condition. If you have or suspect that you have a medical or mental health problem, contact your medical or mental health provider promptly. Also, before beginning any physical activity suggested in or inspired by this book, it is recommended that you seek medical advice from your personal physician.

Thorsons
An imprint of HarperCollins*Publishers*
1 London Bridge Street
London SE1 9GF

www.harpercollins.co.uk

First published by HarperCollins*Publishers* 2017

13 5 7 9 10 8 6 4 2

A catalogue record of this book is available from the British Library

HB ISBN 978-0-00-814793-8
PB ISBN 978-0-00-816640-3

Printed and bound in Great Britain by Clays Ltd, St Ives plc

MIX
Paper from
responsible sources

FSC
www.fsc.org

FSC™ C007454

FSC™ is a non-profit international organisation established to promote
the responsible management of the world's forests. Products carrying the
FSC label are independently certified to assure consumers that they come
from forests that are managed to meet the social, economic and
ecological needs of present or future generations,
and other controlled sources.

Find out more about HarperCollins and the environment at
www.harpercollins.co.uk/green

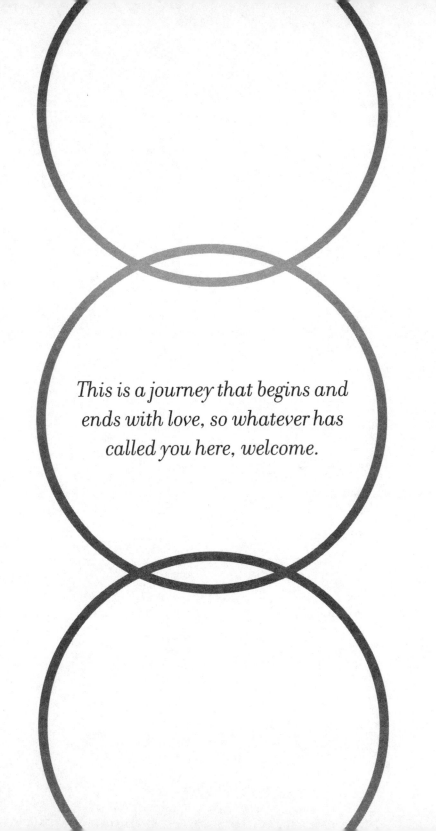

This is a journey that begins and ends with love, so whatever has called you here, welcome.

AN INVITATION TO YOU

'Tell me, what is it you plan to do with your one wild and precious life?'

MARY OLIVER

At some point in our lives, most of us feel the gentle calling of our soul. Sometimes it's so quiet we can barely hear it – a soft tapping. No louder than a leaf falling from a tree.

We may imagine we didn't hear it. Or perhaps it is louder and takes the form of a persistent ache, a nagging sense that there is something missing. 'Is this it?' we wonder when we wake in the dead of night or find ourselves caught in the treadmill of our daily grind.

It may be a hint of loneliness that endures even in the company of friends. Or a sense of injustice and a desire to change things that feels urgent and necessary, but also hopeless before it even begins.

Perhaps our heart tells us there is a better way of living, that we need to stop ignoring what really matters – the suffering of others and our planet's future – but our head insists we're naïve and tells us to knuckle down and get on with our lives as they are.

For others the call may take the form of a crisis – a break-up or break-down, a betrayal or loss. Or perhaps it's addiction, depression or another serious illness.

However it comes, it is an invitation to take a journey. You may resist. Many of us have resisted it for years, even decades. Ultimately it's your choice. But it will wait for you patiently, tapping daily or every so often in small and big ways to remind you that, in truth, you can't avoid it if you truly want to live a meaningful life.

If you've heard that call, this book is for you. It's for women who want happiness and meaning. It will guide you towards inner peace and provide the power to help transform the world in which we all live.

CONTENTS

THE JOURNEY

'Take courage, join hands, stand beside us.'

CHRISTABEL PANKHURST

WE is a journey based on nine principles that have been taught by sages and saints throughout the ages and they have the power to transform your life and the world around you.

It isn't a lifestyle choice to be bolted onto our normal *'me-centred'* way of living; it's a path of radical transformation that puts compassion for the world at its core.

Use this book both as a guide and a source of inspiration. If you're hurting, it will help you heal. If you're lost, it will steer you home. If you're searching for a purpose, it will gently lead you towards fulfilment.

We arrive in this world without instruction manuals and we grow up without an emotional toolkit. So it's easy to lose our way.

As we go through life we amass emotional scar tissue from the knocks that we inevitably take. We become like electrical circuit boards that have got so clogged up by the silt of life that we can no longer connect with ourselves and our core beliefs, let alone with the world beyond.

All of us start out in life with a strong internal value system – a sense of what's right and wrong and what's fair and what's unjust. But then life intervenes. In the cold light of reality our ideals can quickly seem naïve, unrealistic and untenable. However strong and heartfelt our intentions, it's hard to give effect to our beliefs when we're struggling, stressed or in emotional pain.

Before long we've abandoned those values in favour of the rules we're taught by the world. Succeed, compete and accumulate. Deep down we feel conflicted, but at the end of the day we each have to get by, don't we?

A gulf emerges between the values we choose for our personal lives and those we live by in the world at large. In our homes and families we believe in sharing and making sure everyone's OK. But once we step outside our front door the rules change. The common good is replaced with the quest for personal success. Within seconds *we* dissolves into *me* and we're elbowing each other out of the way in the race to get to the finishing line. Only, of course, there isn't one – just a horizon that moves further away the closer we get.

The Nine Principles in this book have the power to heal our wounds and return us to our centre. As you learn to apply them to your life one by one, you will be taken on a journey from *me* to *WE*. Loneliness will evaporate. You will discover a sense of purpose and you will be freed – freed to live a life that is authentic, happy and meaningful.

WHY NOW?

'Politics hates a vacuum. If it isn't filled with hope, someone will fill it with fear.'

NAOMI KLEIN

Our current way of doing things – the 'me culture' – isn't working.

The world we all share is more divided and unequal than ever.

Rates of anxiety, depression and self-harm among women are rocketing. And the hard-fought-for rights that we, as women, thought we'd finally won are once again under renewed attack.

Nearly 800 million people live in hunger and yet those with plenty battle with obesity and depression.

Every minute one woman dies needlessly in childbirth, while elsewhere in the world another woman spends thousands on cosmetic surgery because she isn't able to feel comfortable with how she's ageing.

Violence against women is rising, yet at the same time refuge services – especially for black and minority ethnic women – are being cut.[1]

The gap between rich and poor is widening, causing social division and ill health,[2] but instead of investment and redistribution we have cuts and austerity.

Large swathes of humanity are threatened by climate change, yet our governments fear tackling it lest they offend big business and consumers.

The list goes on and on, and every one of us knows that it's crazy and it's wrong.

Yet instead of joining together, we often find ourselves isolated and in competition. Trying to put a positive gloss on our lives to disguise the huge gap between how things look externally and how they feel inside. Not able to lift our eyes to the horizon and deal with the bigger issues because we each already have so much on our plate.

There is a different way of doing things.

WE is a movement for change, a manifesto for a female-led revolution: a quiet, peaceful about-face that doesn't require the consent of those in power. It just asks each of us, one woman at a time, to be the change and take the journey from *me* to *WE*.

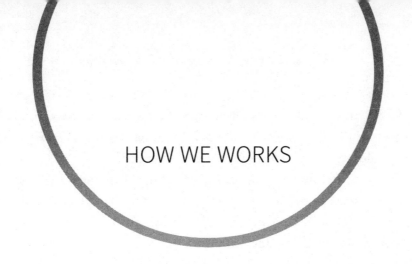

HOW WE WORKS

'We must not wish for the disappearance of our troubles but for the grace to transform them.'

SIMONE WEIL

WE combines spirituality, politics and psychology. We're often taught to compartmentalize them, but they are intimately connected.

Unless we work across all three disciplines, it's impossible to achieve lasting, sustainable change. It's not possible to get happy without getting kind, we can't be spiritually fulfilled without rolling up our sleeves and helping others, and we can't help others without healing ourselves.

This is not a self-help book to enable you to get more out of life or a spiritual text to encourage you to float above your difficulties. Nor is it a lecture on how to try harder! It is an intensely practical guide to healing and activism from the heart.

Each of the Nine Principles in this book can be applied to your own life and to the world at large. Their impact is cumulative. Once you've completed the process, you'll have a set of tools that will enable you to handle whatever life throws your way.

Most importantly, underpinning all WE's principles is an ancient rule that can be found in almost every ethical, spiritual and religious tradition: the Golden Rule.

5

At its simplest, the Golden Rule states that we should treat each other as we would like to be treated ourselves — in other words, with love. It is a simple rule that has the power to change everything.

Our goal in taking this journey isn't individual happiness — though that comes as a welcome by-product. It is to live in a way that is true to our inner calling. A way that is kind and just. That leads to personal fulfilment and helps other women across the planet.

WHY WE WROTE *WE*

'History has shown us that courage can be contagious and hope can take on a life of its own.'

MICHELLE OBAMA

This book doesn't come from lofty heights. It comes from two friends who have stumbled along together, trying, failing, crying, laughing, learning and trying again.

It is about a set of principles that led us out of darkness, from a place where both of us were in despair, into a way of life that has meaning and purpose.

We discovered the hard way that no amount of external success could fix how we felt on the inside. The more we had, the more we felt we needed to get. No matter what we achieved, it didn't make us happy. It made us feel guilty that even with the gifts and luck we'd been given, we couldn't seem to make life work.

In the end we'd both become dependent on a whole host of unhealthy crutches – alcohol, drugs, work, food, abusive relationships – you name it, we tried it. And at the same time we had therapy, did yoga and tried to puzzle life out.

Our crises were severe enough that we had no option but to change. To start a process of complete rebuilding. Root and branch.

We're passionate about the Nine Principles in this book because they've transformed our lives. That doesn't mean we're happy all the time, that we handle every situation perfectly, or that we're saints. Far from it – we are, like every one of us, perfectly imperfect. But, when we're willing to use them, WE's principles give us access to a peace of mind and inner freedom that we'd never even dreamed was possible.

We aren't doctors or therapists or priests. Our principal qualification is that we handle emotional pain so badly that we've been forced to look for answers. For over 20 years we've each searched for what works. The wisdom in this book isn't ours; it's distilled from a myriad of teachers far wiser. We are passing it on with gratitude and in the hope that others might gain comfort and meaning from it.

When both of us started walking this path we were cynical and resistant. But now, from our own experience, we know that transformation and happiness are possible and that miracles do actually happen. Hopefully you haven't hit as bleak a patch as we both did, but wherever your starting point, if you follow this path you will experience profound changes.

I came to the journey that is contained in this book when I was a single parent of two boys working my dream job. I was a network news correspondent who got to tell the world about the issues I cared deeply about. Then one morning I woke up and realized I couldn't go on. I called the news desk and said I was very sorry but I couldn't come in – not that day and, as it turned out, not ever. Unsurprisingly, my life fell apart. I was diagnosed with severe depression and burnout. I began the journey I'd been avoiding for the previous 35 years – the journey to meet myself and to find a way of living that accorded with who I really was at my deepest level. I sought help and wisdom from numerous teachers, support groups and professionals. I met friends like Gillian who were seekers also. Today I am the same person, but I am so much happier. I have meaning, I have connection, I have people that I truly love in my life. Of course, I still hit patches of pain and difficulty, but I wake up each day excited to be alive.

The journey that these Nine Principles map out doesn't ever end. But it contains truth. Truth that I know from my own life has the power to guide us away from doubt, depression and self-hatred, and for which I'm infinitely grateful.

JN

I think I started searching for some kind of deeper meaning to my life when I was in high school, but I don't feel like I properly put solutions into practice until I was in college. By then I had turned to so many outside sources for comfort to deal with my fear and uncertainty, my sense of loneliness, confusion and feeling misunderstood about the world and my place in it that when I started practising some of these principles the effect was dramatic and life-changing. I suddenly felt a sense of stability and grounding, personal power and purpose, and am absolutely certain that had I not had that foundation when I then achieved what turned into international career success, I would simply not have been able to deal with it. That's not to say that I have not struggled or handled things appallingly or turned for long stretches towards unhealthy ways of coping, but what I did learn in those initial years were tools for how to handle life's hardships better. And on a daily basis I get to choose how my life plays out. How do I deal with this rejection, this grief, this fear? With these practices in my pocket, it's my choice.

GA

You don't have to take our word for it. Treat this journey as if it were a scientific experiment. See what happens if you practise the principles as they are laid out. If at the end of these chapters you don't feel better, you can always have your old life back.

The Nine Principles in this book work.

Change is possible.

There's no need to panic or feel overwhelmed. Nothing is asked of you now, other than that you read the book and give the principles within it a try. This is not another thing to add to your to-do list. It is a gateway to an inner freedom and a peace of mind that you may not have known was possible.

You have nothing to lose but your unhappiness, and the world has everything to gain.

WE'S VISION

'Like life, peace begins with women. We are the first to forge lines of alliance and collaboration across conflict divides.'

ZAINAB SALBI

Imagine a sisterhood – across all creeds and cultures – an unspoken agreement that we, as women, will support and encourage each other. That we won't seek to take advantage of another's weakness, or sit in judgement of each other's shortcomings. That we will remember we don't know what struggles each of us may be facing elsewhere in our lives and so we'll assume that each of us is doing our best. That we will do the work to heal ourselves so that together we can create a more compassionate world.

www.wewomeneverywhere.org

PART 1

The Essentials

Getting Started

'You change the world by changing yourself.'

YOKO ONO

You are at the start of a miraculous journey. The Nine Principles within these pages will change your life.

As with any expedition, before you set out you need to get prepared. The essentials in this section are vital for your well-being and will ensure you get the most out of WE's principles.

On this journey you'll be engaged in emotional archaeology – digging down beneath layers of hurt and protection and confronting deep emotional truths to reconnect with your true self. You'll be dismantling the parts of yourself that no longer serve you and transforming your relationship with yourself and the world around you.

These Essential Practices will hold you steady as you do the work. The extraordinary thing about them is that they do far more than just provide you with support for the journey ahead. Each one is also a powerful agent for change in its own right.

Like the principles that follow, these practices are a distillation of what works within innumerable traditions. When they're used together, you'll discover that an alchemy takes place that produces astonishing changes. In fact, if all you feel ready to do right now is introduce these four healthy habits into your life, you will be amazed by the miracles that start to flow immediately.

Taking care of yourself emotionally, physically and spiritually is a profoundly political act. As women, many of us have been conditioned to be caretakers, to measure our worth by how much we do for others. But when we sublimate our own needs we risk ending up dependent on others and vulnerable on many levels as a result.

Martyrdom is for saints. Real women have needs and real giving comes from a place of plenty, not a place of lack. Self-denial only sets us up for failure.

Self-care is even more crucial if you have children. When we harm ourselves or neglect our needs we model that neglect and abuse are acceptable. If we want our daughters to think of themselves as worthy, we need to model self-worth. Similarly, if we want our sons to see women as strong, independent beings, we need to show them that is what we are.

Use the four Essential Practices that follow on a daily basis. They are the foundations for your new life and indispensable for the journey to come.

You'll be amazed at how great you feel when you start giving yourself the care you've longed for from others.

WE's exercises

This is an experiential process. Each chapter contains exercises that will integrate what your mind is learning with what your heart already knows. These exercises are not optional extras; they are essential to the journey you are on, so please don't skip them. Knowing is not enough – you need to experience the principles for them to achieve their full transformative power.

The more diligent you are in completing the exercises, the greater the results you'll see. It is better to do them hastily than not do them at all, so don't let perfectionism creep in. From time to time you will need to write things down, so a notebook or journal will be useful. You may also want to ensure that you have a quiet place where you can work on them without being disturbed. This is a sacred process that deserves a sacred space.

You can return to any of the exercises and repeat them once you have finished working through the principles. Use them if you hit a bump in the path or if you're feeling stuck. Each exercise works on an emotional, intellectual and spiritual level, so take advantage of them. You will get out of this journey what you put in.

Centre yourself before each exercise. Start by taking five deep breaths in and out, allowing your out-breath to last a beat longer than your in-breath to calm your nervous system. If you have the time and space, light a candle to signify the sacred nature of the work you're undertaking. You're doing it for you and for many. Try not to sit on the sidelines, figuring out how to understand the journey by intellectualising it – take the plunge, dive in and experience it!

WE's affirmations

At the end of each chapter you will also find affirmations. These are anti-dotes to the toxic messages we give ourselves on a daily basis. Use them to ward off negativity, as you would use a medicine to prevent an infection. Repeat them to yourself as you go through the day, knowing that each time you say them you are gradually moving away from self-harm and towards self-care and self-love.

Essential
Practice
1

GRATITUDE:
A Mind-altering Substance

'When we focus on our gratitude, the tide of disappointment goes out and the tide of love rushes in.'

KRISTIN ARMSTRONG

Gratitude has the power to transform everything: our perceptions, our experiences and our state of mind.

A lot of us come to this journey with a mountain of disappointments and hurts. Feeling grateful may be the last thing you want when you're unhappy, when you're full of all the things you haven't got, and all the things that have gone wrong. But – however low, angry or despondent you feel – you will start to feel the benefits of gratitude as soon as you allow this tool into your life.

A warning: like many of WE's tools, gratitude may sound simple – way too simple and perhaps not quite complex enough for our sophisticated female brains. Don't be deceived. Remember those connect-the-dot books you had when you were little, where you joined numbered dots together and a picture emerged? This is what we do every day of our lives: we join up events and assign them meaning so that we can interpret the world.

The problem is that very often we join up the wrong dots. As we go through life, many of us notice all the things that seem to go wrong rather than the things that are going right. We focus on the times we haven't got what we wanted, when life has disappointed us, when we may have been ignored or slighted in some way. Like fortune-tellers, who are only capable of negative conclusions, we examine the tea leaves of our life and decide that life is unfair, that we're just not destined to be happy, that we don't have the good luck others seem to enjoy.

Not surprisingly, if you join up these dots, you end up with a depressing picture.

But stop right there. From this moment forward you are going to try a different approach.

'I don't have to chase extraordinary moments to find happiness — it's right in front of me if I'm paying attention and practising gratitude.'

BRENÉ BROWN

EXERCISE: Daily Miracles

This exercise will begin a mind-altering process by showing you how to put the practice of gratitude into your daily life. Make yourself comfortable and close your eyes. Breathe in and out five times, as described on page 17, until you feel centered and settled.

Take up your journal and write down ten things in your life right now that you're grateful for. They can be as small or as big as you like. Notice if your mind leaps in and lodges an objection. It may claim that it can't find anything at all to be thankful for, or it may want to remind you of all the disappointments, trials and losses you are experiencing.

Like a miner panning for gold, try to pick your way through the silt and mud that your mind kicks up to find the treasure that rests in its midst. Keep looking until you find something – anything at all – that you can be grateful for. Perhaps it's that you've got a roof over your head or you have eyes to see your children with. Or perhaps it's that you started your day with a warm cup of tea and have something to eat in your cupboard. The items on your list don't need to be any more complicated than that. In fact, the most basic things are often the most powerful. Imagine what life would be like if you didn't have them.

Your list might also include some of the simple daily events that we so often overlook because we take them for granted – yet if they were suddenly to disappear we'd be lost.

Keep writing until you've got ten. If you've got more than ten, that's great too – you can keep writing until the flow naturally stops. Now read it back to yourself, or, for maximum effect, read it aloud and say, 'Thank you for …' each item on the list. It will likely feel awkward at the beginning, but the more often you do it, the easier it will get.

Gratitude lists will become a staple of your new life. We suggest writing a list daily while working through the remaining chapters. After that, it's up to you, but it's very possible you won't want to stop.

What you'll discover is that as you list the many little things for which you're grateful, the picture you have of your life starts to change. Behind the gloom, a more positive image starts to emerge. One that is tender and full of wonder. One that existed the whole time, just beneath the surface. We're not deceiving ourselves; we're simply joining a different set of dots.

'Gratitude unlocks the fullness of life. It can turn a meal into a feast, a house into a home, a stranger into a friend.'

MELODY BEATTIE

Gratitude is infectious. It creates its own virtuous circle. The more grateful you feel, the more you'll have to be grateful for. Knowing that you'll need to come up with a list of positive experiences each day means you'll start to become more aware of them. When you're on the lookout, miraculously they start to appear far more often.

It is as if your mind is a magnifying glass expanding whatever you choose to focus on. Suddenly you become aware of sources of gratitude that you've never noticed before. A fellow train passenger's smile; the friend who's agreed to mind your child for an hour to give you a much-needed break; the first shoots of spring pushing their way through the cold earth; the warmth of the bathwater we sink into at the end of a tiring day.

'Thank you is the best prayer that anyone could say. I say that one a lot. Thank you expresses extreme gratitude, humility, understanding.'

ALICE WALKER

As the picture you paint of your life starts to change each day, miraculously so too does how you feel about your life. The situations you find yourself in somehow no longer seem so bad. There is some good in almost everything you discover.

And before long, other people start to notice the difference in you and in turn you'll find that they are warmer and friendlier to you. This is the magic multiplier effect.

When you practise gratitude, you exercise a spiritual muscle. Ever wondered why some people seem to be cheerful no matter what is happening around them? It's because of their attitude. Everything that you add to your list and every 'thank you' that you think or utter aloud changes your attitude. It has a profound impact on your mindset and, as a consequence, on your life and the people in it.

Gratitude can also be used as a shield to ward off negativity – either your own or other people's. As you become more positive, those around you – whether they are colleagues, friends or family – may become confused. They may be so used to you despairing or complaining about your lot that they're thrown and don't know how to react to your new, more positive outlook. They may invite you to pick up your list of woes again. Try your very best to resist. Whatever you focus on grows, so keep your focus firmly on the good in your day.

Like any exercise, the more you practise the easier it gets. Before long you'll wonder how you ever managed without it.

TIP: *Keep a small notebook or space in your journal for your gratitude list. Experiment with what time of day you write it. Use it as a spiritual remedy to either kick-start your day or get a restful night's sleep. And you can always refer to it halfway through your day if you need an instant hit of positivity.*

I was very depressed when I first started this practice. I did it to people-please – as someone had told me to – not because I thought it would work. To my cynical intellect it seemed trite and insincere. For the first few days I struggled to find anything I felt grateful for. But somehow each day it got easier and now my list is so full of wonderful things that if I do it too late at night it can keep me awake through excitement. The more good I see in my life, the more good seems to come.

JN

I know it seems absolutely ludicrous with everything that I have that is good in my life, but I have a habit of complaining. I can't believe I'm admitting that, but it's true. I go through stages where I forbid myself to complain. The minute a negative thought is about to leave my lips, I force myself to say the opposite. 'Thank you for getting me here safely,' as opposed to 'Oh my God, the traffic!' The difference it makes in my life is huge. And yet before long, there I am again finding ways to complain through humour or storytelling. Obviously sometimes this has got to be OK – to find humour in the ridiculous – but I have to stay vigilant to make sure that it isn't just another excuse to talk about what's wrong as opposed to what's right in my life. The more I keep up my gratitude lists the less likely I am to complain in a day; it's as simple as that.

GA

Reflection

'Joy is what happens to us when we allow ourselves to recognize how good things really are.'

MARIANNE WILLIAMSON

It only takes a miniscule turn of the steering wheel to change the direction of an ocean liner. When I'm off-kilter or worrying about what I haven't got, I use gratitude to redirect myself. It usually only takes a moment of pausing and thinking of something I have to be thankful for to get back on track. Whatever I focus on grows, so I make sure that I keep my gaze on what is good so that I can open myself up to joy.

Action: Today I will notice all the nice things that happen and I will say thank you.

Affirmation: I am lucky and I am blessed. My life is full of wonder.

Essential Practice 2

GENTLENESS:
Changing the Messages We Give Ourselves

'Peace begins with a smile.'

MOTHER TERESA

Imagine if every morning you woke up with a radio station blaring full volume inside your head. It would drive you crazy. In fact, that very tactic is used to torture prisoners into submission. And yet, that is exactly how we all live – with voices inside our heads telling us crazy, negative, self-defeating messages.

Take a moment to think of some of the thoughts you may subject yourself to on a daily basis, without even realizing you're doing it. We all have our own individual ones, but here are a few favourites: 'I don't fit in', 'I'm too fat', 'I'll never meet anyone', 'I'm going to end up broke and alone', 'I'm a failure', 'I'll never get anywhere', 'It's not fair', 'She doesn't like me', 'He's going to leave me'.

Get the picture? Your voices may be slightly different, but they are all coming from the same place. A place of fear. Fear that there is not enough, that we are not enough, that anything good we may have will be lost, that things are ultimately not going to be OK.

It's as if we each have an internal propaganda machine generating messages of fear and inadequacy so that even when things are going well, the machine is at work warning us that it will never last or things will never be this good again.

> 'We have been taught to believe that negative equals realistic and positive equals unrealistic.'
>
> SUSAN JEFFERS

To compound and complicate things, many of us have come to believe that the messages being broadcast by our negativity transmitter are in fact helpful. We tell ourselves that they protect us from disappointment and loss by ensuring we are realistic. We mistakenly believe these messages are our friends – that they stop us getting carried away and having dreams that will never be realized, that they keep us firmly on the ground.

In fact, the opposite is true. And there's a much better source from which to generate the messages we give ourselves: LOVE. That may sound a little hippy-dippy, but think about it. Would you talk to your best friend, or someone else you love – a child or a partner – the same way that you talk to yourself? You may be quite comfortable telling yourself that you're useless or stupid or a failure, but you'd be unlikely to say it to someone you really cared about.

'You cannot have a positive life and a negative mind.'

JOYCE MEYER

Every time you say something cruel or unkind to yourself you are wounding yourself, whether you are aware of it or not. Think how you feel when you receive a compliment. It's not always easy to let positive messages in, but think how good you feel when you do. Remember that burst of confidence. Now compare that with how you feel when you're criticized.

Just as you can't expect to lose weight if you live on a diet of fast food and sugar, you can't expect to live a peaceful and happy life if you're living on the mental equivalent of an unhealthy diet.

What's more, we often unwittingly pass on these internal messages to others – particularly (if we have any) our children. So the abuse we give ourselves gets handed down the generations – unless we make a conscious decision to intervene.

I love my children more than anything in the world. They are the most important part of my life and when I'm with them I am happiest – and yet, I find parenting hard. I do my very best to carve out as much time to be present and active with them as possible, but I'm not entirely sure that my nerves are built for the noise, the intensity, the constant requirement to be selfless and to remain calm. It takes everything in me not to nag them to quieten down and stop everything childish, which would obviously be devastating for their childhoods!

I see other mothers who seem to find it less of a struggle. Perhaps they have grown up in bigger families or have tougher nerve endings. I have worked extremely hard to practise patience and to pause when necessary before reacting, but, on the other hand, I also have to remember to forgive myself. So, for instance, even when I do the 'right thing' and get down on the floor to play Lego, my kids can sense that it's not the easiest thing for me. I will do it and I will stay there and engage, but somehow it's a struggle, even if I'm pretending it's not, and consequently they can tell. But it has taken me years and years not to feel guilty, to accept that I have limitations in that area and that I really am doing the best that I can. When I accept and forgive my own weaknesses, then I can be lighter in the moment, because I'm not trying too hard to be perfect and in the end, my kids benefit too.

GA

There is growing scientific evidence to suggest that negative attitudes can shape our experience of reality. Just as the placebo effect has been shown to produce improvements in patients' health, there's now evidence of a *nocebo* effect: up to 80 per cent of patients who're told they'll experience negative side effects from a treatment may experience them even if they're given nothing more than a sugar pill. In trials, patients who've been told they are being given chemo when in fact they're being given saline have been known to throw up and lose their hair.[3] It is what we believe about a situation, rather than the truth, that influences our responses.

....

EXERCISE: A New Script
....

This exercise is to help you start reprogramming the propaganda machine in your head.

Pick one of the negative messages that you give yourself. Write it down so you can see it for what it is: mean, unkind, negative, unhelpful. The problem is your brain usually doesn't see it that way. Your brain thinks it is *protecting* you by giving you that message. So, one step at a time, you are going to have to retrain your brain. Later on we'll work with specific tailor-made affirmations (p. 119), but for now let's use a message as an antidote that fits almost every situation.

Underneath the sentence you have written, write this: 'My name is

[_____]. I am a good and kind person. I do not need to please every-one. I do enough. I am enough'.[4]

Now cross out your original sentence and then say out loud the new message you have given yourself. Every time you notice a negative thought coming into your head, repeat your new message until the negative thought has gone.

Each morning and each evening for the next 14 days, when you brush your teeth, look in the mirror and say your message out loud to yourself three times. Look yourself in the eyes and say it tenderly, as you would to someone you care about. Are you cringing? If so, that's good – it means you're hitting a live nerve. Morning and night, eyeball to eyeball in the mirror, three times. Try it. You've nothing to lose but a bit of pride, and everything to gain!

How will you ever know whether there's a better way unless you try?

⋯⋯⋯

This technique for reprogramming our internal message machine can feel incredibly awkward when we begin. 'What if someone hears me talking to myself?' It's ironic that so many of us have no problem with bombarding ourselves with negative messages but then feel embarrassed by the prospect of giving ourselves kind, positive and encouraging ones.

You'll be amazed at how changing the way you talk to yourself will make a difference in your life. For a start, you'll begin to enjoy your own company more – who wants to spend time alone with someone who's going to be mean or moan all the time? But more importantly, it starts to change how you actually feel about yourself. Having positive thoughts coursing through your mind can't help but lift your spirits … and your attitude.

And then, of course, the magic multiplying effect of this exercise starts to kick in. As you feel better about yourself, your perception of the world around you starts to shift, and your relationships start to miraculously improve. And this is just the beginning of the process. Please don't take our word for this: try it out for yourself. The changes may be almost imperceptible at first, but they will accumulate. There is so much more that is good to come.

> TIP: *Write your message on a Post-it note and, if you feel comfortable to, stick it to your bathroom mirror. Otherwise keep it somewhere you'll see it often to remind yourself that you are in the process of learning a vital, life-transforming new habit.*

I've found great benefit in creating an internal intolerance towards self-criticism. Granted, it isn't foolproof and is a work in progress, but it works more often than not. The second a negative thought even reaches the periphery of my mind, I try to banish it – kind of like Dr. Evil's 'shhh' in *Austin Powers* – humour really helps! If I were to let the thought develop, it might look like: 'If only I looked like so and so' or 'If only I was right for that job, but I'm not, so I'm just not going to try'. It doesn't matter how big or small the thought; I let it go before it gets beyond the 'If'. For me, just the act of refusing to let a negative thought into my consciousness is liberating.

I spent years doing the opposite and letting the negativity sit there and grow until it led to further self-deprecating thoughts and inaction. Suddenly, I'd find it was 20 minutes later and I'd forgotten to wish my colleague happy birthday, follow up on something important, or sign up for something that would have been enjoyable or even life-changing, because of self-obsessing and essentially self-harming.

GA

One day my teenage son, who had exams fast approaching, came to me and said he felt ill. 'Push through it,' I told him. 'Just get one more hour in.' His face fell as he dragged himself back to his desk, and as he went I realized I was passing on exactly the lesson I'd learned in childhood – 'Don't stop, ever. Even if you're ill, you've got to keep working or you won't amount to anything'.

I'd carried that same message into my working life as a journalist and it had eventually resulted in my burning out. And yet, here I was, all those years later – despite having worked on myself – passing on exactly the same harmful message to my son.

I boiled the kettle, made him a mug of honey and hot lemon and insisted he close his books and lie down on the sofa and relax instead. The relief and gratitude that swept across his poor tired face reminded me that knowing how to be kind to himself would carry him further in life than any uplift in his grades that the extra hour's study might have given him.

JN

Reflection

'Imagine how much happier we would be, how much freer to be our true individual selves, if we didn't have the weight of gender expectations.'
CHIMAMANDA NGOZI ADICHIE

If I don't take care of myself I can start thinking I am only my job or someone's wife or mother. Or I can think I am my body weight, my looks or my brain. Before long I'm telling myself I'm fat or lazy or dumb or hopeless.

And then I remember the truth. That who I am is not dependent on anything I own, have or do. That I exist beneath and beyond the facts of my life – that I'm a spiritual being on a human quest.

Action: Today I will be kind to myself.

Affirmation: This is who I am and I feel glad to be me.

Essential
Practice
3

RESPONSIBILITY:
Taking Care of Ourselves

'When I was around 18, I looked in the mirror and said, "You're either going to love yourself or hate yourself." And I decided to love myself. That changed a lot of things.'

QUEEN LATIFAH

As women we often find it far easier to give love than to receive it. Culturally we're encouraged to be selfless, putting others' needs before our own. It can feel more comfortable to love our friends, partners and children than ourselves. Being kind to yourself can even feel indulgent, greedy and selfish. But it isn't. It's vital.

Our bodies need love just as much as our hearts and minds – and if they don't get it, they often start filling the deficit by looking for it elsewhere. Perhaps in a partner who's not good for us, in endless box sets, or tubs of Häagen-Dazs. Or maybe it'll play out at work where we crave a disproportionate amount of recognition or online as we develop a low-level shopping addiction.

Ignoring our needs can become habitual. Sometimes we don't even realize we're doing it, and we may not even see it as a problem. Maybe we're comfortable living small – or, at least, we tell ourselves we are. We may give ourselves just enough to get by so there are no crises, but we never actually reach our full potential.

Some of us shove our wants and needs deep down inside so that we can be *nice*. Or maybe we call it being *realistic*. If we don't 'want', we can't be disappointed when we don't 'get', our subconscious reasoning goes. But our needs are still there, gnawing away at us from beneath layers of self-protection. The problem is, we risk sabotaging the good that awaits us if we don't attend to them.

....

EXERCISE: Befriend Yourself

....

This is an exercise to help you identify the things you may be missing in life.

Have your journal handy. Then take five breaths in and out to centre yourself. Now imagine that a close female friend – someone you really love – is having a tough time. You invite her to stay over for a few days and to prepare for her arrival you make a list of things you could do to make her feel loved and cared for. Perhaps you'll run her a hot bubble bath at the end of each day to unwind. Maybe you'll take her to a movie or a walk through the park to your favourite coffee shop. Or perhaps download a comedy that you know will make her laugh or create a special playlist for her to listen to.

Make your own list – put at least ten things on it. Notice what happens to your energy as you write each item. Let yourself imagine how happy and cared for she'll feel. Now circle the three things that you think would be most fun and uplifting for her to do.

OK, here's your assignment: do those three things for YOURSELF. Take out your diary and schedule them in. Notice any resistance – in particular the voice that tells you this is silly or that you're too busy/tired/broke. From now on you're going to cherish yourself as you would someone you love deeply. If you've got time to do more than three then go for it. And don't forget to enjoy yourself – this exercise is about allowing yourself to have fun.

....

The list you've just made is a great resource. You can turn to it when the going gets tough. Add to it whenever you think of something else you'd enjoy and use it whenever you feel needy or depleted. As a rule of thumb, schedule a minimum of one fun or nurturing experience every week. More if you're able.

'I've been searching for ways to heal myself, and I've found that kindness is the best way.'

LADY GAGA

As you do the work laid out in this book, one of your aims will be to treat yourself as if you were your own best friend.

If you find yourself about to do something that might cause you harm, ask, 'Would I do this to someone I love?' If you find you're berating yourself for a mistake, ask, 'Would I talk like this to someone I love?' If you find you're 'comfort' eating or spending money you haven't got, ask yourself, 'Would I want someone I love to do that to themselves?' It takes time to establish new behaviours, but do your very best to interrupt any negative habitual responses that you notice as often as you can.

Don't blame or shame yourself; have compassion, and use your list to come up with kinder ways of comforting yourself. Some may find this harder than others, some may even find it excruciating. But it's really important that the love starts with you, that you start embracing all aspects of yourself from here on out to the best of your ability. It may seem like a mountain to climb today, but we're all in this together and there will be hundreds if not thousands of women on the same path to extend a helping hand.

Precious vessels

'Caring for myself is not self-indulgence, it is self-preservation, and that is an act of political warfare.'

AUDRE LORDE

Our bodies house all that is vital to our existence, yet we judge them and abuse them, and allow others to as well. Eating disorders and rates of self-harm continue to escalate and even those of us who stop short of obviously harmful behaviours often struggle with how we see ourselves.

Billions of dollars are spent each year trying to convince us that our lives would be better if we changed the way we looked. We may think of ourselves as independent-minded feminists, but on average we spend more time and money on trying to look good than ever before. Even the women's magazines that profess to boost our independence and confidence frequently encourage us to compare and improve our bodies, boosting sales by stoking our fear that we're not good enough as we are.

It's not surprising so many of us struggle with how we see ourselves and, by extension, how we treat ourselves.

Criticizing our physical form can also be a way of avoiding our real feelings. It can be easier to hate our bodies than to admit we're feeling sad or lonely or let down. Plus, if we can blame our physical body for our situation, we have an element of control and a scapegoat. Our subconscious thinking goes, 'My body is to blame – and there's something I can do about it – I can starve it or over-exercise it or ignore it.'

How we treat our bodies is an indicator of our emotional and spiritual state. If we're not comfortable in our own skin it means we have internal work to do and emotional wounds to heal. Our ultimate goal is to inhabit our bodies and selves with ease, joy and grace.

As a result of walking this path we will come to see our bodies as unique and precious vessels rather than objects to criticize and compare. But for the principles to work their magic you first need to get some basics in place.

Think of what happens to a toddler who doesn't get enough food or sleep – tantrums. We may be older and more sophisticated, but our bodies have the same needs and our emotions will be affected if those needs are not met.

It can be humbling to discover that quite often when our emotions are out of control it's not because of the complexity of the issues we're facing, but because we've been ignoring a simple physical need – like keeping our blood sugar level steady.

TIP: *HALT is an acronym for:*
H*ungry*
A*ngry*
L*onely*
T*ired*
HALT is widely used in 12-step fellowships, these are free groups set up to help people in addiction or affected by it (p. 57). Whenever we're hungry, angry, lonely or tired we're in danger of our emotions getting out of control and tipping us off balance. So if you notice yourself feeling one or more of those four, HALT and attend to it, fast.

Four essentials to self-care

There are four essential areas that we often neglect or let slide when it comes to our physical well-being. If you want to get the benefit from all that WE's principles have to offer, commit to taking care of yourself in each of them in turn.

Food

It's only human to want to be desired and so most of us at some point cave in to the toxic messages of the beauty and diet industries and mess around with our intake of food. The extent to which we do this will depend upon our self-esteem, our conditioning and how addictive is our personality.

If you find it difficult to regulate your food intake or if your weight tends to yo-yo, fuelling self-hatred, then for the duration of this work we recommend following an eating plan.

Structure and boundaries around what we consume free us up to think about more important things and keeps us from exacerbating the natural highs and lows of our emotional and hormonal circuits.

There's nothing faddy about it – it's boringly sensible, which is why it works. Three moderate-sized meals a day, eaten at regular intervals (between four to six hours apart), with one snack either mid-afternoon or before bed. If you're not sure what moderate means, ask someone else to serve your portion and make sure it contains protein which sustains your energy and doesn't give you the ups and downs that sugary foods do.

Watch for resistance in the form of 'But I'm not hungry', 'I'm just not a breakfast person', or 'Just one more muffin won't make a difference'. Try your best to ignore those voices. Many of us have trained our bodies not to need or want what is actually healthy or to want much more than what is healthy. Try following this simple plan and you'll be amazed by the results.

If you're prone to binge eating, avoid foods that trigger cravings. For some that will mean foods full of sugar or white flour; others have problems with dairy. All of us benefit – if our budgets allow – from cutting out processed foods that are laden with hidden sugars and additives. If your body–fat ratio is above or below the average range you may need more concentrated help. Remember, your own assessment may be distorted. For more information on healthy body weight visit www.calculator.net/body-fat-calculator.html and www.calculator.net/bmi-calculator.html.

When I went into treatment for depression and health professionals told me to eat three meals a day I thought they were trying to make me fat. I'd spent so many years avoiding breakfast to try to shrink my stomach for the rest of the day that I thought the act of consuming a bowl of oatmeal each morning would add another 14lb to my weight. But after two weeks of eating three meals a day I found I'd not only lost 7lb, but that I'd also ended the battle that had raged in my head since adolescence. I was liberated from the almost constant 'Shall I eat this or not?' debate and free to think about things that mattered far more. Plus I started to feel a lot more comfortable and at ease with my body.

JN

For most of my life I have vacillated between carefully watching what I eat and eating whatever I want. The periods where I stay away from sugar and wheat and cut down on or even remove caffeine, I am a calmer, more patient and kinder human being. When I don't I am moody, impatient and grumpy. It's really that simple. And it's my choice.

GA

Physical exercise

When we don't feel comfortable in our bodies, we can view them as separate from ourselves and get stuck in our heads, thinking obsessively about whatever is preoccupying us from one moment to the next.

For many women, food and exercise have ceased to be a form of self-care and instead become another lever we pull to try to change how we look. If we can't starve or eat ourselves into the right shape, then we can exercise our way to it.

Physical activity is, of course, an important aspect of healthy living. It not only gets our limbs moving but it sends necessary oxygen to the brain, helps our organs to function properly and our muscles to stay supple, and maintains bone strength. We know we should do it, but often we either don't do it at all, exercise like crazy or swing between the extremes.

If you find it hard to exercise, starting small can sometimes be the only way in. Committing to just ten minutes a day is enough to make a real difference. Try a brisk morning walk, or if you're short of time get off the bus one stop early so that your exercise uses up time you'd be spending in transit anyway. There are also hundreds of mini-workouts available online that are free to download. It needn't cost you anything to feel better inside your own body.

If you're at the other extreme and think you might be over-exercising, try cutting back and notice what happens to your anxiety levels. If there's an increase in self-judgement and panic that you're going to put on weight, it's highly possible there are feelings underneath your regimen that you're suppressing. Again, start small by cutting down on the intensity of your workout or the hours you spend at it per week and see what comes up. This is a good place to start getting honest about what's really going on for you, because that's a big part of what this journey is all about.

Rest

We know we need rest, but the pressures of modern life often make it impossible to prioritize it. It may simply be that we're working too many hours or nursing a waking baby, or we may resist rest because of our own internal resistance to self-care, but like nutrition and exercise, your brain needs rest to function effectively.

Do you have enough energy as you go through your day or do you find yourself feeling sluggish or falling asleep? Do you push through exhaustion so that you're stuck in an adrenalin-fuelled cycle or do you take breaks as needed? Do you keep your sleeping space safe from the stresses and strains of daily life? If you have trouble sleeping, is it because you're using your laptop or phone in bed? That alone can lead to stress and sleep disturbances.

Even when we know what's missing, it can still be hard to change our behaviour around it. Try to imagine you had a daughter with the same issues around sleep. What would your advice be? Really think about it. Don't take your phone or laptop to bed? Head on the pillow before midnight? No caffeine after 4pm? Whatever your loving advice might be, follow it yourself.

It's also really important to take at least one break in the middle of the day. If you can't take a lunch hour, make sure you take a pause of some kind. Notice the sky, notice the temperature, breathe deeply and return yourself to centre before engaging in your next round with life.

Appreciation

How do you feel about your body?

Try asking yourself that question while standing naked in front of a full-length mirror. 'What?!' you might ask. Once you've moved through the shock and the fear and are actually standing before your reflection, notice your reaction to what you see. Hopefully you feel happy and fond of your physical form – that's certainly what we're working towards. But many of us are not only uncomfortable, but also highly critical. We focus on the parts of our body that we don't think are perfect – like our thighs, our tummy, our breasts. We feel vulnerable and even ashamed. Our poor bodies endure some harsh judgements, whether we are naked or fully clothed.

Now, take in your whole reflection again, spend a moment centring yourself by breathing in and out deep into your belly. Instead of thinking about what your body looks like, think about what it does for you. This magnificent vessel before you enables you to live this life. Look at your legs, which carry you every day; your arms and hands, which perform so many tasks; your torso, which contains your vital organs: your heart, your lungs, your stomach.

This body houses you. It has grown with you. It sounds like an obvious statement, but so often we forget that it is the same body we came into this world with. Would we forgive it more if we remembered our newborn selves? Try to connect with the kindness you'd feel if it belonged to that baby or to someone else whom you love.

Run your hand over the parts that you find hardest to love. Breathe deeply, take your time and consciously release each negative thought that crosses your mind.

This is a powerful experience. If you can, try to commit to doing it a couple of times a week until the habit of praise for what you have overrides the habit of shame. One day this body will be gone. The time you have with it is precious. From now on, commit to treating it with kindness and care.

For a large part of my life I hated my body. Even when I was at my skinniest, which was really underweight, I thought I was fat. At the depths of my despair I used to self-harm as a form of punishment for being what I thought was ugly. Now I'm deeply happy to be me. I'm older (of course!) and heavier than I've ever been, but I wouldn't be any other way. However, I still have to put in the right action on a daily basis – it only takes a missed meal or too many late nights and my mental state starts to slide and suddenly I'm looking in the mirror and checking my tummy to see how many inches I can pinch. Now, though, I know exactly how to get back on track. And I do. Fast.

JN

So many of my living years have been spent engaging in one form of self abuse or another. I've often wished and prayed that it wasn't so easy to escape. Denegrating oneself is a form of abuse and a way to hide because, in doing so, we refuse to see and acknowledge the beautiful being we are just as we are. What if we could make a commitment to ourselves and to our daughters that we will stop abusing ourselves and our bodies in thought and in action? When we abuse ourselves we teach others that we are worthy of being treated badly. We show our daughters that we think we deserve to be abused and therefore they deserve it too – which is not true. Nobody deserves to be abused.

GA

Beauty really is an inside job

'A mother who radiates self-love and self-acceptance actually vaccinates her daughter against low self-esteem.'

NAOMI WOLF

Taking care of your body will make the work ahead infinitely easier and more pleasurable. When you write your gratitude list each day find at least one thing you're grateful to your body for. And as you go through your day, find ways to say thank you to your body through your actions. Notice how your relationship with it starts to shift as a result. You may also start to feel more confident in the process, because you know that you are doing right by yourself. Self-assurance will come more naturally and your relationships with others will change for the better. If we don't care for our body, how can we expect anyone else to?

A woman who is truly comfortable in her own skin radiates an inner beauty regardless of whether she conforms to cultural norms of beauty. When someone is genuinely joyful and at ease with herself we gravitate towards her – and feel better about ourselves for being in her presence.

In my twenties I was quite consistently in the public eye. I remember doing one particular photoshoot for the cover of a magazine and being completely focused on, and distracted by, the fact that I felt fat. It wasn't so much that things weren't fitting, which has happened, too, on many occasions – in fact, one time I ended up wearing a tarpaulin over my shoulders because nothing else was working – but on this day I just felt unattractive in myself, and I remember turning inwards and being uncommunicative and allowing my negative thoughts to essentially ruin my (and maybe for all I know other peoples') experience of that shoot. Now the pictures that were created that day expose not a hint of my inner turmoil – many over the years have been more revealing. Today, what I see when I look at those photographs is a very young, fresh-faced, beautiful young woman who had no sense or appreciation of how lucky she was in so many ways.

GA

Hormones

For many of us the onset of puberty marks the beginning of a monthly hormonal rollercoaster. Menstruation affects each of us differently, but mood swings, pain and changes in weight and libido can leave us feeling scattered and crazy each month. In fact, half of all women's suicide attempts are made during the four days just prior to menstruation, or during the first four days of menstruation.[5]

A few pioneering companies have introduced a 'period policy', so that their employees can take sick leave if they need it, but most of us have learned to just 'deal with it'. This may mean going to work when we're in pain, rushing around doing chores rather than resting or feeling guilty for being bad-tempered. During your next cycle, consider listening to your body more carefully and responding to yourself with more compassion and kindness.

Pregnancy, miscarriage, oral contraception and fertility treatments can also create hormonal chaos in our lives and then, as we get older, there is another journey that we all end up taking as women and that's the menopause.

The menopause

It's astounding what a taboo topic the menopause – the cessation of periods – continues to be when it affects 50 per cent of the population. Women commonly experience the menopause between the ages of 48 and 55. Each woman's experience will be unique, but common symptoms include hot flushes, night sweats, difficulty sleeping, reduced sex drive, memory and concentration problems, vaginal dryness and pain, itching or discomfort during sex, headaches, mood changes, palpitations, joint stiffness, reduced muscle mass and recurrent urinary tract infections. The symptoms often arrive several months or years before the menopause itself, during the perimenopause, and can continue to affect women for up to 12 years after their last bleed.

For me the perimenopause was a sudden inability to cope with anything when I had been seemingly able to cope with everything simultaneously for years without many hitches. It came in the form of sudden uncontrollable emotionality and hysteria and feeling like someone else's brain had replaced mine. I honestly think I have been in gradual perimenopause since my thirties, and when I finally identified and acknowledged what was going on for me – or I guess when it finally got so bad that I needed to seek out a solution: bio-identical hormones – I could not remember when my brain had felt that 'normal'. I started to realize how long I had been living with some of the symptoms.

When I began discussing it with my female friends I was amazed by two things. One, how many women had been through it, but it had never been a part of our conversation. I felt like we were whispering in covens, discussing the best witchdoctor to go to in order not to turn into a toad. And two, how many women had no idea it was coming or that some of their 'symptoms' might be related to it. If someone had told me sooner, if the subject had been less taboo and I had understood earlier what to expect and what lifestyle choices could make it worse, I might have saved myself years of emotional turmoil.

How great would it be if we as women didn't feel embarrassed talking about the menopause and perimenopause? If we embraced this transition as one of the natural rites of passage of being a woman? How wonderful it would be if we were able to immediately identify the signs because we had been educated about them, know that we are not alone, and could seek early help?

GA

There are a range of natural remedies, dietary changes and hormone replacement therapies out there, but unless we know we need help we can't access them. Too many women suffer either in ignorance or shame.

We should no longer feel obliged to just 'deal with it' or educate our daughters to do the same. If women started to speak about it more openly, we would embrace our hormonal experiences with curiosity and fearlessness as another example of what joins us together.

Reflection

'When a woman becomes her own best friend life is easier.'

DIANE VON FURSTENBERG

I used to think that it was selfish to take care of myself. I wanted others to love me so I spent my time caring for them. I abandoned myself in pursuit of my quest for love and acceptance. Now I know that the relationship I need to foster, especially if I'm feeling low, is with myself. The longer I spend developing a relationship with myself, the more rewarding and fulfilling are the relationships I have with others. When I treat myself kindly I'm able to relate to others from a place of wholeness rather than a place of need.

Action: I will notice my needs and attend to them.

Affirmation: I love and care for myself.

Essential Practice 4

MEDITATION:
Creating a Safe Space

'When you find peace within yourself, you become the kind of person who can live at peace with others.'

Many of us spend our lives searching for safety in one form or another. Some of us have looked for it outside of ourselves – in partners, in jobs, in families, in material possessions. Others have tried to keep safe by putting up a barrier between ourselves and the world around us.

But there is a genuinely safe place that each and every one of us can access. It's a sacred space that we can enter at any point during our day – regardless of what is happening around us. In that place we find peace and we find healing. We create this space by meditation.

Like the habit of gratitude, meditation creates a new muscle group that will enhance your emotional balance and intuition while cultivating the resilience to handle whatever life throws your way.

Making way for the sacred

Most of us spend our lives rushing. If we're not physically racing around, our minds are full of mental hurry. We're thinking of what we ought to do, what we've done wrong, what we should have done better, what we're going to do, and so on and so on. When we meditate we get a break from those thoughts. We create distance and the chance to connect with what lies underneath the bustle of our chattering minds and our ever-lengthening to-do lists.

> *'I am not afraid of storms, for I am learning how to sail my ship.'*
>
> LOUISA MAY ALCOTT

You may already have your own meditation technique and, if so, you know what we're talking about. But if you don't have one or you're new to meditation, this section will get you started with a practice that you can use for the rest of your life.

For now, just think of meditation as a moment away from the rush of your day and the clutter of your mind. A moment of stillness.

Of course, stillness can't be forced, just as healing can't be made to happen. But what you can do is create an environment in which stillness and peace are fostered and can grow.

> *'As your mind grows quieter and more spacious, you can begin to see self-defeating thought patterns for what they are and open up to other, more positive options.'*
>
> SHARON SALZBERG

When you get to the Sixth Principle, Peace, you'll learn how to deepen and strengthen your meditation practice, and the Eighth Principle, Joy, will introduce you to prayer, which you can use whether you have a faith or not. But for now all you have to do is decide to commit to taking a few minutes out of your busy life at the start of each day. And when we say a few minutes we mean just that. Two minutes each day. That's all you need to begin.

Even though all of us can manage to find two minutes, it's quite likely that at this point you'll experience resistance or even self-sabotage. You may start to find excuses before you've even read through this section. Perhaps your mind is defending how busy or tired you are. Or maybe you've just remembered that you took a meditation course once before and it didn't work. Or that there's meditation at the end of your exercise or yoga class, but you just fall asleep each time.

Be aware of all these rationalizations and do this exercise anyway.

....

EXERCISE: Daily Meditation Practice
....

This exercise is to help you establish your own daily meditation practice. Two minutes, that's all. You can download one of many free meditation timer apps or use the regular timer on your phone. Leave it to the bell to remind you when the time's up. Tell your mind that it can return to thinking as much as it wants as soon as this brief exercise is over.

Then, when you are ready, sit cross-legged on the floor or on a chair. Make sure you're comfortable before you start. You can close your eyes or keep your focus fixed on a point just in front of you – placing a candle in your sightline is both helpful and calming. Try not to let your gaze drift around the room looking for distractions. Remember, this short time is about peace of mind.

Now just breathe, in through your nose and out through your mouth, slowly and gently.

Try to let your out-breath take slightly longer than your in-breath. Notice the gap between each inhale and exhale. Relax. Don't worry about any thoughts that come – just try not to engage with them, gently returning your attention to the rise and fall of your breath.

Although two minutes may not seem very long it is enough to start creating a very important space and a very important habit. Remember that from tiny acorns grow mighty oaks.

....

If your mind objects to this practice, that's great news. It means it knows it's about to be rumbled. The mind likes to pretend it knows everything and sadly, too often, we believe it. The truth is that the mind is an excellent servant but a terrible master. It's great at solving crossword puzzles or reading train timetables, but it's not so good at helping us to find fulfilment or love.

So for just two minutes every day you're going to suspend its operation. You're going to ask it to take a short break and then see what happens when you give yourself just that small amount of time away from your thoughts.

Don't worry if this doesn't make any sense. Don't worry if nothing seems to be happening. This is not about sense or meaning, and there is no right or wrong way of doing this. It is about very gently starting a new and vital habit: training your mind and body to get used to being still.

Each day, when you have finished your two minutes of silence, read the affirmation that corresponds to the chapter you're reading. Allow what's written there to seep in gently as you continue to breathe in and out. Then softly say the affirmation to yourself.

You might like to commit it to memory or jot it down in your journal so that in moments of doubt and indecision you can return to your affirmation and use it as a way of keeping yourself calm and centred. It will help you to recall your safe place, as well as reinforce the lesson contained in the chapter you've just read.

It's simple. All you have to do is do it!

TIP: *Try to meditate in the same place each day. Create a special place for yourself to sit, whether it's cross-legged on the floor in a corner of your bedroom or on your favourite sofa. Try to make it feel special. Lighting a candle before you start helps to create a ritual around the process. Or you could burn incense, if you like it, or place a fresh flower in a vase just in front of you. Assail your senses so that your body and mind learn that when you sit in your special place and the candle is lit this is their time to switch off and allow something else to take over.*

Before I started meditating I used to think, 'When I'm in the right apartment, I'll create the perfect space and then I'll do it on a regular basis.' Eventually I started anyway and then it became about the perfect conditions. I had to be facing in the right direction, there could be no distractions, the candle and incense lit, my legs crossed. Then at one point I was away working and had none of my usual crutches. I remember sitting on a hard floor in a fluorescently lit corner of a kitchen and experiencing one of the most blissful meditations of my life. Now I do it anywhere – in the midst of a crowd, on a bus, at work. My need for meditation to be a part of my life is greater than my need for it to be perfect.

GA

When I first tried to meditate I was scared of it. It felt like I was being put in a torture chamber where all the thoughts I'd been trying to repress would appear and torment me. But knowing that I only had to sit for two minutes made it possible. It might not have sounded like very long to anyone else, but to me it was a lifetime. Over time my mind learnt to quieten for that period. Just that brief respite gave me a glimpse of what was to come. Peace of mind and a way of being in the world without the noise in my head constantly destabilizing me.

JN

Reflection

'It feels good. Kinda like when you have to shut your computer down when it goes crazy and when you turn it on it's OK again. That's what meditation is to me.'

ELLEN DEGENERES

Meditation is the way I achieve real, lasting change. I breathe in deeply and I breathe out, and as I do so I return to the present moment and remember the truth: I am a spiritual being on a human journey.

Action: Today I will take time out. No matter how busy things get I will create a moment to honour myself and the spiritual path I am on.

Affirmation: As I breathe in and out deeply I feel myself return to who I truly am.

A NOTE ON ADDICTION

An addiction is any behaviour you are unable to stop repeating despite its negative impact on your life. It's a medical illness, like cancer or hepatitis – not something you can heal through willpower alone – and it's impossible to make much real progress if you're in active addiction.

The good news is that there is great help out there. There are now 12-step fellowships that can help with any addiction you might have. At the back of this book are links to their websites where you'll find self-diagnosis questionnaires and information about how to access the support that is freely available (pp. 304–6).

One of the most cunning symptoms of addiction is denial. If you find yourself tempted to minimize your behaviour, please don't. Ignoring it will cheat you out of a whole new way of life.

Addiction to substances like drugs, alcohol or food are widely known, but you can also be addicted to behaviours like shopping, exercising, gaming, gambling, care-taking, loving and sex. Basically you can become addicted to anything that changes how you feel. A temporary period of abstinence from a substance or behaviour doesn't mean you no longer have a problem. Addiction is a progressive illness, so in its early stages you may be able to kid yourself that you've got it under control. Long term, though, it only gets worse. So if you find you're unable to control yourself around a particular substance or behaviour then you should jump straight to the Resources section on pages 304–6.

Congratulations. You now have four Essential Practices in place that will hold you steady for the journey ahead and, we hope, for the rest of your life.

Often we start this journey feeling alone. But the truth is that there are many of us – across the globe – searching for a happier, more meaningful way of living.

PART 2

The Nine Principles

The Path Ahead

'Look into your own heart, discover what it is that gives you pain, then refuse, under any circumstances whatsoever, to inflict that pain on anyone else.'

KAREN ARMSTRONG

The Nine Principles in this book provide a compass. Without them life can feel like a losing battle. We can thrash around trying to satisfy conflicting wants and needs. At times we seem to make headway in the 'want' department — we get the job or the partner or the home — and yet our deeper needs get buried. Other times we feel like we're in a boat with one oar, paddling as hard as we can while spinning in circles.

The Nine Principles in this book guide us forward. They guide us home.

When you've learned to practise them in your life you'll be able to live from a place of authenticity and love wherever you find yourself and whatever has happened in your past.

'Only if you are ready to change yourself can you be ready to change the world.'

EDIT SCHLAFFER

The work of transforming our world begins with healing ourselves. If we don't do the work, we risk allowing our egos to run the show. We can wind up acting out our own unresolved issues on those we seek to help, or taking up a cause from a need to feel important rather than from a place of genuine passion and concern. Our world is full of people who inadvertently cause harm while trying to do good.

You may feel tempted to flip through the book until you find the part that deals with a particular issue that you feel relates to you — like relationships, for instance — but don't. The Nine Principles are laid out in an order. Each one builds on the last and if you skip through the others, you'll short-change yourself. When you finish the book in its entirety you may want to keep it close for reference, but before then give yourself the gift of committing to the whole process. You may choose to complete a chapter a week or take it more slowly. You can also work through the chapters with friends or other women who are also interested in taking the journey (p. 319).

There's no timescale, but the sooner you do the work, the sooner the miracles will manifest.

'Action is the antidote to despair.'

JOAN BAEZ

Doing vs thinking

WE is an experiential rather than an intellectual process. Most of us exert a lot of mental energy trying to understand ourselves, but with little permanent result. We may have plenty of insights, but insights alone rarely lead to change, just as reading a recipe sadly doesn't result in a cooked meal — there's still all the measuring, chopping and stirring to do.

For change to work, ACTion is necessary. ACT is one of the acronyms we'll repeat again and again:

Action

Changes

Things

Right action leads to right thinking. Not the other way around. It's not enough merely to know or understand. You don't get to experience swimming by sitting at the edge of the pool. And once you're in the water, if you want to stay afloat, you'll need to move your arms and legs rather than just think about it.

Action is also what will enable you to make the journey from the head to the heart. So throughout this journey you'll be reminded to ACT.

The exercises that each chapter contains are actions in their own right. They are an integral part of the journey as they help you to action what you're learning.

For decades I tried to work things out in my head. I lived with a mountain of self-help books by my bed. I'd read a chapter or two until I found an insight that made me feel momentarily better. Then I'd recommend it to someone else as a brilliant read. I thought I could get rid of my pain by understanding and knowing. I'd lie awake at night looking at things from every angle, stuck in analysis paralysis. In the end, a combination of whisky, sleeping pills and tranquilizers was the only way I could get any peace from the constant noise in my head. It was revolutionary to me when someone suggested I move a muscle to change a thought. I thought I had to wait for my thoughts to change before I could act. Now I know it's the other way round. Right action creates right thinking and self-esteem to boot.

JN

I have to say that even though I was introduced to these practices decades ago, I still find the doing of them hard. Even though I know what's best for me and have experienced first hand the difference they make to my entire life, my brain still wants to forget that I feel better when I practise them daily. Maybe it's the fact that they work that makes the challenge greater – my ingrained, stubborn self-sabotage doesn't want me well, or maybe it's my internal rebel that says, 'Don't tell me what to do!' or perhaps it's just plain laziness. Whatever my resistance is, the fact is, when I do them, they work.

GA

Commitment

There's only one thing you need to agree to for the principles in this book to work. It's a commitment to be willing. Willing to try. Willing to pick yourself up when you mess up (which we all do) and to try again.

Anyone can make this commitment. It doesn't require education, status or wealth. And it certainly doesn't require perfection.

Nothing in this book needs to be done 'right' or 'perfectly'. The P-word, perfectionism, should be banned. It causes all of us monumental problems – in society's expectations of us and the demands we make on ourselves. We are not cardboard cut-outs. We are individuals. That means each one of us is complicated and real, with our own unique and often messy layers of emotional wounding.

Your head will present you with a thousand excuses, but you can and will find the time. You can and will find the space. You can and will find the courage. That which is no longer necessary to your well-being will fall away.

The Nine Principles that follow are for you personally and also for the world you inhabit.

They are not just for your yoga mat or your place of worship. They are for the big decisions and for the small. They work just as well in helping you choose how to vote as they do in the grocery store aisle as they do in your intimate relationships. Nothing is too important or too mundane for them to have an impact on. Don't keep them just for crises – they will work in every aspect of your daily life. We promise.

This is a journey towards love.

Prepare to be amazed.

Principle
1

HONESTY:
Getting Real

'To be oneself, simply oneself, is so amazing and utterly unique an experience that it's hard to convince oneself so singular a thing happens to everybody.'

SIMONE DE BEAUVOIR

Honesty is the guide that leads us home. It returns us to our true selves and enables us to live authentically, courageously and congruently.

Most of us do our best to tell the truth. We might tell the occasional white lie to avoid hurting someone's feelings or exaggerate a story for the sake of effect, but aside from that we try to be honest.

And yet, there is one person we lie to on a regular basis, perhaps even without realizing it – ourselves.

We all do it. We tell ourselves we're OK when we're not. We tell ourselves we don't mind when we do and that we can't when we can. We say yes when we mean no and no when we want to say yes. We override our instinct in the name of being practical or polite. We bury our dreams and then help others fulfil theirs. We disguise, shave and shape ourselves to conform to an artificial feminine ideal only to suffer the consequences: depression, relationship problems, anger issues, addiction and despair.

WE's First Principle takes us inwards. It involves digging down beneath the surface of who we think we are, in order to reclaim our true selves.

It's a process that involves discovering and discarding the lies and myths we've accumulated over the years, which have resulted in us becoming estranged from ourselves. It requires courage, commitment and self-care.

Most of us are called to this journey when we hit an obstacle in life – a relationship that's ended badly, a betrayal or disappointment, or when one of the distractions or addictions we use to cope stops working. When our lives are ticking along and appear to be functioning, it's easier to ignore that niggle deep in our soul, pleading for our attention.

But wherever you are in your life, and whatever is happening, WE's First Principle will bring an enormous sense of relief and freedom. There is nothing quite like being able to say, 'This is who I really am,' and to feel truly glad about it.

Losing ourselves

'Severe separations in early life leave emotional scars on the brain because they assault the essential human connection: the [parent—child] bond, which teaches us that we are lovable.'

JUDITH VIORST

From early childhood most of us start to lose touch with our authentic self.

Our instinctive need to be loved, feel safe and belong leads us to adapt. Sometimes consciously, sometimes not, we shift in response to our parents', teachers' and peers' perceptions of who we are and what we should be. And in the process we naturally abandon parts of ourselves.

The extent to which each of us does this largely depends on how well we are cared for in our early years. We rely on the world we're born into to reflect back to us who we are. If the message we receive as babies and toddlers is that we're loved and 'enough' just as we are, we'll have a much greater chance of developing a resilient sense of self. The less secure we are during those early years, the more we adapt ourselves to try to get that missing approval.

We create false selves to ensure our emotional and sometimes physical survival – sub-personalities that are almost us but not quite. They help us to get our needs met at a time when we are too young and dependent to have any other choices. The problem comes when we continue to rely on them long after they've fulfilled their useful purpose. Often they become so habitual that we no longer realize they're not who we really are.

EXERCISE 1: Would the Real Me Please Stand Up

This exercise will help you begin to reconnect with your authentic self.

Pause for a moment and think about which false selves you may have developed over your lifetime. Remember that each one of them came into existence to keep you safe. They're not bad, they've just outlived their purpose and they prevent you from living authentically. Take out your journal. Close your eyes and allow yourself to slide backwards along the timeline of your life. Be as honest as you're able about the sub-personalities you've developed.

For example, perhaps as a girl you relieved household tensions by making people laugh, so as an adult you continue to clown your way through life — never showing your tears and keeping everyone else smiling at your own expense. Or maybe you were the 'good' girl who was rewarded for working hard, and now you're at the top of a career ladder and you have no idea why you climbed it.

Perhaps you gained your sense of worth by care-taking an alcoholic or otherwise sick parent and now continue to give more than you have and wonder why you are always running on empty. Or maybe you grew up in an environment where there was nobody you could rely on and so you developed a mask of independence that leaves you seemingly invincible but horribly alone.

It may be difficult to draw sharp distinctions between the characters you've played, whose boundaries may conflict and overlap. Were you Mummy's little helper or Daddy's princess? Were you the intellectual or the dropout? Were you the peacemaker or the truth-teller (or both)? Were you a people-pleaser, a party-girl, a loner or a saint? Were you Miss Perfect, a rebel or a critic who sat on the sidelines? Or were you invisible? Write down every sub-personality you find.

Each of us will have developed a number of selves to ensure our survival.

68

Normally you'll find five or six dominant ones that are still with you in adult life.

Now take every one that you've found and visualize her as a separate person. Greet her and thank her for the protection she has given you. Each of them has helped to keep you safe.

When you've worked through your list take five deep breaths in and out and congratulate yourself. This is an important step you've taken. Even though these sub-personalities will emerge and sometimes still be useful, from now on you will see them for what they are – masks that you've needed to wear – and you will not mistake them for yourself. Who you truly are lies beneath and beyond them, and you are now on your journey to meet her.

....

As you go through your day try to notice when you slip into one of your sub-personalities. Practising honesty will enable you to identify them and then let them gently drop away, in the same way that a husk drops from a seed.

When I told the school careers advisor that I wanted to be a secretary at the BBC (I didn't dare tell her that I wanted to be a reporter because I didn't think it would ever be possible), she laughed at me and said, 'Don't you think every girl wants to do that? Why don't you be a bit more realistic and work at the insurance company? They're always looking for typists.' When, years later, I found myself reporting for the BBC, I always carried a sense that I should be in the typing pool rather than on air. While the men around me had a sense of entitlement and clearly planned their career progression, I always felt as if I was begging to be allowed to do what I loved rather than claiming my rightful place at the table.

JN

Other people's stuff

'When she stopped conforming to the conventional picture of femininity she finally began to enjoy being a woman.'

BETTY FRIEDAN

How we are seen by others and society as a whole informs how we see ourselves. The messages we're given as women about what it is and isn't OK for us to do, feel, look like or want, get absorbed.

Whether the message is that we need to be passive and wait to be chosen or that we should try to have it all – children and the seat in the boardroom – the complex truth of who we are gets obscured. Our sense of what is possible is limited and we bury parts of ourselves, fearing we won't fit into the world as it is.

Similarly our perception of our physical self gets distorted by the constant messages we receive about what we should and shouldn't wear, weigh and eat, and how we should or shouldn't look. No matter how hard we try, it's difficult not to be affected. They're all around us in what we read and hear, and in the images we see on a daily basis. Whether it's scantily clad, airbrushed models staring down at us from billboards or magazine covers, or images on social media, the message is the same: it's not OK to be who we are.

....

THE PRICE OF SOCIAL MEDIA

The stress that social media is causing young women is heavily implicated in a dramatic rise in mental illness. Levels of self-harm, post-traumatic stress disorder and chronic mental illness are all on the increase.[6] A quarter of 16–24-year-old women have anxiety, depression, panic disorders, phobias or obsessive compulsive disorder according to UK government-funded research.[7] And the proportion of young women self-harming has trebled between 2007 and 2014.

....

At this stage of WE's journey your goal is to discover and know your true self. Becoming conscious of those messages is the first stage to escaping their toxic power.

When I was broadcasting I felt obliged to don the 'uniform' – power suit and heels – that my news editors and the industry expected. I was very conscious that I was perpetuating the stereotypes I hoped my work would dispel, but I felt trapped. If I didn't look the part I wouldn't get to play the part. And I desperately wanted the part. So I dressed up and pretended to be someone I was not in order to get the chance to tell the truth – one of the many acts of hypocrisy that I engaged in to become 'successful'. I became part of the problem that I was hoping to solve and each time I put on my work suits I felt myself getting more and more estranged from my real self and my levels of internal self-hatred grew.

JN

I agreed to participate in photoshoots when I was younger that I would advise myself against in retrospect, where my desire to be liked or found attractive overrode that small voice that wanted to say, 'I'm not OK with this'. Whether it was not wanting to upset the male photographer or letting my ego get caught up in the attention, I hadn't yet found that part of my brain. Not just the part that could stand up for myself and say I will not participate in an act that feels shameful because it is exposing too much of myself for a stranger's gaze, but the part that might recognize that what I was participating in was a bigger issue and that by agreeing to do the shoot I was colluding in a far darker message about women and our objectification.

GA

It's easy to forget how relatively recently women – even in the developed Western hemisphere – won basic legal rights. A hundred years ago, women in the US and UK weren't allowed to vote and it wasn't until 1920 and 1928 respectively that women gained voting parity with men. And until the 1990s our husbands could legally rape us. For the bulk of legal history we've been treated as inferior and the legacy of centuries of inequality continues to exact its toll on our sense of who we are.

Leading female scientists, politicians and commentators still find that if they speak publicly, their looks and clothes are dissected in ways that simply don't happen to men, reinforcing the sense that beneath the talk of equality we remain objects to be lusted over, dominated and possessed, rather than equals.

To get a snapshot of the extent to which equality is still resisted take a look at the comments that women who write about equality generate online – threats of sexual assault and even death are commonplace. As a result, whatever strides the world is making towards equality, the mirror we're reflected back in is distorted and, in turn, can corrupt and limit how we perceive ourselves.

UNDER COVER

Too often we can feel we have to disguise our real physical self to match artificial notions of femininity that have largely been created by men. Whether we're forcing our feet into heels so high they damage our backs or suppressing what we think or feel in order not to upset our other half, we're often left feeling worse about ourselves.

The rise of porn has compounded the problem, giving both genders warped perceptions of what is normal. Young men expect girls to look and behave like porn stars, and girls find themselves under pressure to oblige. Plastic surgeons have seen a surge in the number of women seeking labiaplasty – a painful procedure that can permanently damage nerve endings – as women try to conform to damaging cosmetic norms perpetuated by the porn industry to make themselves desirable.

Of course, changing our outside appearance doesn't get us any nearer to being loved and wanted for who we authentically are. Applying WE's principles enables us to know our identity from the inside out rather than the outside in. We realize that who we are lies beyond what we do, how we look and what we own.

....

When you are clear about who you are and who you are not it's a lot easier to be clearer with the outside world. If you adopt rigorous self-honesty as a way of life, the false-selves and labels that have disguised your true self will gradually start to fall away.

'Curiosity is our friend that teaches us how to become ourselves.'
ELIZABETH GILBERT

As children we're all emotionally super-porous. In addition to the messages we receive from our families, peers and society at large, we also absorb our caregivers' fears, frustrations and beliefs, and mistake them for our own. We start receiving most of them before we're old enough to be able to scrutinize and reject those that don't serve us or belong to us. This will especially be the case if you come from a family in which there are secrets or traumatic events. You may not know the facts, but you'll still absorb the feelings. It's possible to carry emotions like shame, fear and sadness for decades, even though they have nothing to do with you.

> I've always lived with a fear of catastrophe and could never define what that 'terrible' thing I feared might be. As a girl I'd squirrel away my pocket money so that I'd be ready for whatever it was that was going to happen to us. It was only years later, when I discovered my father's secret past, that my behaviour made sense and my fear started to evaporate. When my father was a child, he'd fled from the Nazis during the Second World War and, wanting to protect us from anti-Semitism, never told us that he was Jewish. But it turned out he inadvertently left me a different kind of legacy: a sense of impending catastrophe and a fear of saying who I really was.
>
> *JN*

GENES WITH MEMORIES

The new and fast-evolving field of epigenetics research suggests that trauma can be inherited genetically. In one study, male mice that were taught to fear a smell passed that fear on to their offspring – which in turn would bequeath the same sensitivity to their offspring.[8]

Another study found that baby rats that received insufficient nurturing from their mothers matured to be more prone to disease and anxiety than their well-groomed counterparts, and then passed on that predisposition to their descendants.[9]

We can live our whole lives with a particular sensitivity, fear or trait that doesn't belong to us – that's been internalized from the outside world. Now we can start challenging the assumptions we've made about ourselves and ask, 'Is this mine? Do I own this? Is it part of me? Is it serving me?' or 'Can I let it go?'

EXERCISE 2: Getting Beneath the Surface

This exercise is to help you discard the ideas about yourself that no longer serve you. Think about the labels you'd use to describe yourself. They might be about your job, how you look, your race, your background, your sexual orientation.

Now think of the messages about yourself that you were given growing up. It doesn't matter whether they were good or bad – we internalize them when we're young and impressionable, and as we get older they can be hard to shake.

As a child, were you told you were lazy, smart or a show-off? Were you criticized or praised for how you looked – told you were too fat, too skinny, too tall, too short? Or maybe you were ignored and grew up with the belief that you were worth nothing at all.

Write a list of the ten most prominent messages about yourself that come to your mind – from your past and your present. Look at each label on your list. Really ponder it. Is it true? Does it really represent who you are inside?

Now make sure you are comfortable and have time to sit for a few moments. Close your eyes. Breathe in and out five times, letting your out-breath last for five counts and your in-breath for four. Imagine you are in a boat that is floating far out at sea and that you take the labels you have written and scatter them onto the surface of the ocean. Watch the words floating there, bobbing up and down on the waves. Now imagine diving into the water so you're beneath them. As you look back up at them, you see that the paper is wet and the writing is starting to smudge so you can no longer read the words.

Dive deeper and look back up again. The paper is dissolving into the ocean and now it is gone. As you swim deeper you find yourself resting on the seabed. It is calm and peaceful and still down here. No turbulence, no waves. Any notion of who you are or are not is just a distant memory left on the surface. Inhale and exhale. You are free. Deep down, beneath the words, beneath the ideas and judgements of yourself and others, you are perfect and whole just as you are. Allow yourself to really embrace what that feels like. To be truly free, to be truly yourself.

When you are ready, slowly float up to the surface and open your eyes.

Take your list and scrunch it up. If you'd like, you can throw it in the trash or even burn it and scatter the ashes. You don't need those labels any more. Your true self – the part of you that dived into the water – exists beyond and beneath all words. When you reside in her, you will feel utterly safe and loved.

....

This is a great exercise for when you're feeling off balance or upset. It's not necessary to repeat all of it, just imagine yourself diving deep down into your own internal ocean and resting there for a while until you feel restored. You can even add this calming imagery to your daily meditation practice.

Finding ourselves

Now that you have started to shed who and what you are *not*, the really exciting work of discovering who you really *are* can begin in earnest.

*'My true identity goes beyond the outer roles I play ... there is an
Authentic "I" within ... a divine spark within the soul.'*

SUE MONK KIDD

It's time to get curious – about yourself. Forget all those messages you may
have been given as a girl about not being nosy or not asking too many questions. Give yourself permission to question everything, assume nothing
and be ready to be amazed.

In my working life I was dedicated to uncovering the truth in the world
around me – first as a barrister, then as an investigative journalist – but it
was a whole new journey when I was told to start asking myself the
questions that I'd normally throw at others. I realised there were all sorts
of truths in my own life I didn't want to get too honest about for fear of
unravelling. Eventually I did, and that's when I discovered a new level of
emotional freedom.

JN

This is not a straightforward, linear process. You'll find false leads and dead
ends. You'll have surprises and tough choices.

Think of yourself as an archaeologist in your own life. Let curiosity be
the tool you dig with. Ask yourself questions as you would someone you were
studying. When was the last time you were really happy in your life? Why was
that? What music did you love in your teens and do you ever allow yourself to
listen to it now? What is your favourite food? What do you hate about your
life and what do you love? Write down your answers in your journal.

Sometimes we simply don't know. We've dulled our longings and our
wants out of necessity. They've become what often feels like a painful luxury.
But the truth is they are the nerve endings we need to bring back to life. So
listen out for the stirrings of what you love and what you want and then
expose and explore them.

There are no rules, and there's nothing that says what you discover has to be coherent or logical. Whoever said we had to make sense? We are all complex and multifaceted.

> Born in the US, I lived in London from the age of two. I naturally spoke with a British accent and felt British but was teased in school for being a 'Yank'. I wanted to fit in but was confused about where my loyalties lay because my parents were American and I loved the US – where the sun always seemed to shine and I was plied with candy. When I was 11, we moved to Michigan. I was so excited at the prospect of living in the land of milk-shakes and hamburgers. But the reality was, I was still the kid with the 'funny' accent. I eventually modulated my speech to fit in, but I still felt like the outsider and I deeply missed my other home.
>
> Today, I still feel torn – the UK has my heart and soul, but the US is in my genes. I've lived in London again now for 15 years and it is second nature to go back and forth with the accent depending on where I am and to whom I'm speaking. This has confused people along the way and the question of falseness has meant that I've had to look at it closely. It would be easy for me to attach a 'bad' label to my intentions or to judge myself as being disengenuous, but I've come to accept that adapting to my mixed cultural identity has been vital to my well-being, and despite the fact that it's confusing and awkward sometimes, I have come to own the reality that they are both the authentic me.
>
> *GA*

You may discover that you've abandoned your own desires and even your tastes for those of your family, friends or partner. Maybe it was easier that way or perhaps you never allowed yourself the space to develop your own likes and dislikes to begin with, and it was a relief to have a ready-made set of preferences handed to you. Or perhaps you never allowed yourself the chance to hope for what you really wanted because it seemed impossible to achieve.

Ask yourself: 'Whose life am I currently living? What would my life look like if I could have anything, be anything, do anything?'

These can be really scary questions to answer truthfully. Don't censor your answers or limit them with personal considerations. During this early stage, getting to know yourself can feel unsettling, daunting, even frightening. What if you're overwhelmed by longings and hopes that you suppressed in childhood? What if you discover you're married to the wrong person or that you hate what you do for a living? Or maybe you worry that you won't be able to do anything about what you find. Change of this magnitude can feel terrifying, but see if you can start to take small steps to move towards where you want to be. Fears will inevitably surface, and they can at first seem paralysing or overwhelming. Do your best to move through them at your own pace. Trust, just as you would if you were pregnant, that within you is a living, breathing being whom you are absolutely going to love.

Allowing yourself to discover your true longings will reset your internal sat nav. You can't even begin to get to where you'd love to be if you haven't yet entered the real destination.

Noticing and naming

'Seldom can it happen that something is not a little disguised or a little mistaken.'

JANE AUSTEN, *EMMA*

Noticing and *naming* are two of WE's most important tools. You'll be using them for the rest of this journey and hopefully the rest of your life. The answers lie within each and every one of us, and noticing and naming provide the mechanics with which we start finding them. Your journal will continue to be a valuable tool throughout this whole process, so keep it close for all these new discoveries.

Noticing

Noticing is like a flashlight in the dark – it leads you to awareness. Allow yourself to notice what's going on inside and around you. Don't judge it or be impatient for answers. Just be curious. You can't be honest about something you don't know exists. Noticing will bring insight. You'll spot contradictions, you'll spot inconsistencies, and then over time you'll start to spot what's congruent with the real you and what isn't.

Perhaps you don't actually want the promotion you've applied for because it will leave you with even less time with your kids, but you're scared to admit it lest you look like you're giving up on your feminist ideals.

Or maybe deep down you know you don't want children, but you pretend to be broody because you fear the dismay and pain coming clean will evoke in your parents or partner.

Remember ACT – Action Changes Things. Well, noticing is an action, so notice what you tell yourself, notice what you tell other people, notice how you feel, and allow yourself to become aware of what the reality of your life is.

Naming

Once you've noticed an uncomfortable reality, it can be easy to want to slip back into denial. If you spot buried and painful emotions or truths, it can be tempting to sweep what you've noticed right back under the carpet. Naming is how we stop denial from creeping back in.

Sometimes acknowledging what you've noticed feels like it will be enough, but it isn't. Things become more real when you name them. Write it down in your journal so it's there in black and white. If you have someone safe to talk to – a therapist, a non-judgemental friend, then say it aloud to her too.

Out the truth. Notice it and then name it – in writing and, if you can, out loud.

Of course, notice and name what brings you joy and peace too. Take nothing for granted. You are on a mission to chart your own internal territory. It is an eye-opening and profound experience being this honest. Do your best to embrace the process and enjoy the wonder of meeting yourself anew.

....

PEOPLE-PLEASING

It's natural to want to be liked and to want to be kind. But people-pleasing – saying yes when you mean no or pretending you like something when you don't – is a form of dishonesty. We all do it, but if we do it without noticing and naming it, sooner or later we lose sight of what we do actually want and need.

When we deny any aspect of ourselves we almost always pay a price further down the line. We may think we're being nice, but, as you'll discover when we get to looking at anger in the Third Principle (p. 115), often you're furious, boiling with rage, but simply don't know how to recognize or access it.

....

In 2016, I made public that I was offered half the amount my male co-star was offered for a job that is famously a 'duo' and an equal amount of work. I eventually got parity, but I knew that one day I would have to 'out' what happened for the sake of, well, women. I can't tell you how nervous it made me. Even though everyone on my team and everyone I had told since was shocked and appalled at the audacity, until the moment when it slipped out in an interview, every time I even thought about saying it publicly I felt afraid and nauseous. It was, I think, purely the fact that the subject of pay equality had been broached fairly recently and on a very public scale by numerous well-respected women in my industry that gave me the strength to get into it. Even though I'd had the same 'fight' for parity with the same network two decades earlier and won. Even though it was insulting and disrespectful and sexist of the company that I'd helped to accumulate billions. Even though it was the truth! I was afraid of angering The Man and embarrassing the WOMAN in charge.

GA

As you use noticing and naming to become more honest you'll inevitably discover parts of yourself or your life that you want to change. Try to resist doing anything right now. This early stage isn't the time to make major changes. This is simply the time to get honest with yourself about what areas of your life might need attention.

When you've completed all nine principles you'll be able to make whatever alterations you need. Answers to problems that at the moment seem intractable will come. For now, your job is just to notice and name what's within you.

It's no longer necessary to hide from truths that are inconvenient or difficult, because you are now on a path that will enable you to resolve them.

....

EXERCISE 3: Inconvenient Truths

....

This exercise will help you identify truths you may have had to bury. Take a moment now to write down in your journal anything in your life that you find difficult to be honest about because you wish it wasn't there. Ask yourself what you'd change if only you could. Maybe you don't want to stay in your job, but what on earth can you do about it? Maybe you haven't enjoyed sex with your partner for months or even years and don't know how to stop pretending. Or maybe you don't like the way a close friend treats you, but you don't want to have a row.

Maybe it's an aspect of yourself that you would rather avoid facing. Perhaps you keep ignoring the voice inside you that says you're drinking too much, or there's a conflict between how you think of yourself and how you behave.

Whatever it is, write it down. Don't let denial creep in and mask the truths that will lead you to a more fulfilled and meaningful life. The act of noticing and naming is all the action that is required of you right now. As you work through WE's principles you'll discover more truths – add them to your list whenever you spot them.

Don't panic about the things that feel wrong or impossible to deal with. The principles that follow will guide you to solutions. But all meaningful change begins in the same place: becoming honest with yourself. The truth will set you free, but only if you allow yourself to see it.

Feelings – the good and the bad

As you uncover issues and parts of yourself that have lain buried for years, you'll find some challenging feelings come with them. If you notice yourself feeling unusually sad, anxious, irritable or needy, these are signs that the process is working.

In the next principle you'll also be shown how to release difficult emotions, but for now focus on becoming aware of them by noticing and naming. The more conscious you become of your own internal landscape, the easier it will be to live with integrity.

To nurture yourself during this process try to be rigorous about your self-care. Make sure you're allowing time for the Essential Practices you learned earlier. Go through your checklist: have you written your gratitude list? Are you keeping to your two minutes (or longer) of meditation? Have you said your affirmations and are you getting enough food, rest and exercise? Now isn't the time to cut corners.

Taking care of yourself is the substructure of this serious work. That includes making sure you have the support around you that you need. That could be a counsellor, a support group or like-minded friends. Or if you know other women who want to apply these spiritual principles to their lives, you can explore supporting and encouraging each other. It's common for women in our culture to think it's strong to be self-reliant, but it's a signal of great strength when you are able to truly open yourself to receive. This is a *WE* process, not a *me* process – there are no medals for going it alone.

If you haven't found your sister travellers yet, you will. As you practise the principles in your life you'll find like-minded women are increasingly drawn to you. You don't need to make it happen. Keep walking this walk, stay open and it just will.

But remember, there's an important person who is already on this journey with you who can nurture you and encourage you through it – yourself.

Inner girl

When we're hysterical it's often historical. It's been estimated that 90 per cent of the distress we feel in the present can, in fact, be attributed to our past.[10]

Inside every one of us is a wounded self, carrying hurts and needs. If we're to have any hope of living honestly and happily, we need to learn how to soothe and heal ourselves.

Picture that wounded part of yourself as a small girl. You may think her feelings don't have influence because you've adapted so effectively to the adult world, but they're still there – just beneath the surface. Until they're uncovered and taken care of, you're at their mercy.

The time to get childhood needs met from your caregivers has now passed, but you can do the work yourself by showing that wounded inner girl the unconditional love she didn't get the first time round.

Talk to her – the frightened, hurt part of yourself. Encourage her, praise her and coach her through situations as you would your own child. Tell her she doesn't need to be scared, she's not alone, she's not abandoned – you are there to love, support and protect her. Talk to her out loud or if you're in public have a silent internal dialogue with her. This is your chance to re-parent yourself by replacing any harmful messages you got as a girl.

Take this process gently and at a pace that feels right for you. Powerful emotions can surface as you uncover these past wounds – and that's normal. If you feel at any time that it's becoming too much, it's important to seek support from a friend or a professional.

Just as with a real child who's clamouring for attention, if you take the time to meet her needs you'll find she settles down and lets you get on with whatever it is you're doing.

> When I find myself reacting to a situation in a way that is out of proportion to what is actually happening (which is still way too often) I try to have a silent dialogue with myself. I ask myself how old I'm feeling. An answer normally comes back pretty swiftly. Often it's three, sometimes it's six and sometimes I feel like a newborn baby. I then ask that younger part of myself what she needs, and I try to find ways of soothing and comforting her that are age-appropriate. It sounds crazy, but it really does work. Often I want to be held, so I'll either ask a friend for a hug or I'll wrap my arms around myself and give that younger 'me' a loving embrace. I'll chat to her (i.e. the younger part of myself) and tell her everything is going to be all right and that I'm here for her and that I love her – just as I would a real child. Once her needs are met I find that I've miraculously grown

myself back up again. The adult part of me can then get on with my day or respond to whatever is happening with the grace of a woman rather than with the tears or rage of a wounded child.

JN

Picture your inner girl each morning before you meditate and then try to carry a mental image of her held tight and safe in your heart as you go through the day. You could even start carrying a real-life photo of yourself at a young age in your purse.

Take your inner girl out to play whenever you can. The healing benefits are miraculous. Be curious. Find out what she likes and doesn't like because they will be clues to unlocking your joy. Try to give her a treat at least once a week. Maybe she likes to spend time in parks or listen to live music. Maybe she likes baking cookies or shaping figures out of clay. Have fun with her and allow her to breathe and be happy. Really get to know her as you would if you were fostering a young child. If you have children, let her play with them. The better care you take of your inner girl, the better you'll be able to respond to life's challenges with grace and maturity.

Both the good and the bad news about this journey is that you get to connect to a whole palette of feelings. Some are pleasant, some painful, but all of them are absolutely vital. They are the clues that will lead you back to yourself.

One of the main reasons we abandon parts of ourselves in the first place is to avoid painful feelings – not realizing, of course, that we're paying a far greater price in losing ourselves.

At some point along the way a therapist referred to my lack of self-care as neglect. When she said it I was shocked. That's a strong word. But she was right. I am and always have been the last person I take care of, if at all. I push myself so hard and pile so much onto my plate and have for so long that I don't know how to do it differently. I've barely paused to ask my adult self what I need, let alone my inner girl. But it is my inner girl and her fear from decades of being neglected by her adult self that is the real victim here. It is only when I stop to ask what she needs and how she would like to see things play out that I can see another way that involves space and gentleness and laughter.

GA

Trust the process

Some of us live in cultures, countries and communities where it simply isn't safe to be honest. Some of us grew up in families where we had to hide who we were to survive emotionally, and even decades after we've left home and the danger's long gone we can still struggle to reveal the truth. Sometimes it takes a lifetime to say, 'This is who I am. This is what I think. This is what I feel. This is what my body looks like and – you know what? – I'm happy about that!'

It takes as long as it takes. This journey back to ourselves is not over and done with in a finite period of time. More will be revealed to us about the parts of ourselves we've buried or abandoned, as well as the parts we thought were integral to us, but which it turns out were actually just ways of coping with life.

Ultimately our intention is to be ourselves wherever we are. We'll still be complex and multifaceted, but each aspect will be a reflection of our true selves, rather than characters we pretend to be. We may be less perfect, but we'll be a lot happier and a lot more real.

Honesty in the wider world

'There are no short cuts. Being true to yourself and what really counts is the only route that leads anywhere.'

DR SARAH FANE

Ultimately, telling the truth is for many of us a political as well as a personal act. It says, 'I'm real – not a stereotype.'

As women we've been obliged to hide our feelings and our desires for centuries. Although many of us now live in societies that are – on the face of it, at least – a lot more equal, it is still difficult for us to tell it as it is. To really be honest out loud with others.

It's a new muscle. Many of us have been conditioned to seek consensus rather than challenge it. That's one of the things that makes women so awesome to be around – we're not constantly picking fights for the sake of it, or entering into unnecessary competition. But it means that often we've lost the habit of speaking up.

At this early point in our journey our primary responsibility is to be truthful with ourselves, not to slip back into denial and lose ourselves again. But when you're ready you can start practising honesty out loud.

A good starting place is with the truths that are nearest to home. Imagine what it would be like if we all told the truth about what it is to be female.

If we stopped pretending to be fine when we felt vulnerable.

If we stopped hiding our needs so as to appear 'likeable'.

If we could say we found being a mother tough or that we hated breast-feeding while everyone around us said they loved it.

If we could speak openly about the menopause and what it involves.

If we could say that we hate online dating but are afraid of loneliness.

If we could talk about how it can be difficult or impossible to orgasm.

If we could talk about stress incontinence.

Imagine what would happen if we collectively decided it wasn't OK that we had to make ourselves look sexy in order to feel accepted; that we had to pretend we don't bleed or have body hair or unequal-sized breasts.

If we didn't feel we had to interrupt the ageing process to hold our place in the workforce or society.

Imagine if we each – one woman at a time – kindly but firmly said, 'Enough. No more pretending. This is who I really am.'

And once we've started to tell the truth about those aspects of ourselves that we've been made to feel aren't acceptable, we can start to tell it as it is in all sorts of other areas.

In the past, many of us tolerated injustice, discrimination or abuse for fear of rocking the boat. Increasingly we find we can no longer tolerate the unacceptable – we see it as a distorted form of people-pleasing.

It may not always be necessary to tell our truth out loud. We don't need to grandstand or court attention. Not all of us will be physically or economically safe enough to speak out. But when we are, and truth and honesty are called for, increasingly we'll find ourselves telling it as we see it.

Slowly but surely we'll find it harder not to speak out, and we'll discover that as we change, the world changes too.

Reflection

'Self-respect has nothing to do with the approval of others.'

JOAN DIDION

People-pleasing is a dangerous game. When I focus too much on others I abandon myself. I may start off by trying to be nice, but before I know it I'm just trying to be whoever I think the other person wants me to be.

Often my need for approval comes from unmet childhood needs. But if I spend my life trying to manipulate others into making up for it I will lose touch with who I really am.

Action: Today I will have the courage to be me, irrespective of what others think.

Affirmation: I am true to myself.

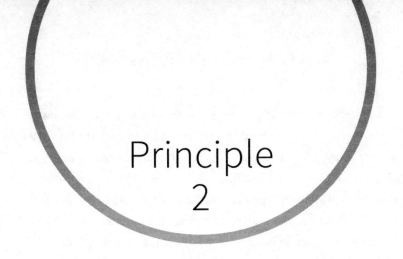

Principle
2

ACCEPTANCE:
Making Friends with What Is

'How wild it was, to let it be.'

CHERYL STRAYED

Acceptance gives us the ability to handle whatever life throws our way. It asks that we sit with what is – even when it's painful. In return it transforms our relationship with reality and enables us to find peace.

Life hurts. Sometimes it hurts unbearably. Few of us are called to this journey unless we've suffered heartache, and many of us arrive at its start laden down with loss and disappointment.

As adults we know that painful emotions are an inevitable part of being human. But what many of us don't realize is that much of the suffering we experience isn't inevitable at all. It comes from our not knowing how to use a vital spiritual principle – acceptance.

Like all of WE's principles, acceptance works just as well for the small things in life as it does for the big. You can use it to deal with minor irritations or howling pain. Whenever you find yourself struggling with difficult emotions or obsessing about how to change something, acceptance is the principle to reach for.

Surrender to win

'Surrender affirms that we are no longer willing to live in pain.'

DEBBIE FORD

Without acceptance we find ourselves in conflict with reality. We resist what is and then make ourselves the victims of it. We get stuck in the drama, the pain, and the rights and wrongs of what *should* and *could* have happened.

We spend our precious energy begging, pleading and fighting against our lot rather than working out what we can do about it, and in the process we generate a lot of unnecessary pain for ourselves and others.

This is true even when we have the best of motives. 'If you loved me, you'd stop drinking,' we tell an alcoholic loved one whom we know is powerless over their addiction to alcohol. 'Please come back,' we beg an ex who's clearly moved on. We become attached to outcomes and when we can't make them happen we're miserable. Even if it's just the rush-hour gridlock or the rain, our default response is to rail against it and want it to be otherwise.

This approach to life doesn't work. It leaves us emotionally battered and unhappy.

Being in conflict with reality is no different from banging your head against a brick wall and wondering why it hurts. Until you accept that the wall is there, you'll get bruised again and again and again. But once you accept it's there, you begin to have choices. You can work out how to get over it, under it or round it. Or you might decide to grow roses against it or to use it for shade.

···

SERENITY, PLEASE

The Serenity Prayer by Reinhold Niebuhr is used by millions of people all over the world. You don't have to have any sort of faith to benefit from it. At its heart is a simple formula – change what you can and accept what you can't. When you apply it to your life you can feel at peace no matter what is happening. If you find yourself obsessing about a problem, instead of trying to work it out in your head, repeat this prayer to yourself:

'Grant me the serenity to accept the things I cannot change, the courage to change the things I can, and the wisdom to know the difference.'

···

Acceptance is a process that we often have to repeat again and again.

You don't need to believe that acceptance will help for it to work. You just have to be willing to give it a try. When you apply it to your life – no matter how imperfectly – things miraculously get a whole lot easier.

Acceptance takes real courage. It ultimately involves grieving losses you'd rather deny. It involves hitting the pause button, so that you can feel whatever you need to feel and then not only let go of how you wish reality was, but ultimately make friends with it, just as it is.

Until you accept things as they are rather than as you'd like them to be, you'll remain stuck in a prolonged emotional tantrum, battling with what's happened. It doesn't mean you like how things are. Acceptance isn't capitulation or resignation. It's a vital step in the process of transformation and finding peace.

It's only once you've accepted reality – shorn of your wishes and wants – that you can start to bring about change.

Whether you're struggling with a break-up, a loved one's habits or behaviours, or just the daily rough and tumble of living, acceptance provides a new way of handling life that brings lasting emotional freedom.

EXERCISE 1: The Acceptance Cup

For this exercise you'll need your journal and a cup (an empty pot or jar will do just as well). Draw a large 'A' on the front of your cup – nail varnish works a treat – and, if you have the time and inclination, decorate it.

Take a moment to centre yourself and then make a list of anything that is upsetting you right now. It can be large or small. A rejection or a loss. Anything that, when you think of it, makes you feel a live jolt of emotion. You don't need to write explanations – just a word or name to denote what you've found that hurts.

You don't need to re-feel what you're writing down – this isn't about getting stuck in your emotions – think of it more as detective work. What you're jotting down are clues. Keep going until no other charged thoughts come to you.

If you do find yourself becoming upset, pause to do something kind for yourself – perhaps take a short walk or make a cup of tea.

If you're someone who shuts down and finds it hard to know what you feel, then ask yourself, 'What would I be feeling sad about if I let myself?' Perhaps a bereavement or loss, or something you wish had turned out differently.

Once you've come to the end of your list, it's time to start the acceptance process. Look over each item and ask yourself this one simple question: 'Is there anything I can do about this situation?'

If there is, jot down on a separate to-do list any actions you could take. Try to be brutally honest. Often we're tempted to imagine we can change things we have no control over. You may want to check your to-do list with someone you trust to make sure that you're being really honest.

If there is nothing you can do – or you're not sure – write the letter 'A' beside the entry: 'A' stands for Accept.

Now look at every item that has an 'A' beside it. You'll find they are all linked by a common characteristic: they are all things over which you have no control. Absorb that fact. When we're most in pain it's often because we're trying to change something that we are powerless over.

One by one, tear off each item that has an 'A' beside it and place it in your cup. As you do, take a moment to acknowledge that it is painful to accept this loss or sad feeling, but that there is nothing you can do. Try not to get sucked into the pain. Just nod to it, as you would to a familiar face or acquaintance, and say, 'This is as it is.'

Accept with your heart as well as your mind that you are powerless. Surrender. Give up the fight and allow yourself to experience the relief of not having to be in control.

You are handing over the person, situation or event to the flow of life, which is deeper and stronger than you are.

Put your Acceptance Cup somewhere safe and use this process whenever you bump up against a situation you can do nothing about. If you find yourself dwelling upon any of the items in your cup, remind yourself that it is not yours to worry about or to fix now.

When we let go of a problem it creates the space for solutions to appear.[11]

Accepting 'what is' is like letting go of the rope in the middle of a tug of war. You remain standing and what you've been battling with falls to the ground.

Once you agree to stop being in conflict with reality and accept it just as it is, you'll experience a huge shift.

That doesn't mean you like or condone what is. It isn't about saying something is OK when it really isn't. But peace of mind will elude you until you let go of bargaining with things that you can't change.

The things we can't change

We can't change the past and yet many of us spend years thinking about how things could or should have been. When we accept that the past has happened and there's nothing we can do about it we give ourselves permission to move into the present.

Similarly we can't really change people, places and things. When we try to control someone or something, even if it's with the best of intentions, we often end up being controlled by that other person, thing or situation. We abandon ourselves in pursuit of an outcome and rob ourselves of the chance to find peace.

So if you find yourself struggling with one of these, ask yourself whether there's something in the situation that you need to accept and if there is, get your Acceptance Cup out and use the process you've just learned in the exercise to free yourself.

The more we start to accept the things we can't change in our lives, the more effective we become at changing the things we can – our own attitudes and actions.

When we're able to bring the focus back to what we do have power over we can then connect to our own sense of power and grace.

EXERCISE 2: Step into Your Light

This exercise will help you to stay in your personal power. Find yourself a space where you won't be disturbed. Stand with your feet hip-width apart so you feel stable and grounded. Close your eyes and imagine that a spotlight is shining down on you. The light is warm and bright and full of love. You are standing in a shower of affection and warmth. You are standing in the glory of being you and it feels right, enough and very, very good.

Now imagine drawing a circle on the ground around the edge of where the light falls. If you were to hold out your arms and turn in a circle, the light would reach about that far from you in all directions and encircle you. Inside your circle is what you can control – yourself.

On the other side of the line is darkness and, within it, all the things that you can't control. Every time you step outside of your light to try to change a person, place or thing, you abandon yourself and step into darkness. Sometimes you may mistake someone else's light as your own for a time. When you enter the dark you lose yourself and your power. When you stay in your light all things are possible.

Imagine for a moment that you are stepping out of your light to try to force someone else to see things your way. Feel how destabilizing it is and how your power fades. Now step back into your light and re-experience the feeling of standing in the warmth of love and wholeness. Feel how empowering it is. Enjoy standing there for as long as you like. Breathe it in. Savour its richness. Try to connect with this feeling during your daily meditations.

As you go through your week, notice when you step out of your power. For instance when you find yourself experiencing pain or discomfort, look at where your feet are – have you stepped into someone else's circle? If so, step back into your own light. Return home and know that you are loved and that all things are possible.

Accepting responsibility

As women, we often accept responsibility for things that aren't our fault. This can be a convenient but destructive way to avoid reality. If you label something as being your fault, then you don't have to accept that the other person just may not be able to give you what you want or need. If you pretend to yourself that you're the cause of another person's dysfunction or cruelty, you may be keeping hope alive but the waltz of denial will have you avoiding responsibility for yourself and likely causing yourself excruciating pain.

Acceptance allows us to stop making excuses and start making tough calls. Do you want peace of mind or just to carry on taking the path of least resistance? Yes, you can go to a party your ex is throwing, if you really *are* OK with the pain that will induce. You can say yes to a promotion you don't want in order to get the pay rise, but you have to be willing to accept the frustration, stress and lack of spare time that comes with it. You can date someone you're not attracted to, in order to avoid feeling lonely, but only if you're willing to deal with the pain that it will generate for both of you further down the line.

Acceptance asks that we get real about what we're up to and accept our truth now, rather than spinning fictions for ourselves, or others.

Accepting reality

The principles build upon and support one another. For instance, honesty and acceptance walk hand in hand — you can't solve a problem unless you admit it exists. And you can't get over an emotion that you're denying you're even feeling, so stay vigilant for any signs of self-deception.

Whenever you feel uncomfortable, notice and name the feeling and then get honest about what you might not want to accept. For example, if you notice you feel really crazy when you spend time with a particular person or in a specific environment, name it to avoid slipping into denial or self-blame, or trying to fix it when it may have nothing to do with you. When you find yourself constantly excusing someone else's behaviour, notice and name it. Again, you may quietly think, 'It's me,' when someone repeatedly disappoints you or stands you up. Noticing and naming opens you up to accepting the reality that he or she is unreliable.

None of this is about blame or judgement. It's just about getting truthful, connected and real. That's not to say you won't feel furious and rebellious about what you're noticing and naming. It's entirely natural not to want to accept that your partner is an addict, that someone you love is ill, or that you can't change a decision that an institution or a politician has made.

If you find that you're experiencing a lot of resistance, try accepting that you are refusing to accept. Often *wanting to want to* will be enough to begin the process.

Feelings – the price tag for acceptance

'No one likes crying, but tears water our souls.'

XINRAN

Acceptance is the gateway to peace of mind, but there's one very powerful reason we resist it – our feelings.

The majority of us try to avoid or minimize our emotional pain. In fact, for many of us, avoidance of our feelings has become a way of life.

But as difficult and as painful as those emotions are, in order to access the miraculous peace that acceptance brings we need to learn how to negotiate them.

Living on the run – avoidance

'We bury things so deep we no longer remember there was anything to bury. Our bodies remember. Our neurotic states remember. But we don't.'

JEANETTE WINTERSON

Often instead of feeling our pain we act as though emotional discomfort is some kind of subterranean monster we can trap beneath constant activity and motion.

Maybe we do it with substances, over- or under-eating, or spending hours online. Perhaps we avoid it by compulsively socializing or over-scheduling so there are no nasty gaps through which the pain can emerge. We might hide in work or parenting. If you're already on a spiritual path, you might use your journey as a form of avoidance – constantly looking for new tools and new teachers to help you avoid pain rather than feel it.

Even self-hatred can be a form of avoidance. The pain hits and you immediately start trying to work out what you've done wrong. You beat yourself up and imagine that if you were smarter or prettier or luckier you wouldn't have to feel what you're feeling. Maybe you try to change your body so you'll be a bit more lovable. Perhaps you buy another self-help book and make a fresh set of resolutions that you fail to keep. We thrash around us looking for answers to give the illusion of control.

Other times we get drawn into the drama of our story and find ourselves bogged down in blame and self-pity. We feel hard done by, wronged or rejected. We start to believe that fate has stacked the odds against us. We'll never get what we want and need. 'See?' we say. 'I'm not worthy of good things' or 'Nothing good ever happens to me.'

We blame ourselves and we blame others. We may blame our parents, our friends, politicians or life events. We try to change things. We try to find satisfaction, and when that doesn't work, if we're not careful, we descend into a negative spiral of despair.

In an attempt to avoid feeling we obsess about what might have been and torture ourselves with thoughts of 'if only'. We make deals in our head as if we can control reality with our thoughts alone.

Some of us deny we're hurting at all. 'I'm OK,' we'll say. 'It doesn't bother me really.' Then, when the pain breaks through our protective wall of denial, we deny it all the more vociferously.

The problem is that not only does avoidance not work, but it actually makes things worse.

The two types of emotional pain

When it comes to emotional pain there are no shortcuts. It has to be felt. If we try to duck out of experiencing our natural feelings, we don't escape them at all; instead, they just mutate into something more damaging.

Also, what many of us don't realize is that there are two kinds of emotional pain. One is the legitimate pain of being alive – *real pain*. The other – *synthetic pain* – is highly toxic and yet most of us live with it on a daily basis.

Real pain

Real pain is the price we pay for being members of this extraordinary race. At its most extreme it is the anguish at the loss of a loved one or the betrayal of a lover. It can sweep over us like a storm. At other times it's a prick of disappointment that burrows under our skin like a splinter.

The only healthy way out is to move through it. But as difficult as that path can be, when we emerge we find that not only can we endure and survive, but we are infinitely stronger for it.

Synthetic pain

Synthetic pain is an impostor. It is real emotional pain's toxic clone, and while it feels urgent and necessary, there is nothing noble or inevitable about it. While feeling real emotional pain is ultimately healing and leads to growth, compassion and wisdom, synthetic pain leaves us stuck and riddled with anxiety, resentment and regret.

Synthetic pain is what we experience when we try to bargain with or avoid reality by refusing to accept what is. It is to real pain what self-pity is to grief, or resentment is to anger. Think of real pain as being akin to the pain of giving birth – it's agony but productive. Synthetic pain is what you'd feel if you crossed your legs and tried to prevent yourself going into labour.

Telling the difference between real and synthetic pain

When we're in real pain we feel it in our body: our guts, our solar plexus, our hearts. But synthetic pain resides in our heads.

Obsessive thinking – replaying an event or situation – is a symptom of synthetic pain. Our minds can resemble a tumble dryer, tossing things around and around and around to try to get a different outcome. We can think we're trying to solve a problem through the power of our intellect, but usually we're digging ourselves deeper and deeper into a painful mental rut.

Obsessive thinking is an attempt to bridge the gap between how we wish things were and how they actually are. We keep a fantasy alive in our thoughts to avoid the feelings that need to be felt and the actions that need to be taken.

For example, instead of leaving an abusive situation, we may obsess about how we wish it were better. Instead of accepting that something we longed for hasn't happened, we may replay events over and over again, hoping that we can make the outcome different through the sheer power of our thoughts. Bargaining is a natural part of the grieving process, but if we're not careful we can get stuck in it, avoiding legitimate sorrow and replacing it with layers of toxic synthetic pain.

....

THE FIVE STAGES OF GRIEF

While each of us will find our own unique way to journey through grief and loss, most of us will go through what are now commonly known as the five stages of grief: denial, anger, bargaining, depression and acceptance. Often we find ourselves moving back and forth among the first four stages before we finally get to number five. Acceptance won't reverse our loss, but it does bring us peace.[12]

....

A toxic legacy

When we fail to feel our *real pain* it remains buried alive inside us. Sometimes we suppress our emotions so effectively that we don't know they're there – but our bodies always know. These feelings manifest in our lives as illness, chronic unexplained pains, anxiety or rage. They lie dormant until they're suddenly ignited and we find ourselves losing all perspective and self-control.

The good news is that when we step out of avoidance and into acceptance, we can begin to defuse the emotional landmines from our past that can trigger distorted emotional reactions in our present. As we release the bottled-up pain gradually and appropriately, we find we are no longer victims of our histories.

When emotions are functioning healthily they act as your guide. They'll tell you when to protect yourself and when to let down your guard and become intimate; when to say yes, when to say no and when to say you're not sure.

Notice, name, feel and release

Hopefully you're starting to get the hang of noticing and naming as initial steps to identifying your feelings. The next steps are to actually *feel* and then *release* them, enabling you to access a whole new level of emotional freedom and making it much easier to practise acceptance.

Notice, name, feel and release is not an intellectual process, it is physical. To practise it you need to become present to what is happening in your body so that you can start to expose the truth of who you are. It is a tool we should all have learned at school, but instead most of us were encouraged to bury our feelings and pull ourselves together.

In order to feel and release emotions you have to allow yourself to experience them without a story, with only the physical sensation in your body as your guide.

Initially, you can use the following exercise to feel and release. In no time at all, you'll find yourself incorporating the process into your everyday life. Sometimes you'll do it in the moment, while at other times you may have to pause and wait until you have the space and safety you need. But from now on you'll have a technique that will enable you to feel your emotions and move through them to a place of acceptance of what is.

EXERCISE 3: Feeling and Releasing

This is a great exercise for any time you need to free yourself from difficult or painful emotions.

Lie down somewhere quiet and safe. Close your eyes and take five deep breaths in and out. Now imagine that your mind is a laser and send it down into your body to explore. Allow it to scan, looking for areas of tension. When it finds one, let its light rest there. Try to breathe into it, into the knot of tension that it has found. If that knot were a feeling, what would it be?

Eastern medicine practitioners would say that if it is in your neck or shoulders it might be anger, as this emotion often gets trapped there just before the point of release – that is before it gets out of your mouth. If it's in your chest it may be sorrow – that's how heartbreak got its name. If it's in your stomach, it's likely to be fear – no different from having a knot in your tummy before an exam or presentation.

Breathe into each feeling that you encounter. Let your mind remain silent. If you're stuck as to what you might be feeling, see if your inner girl is around (pp. 84–7). She's likely to know the answer. Ask her if she's OK. If not, what is she feeling and why? Trust the first answer you get back; it's often right.

When you've worked out what feelings your tensions are holding, breathe deeply into every one of them until each knot has started to diminish. You might need to release a few tears as well. Let them flow. There's no need for thoughts to get involved. Now isn't the time for words. You're diving down beneath the narratives you tell yourself. Just feel and release. Feel and release.

It's important to take this work at your own pace and pause if you start to feel overwhelmed. There's no need to push yourself – it's important to take this journey one step at a time.

Pause for a moment to congratulate yourself each time you allow yourself to notice, name, feel and release your emotions. You're doing a beautiful thing, not just for yourself, but also for the people in your life. Imagine how many times you have said or done something hurtful because you haven't taken the time to address what's really going on for you. Imagine what it might be like to make this a regular practice so that you can move into your life from a more grounded, connected and less agitated or distracted place.

This is an exercise you can come back to whenever you have noticed and named feelings that need to be felt and released. If you have limited time or are worried about being overwhelmed you can set a timer for 5–10 minutes. Or you may choose to take as long as you need to process what surfaces. Either way, release whatever comes up and be gentle with yourself when you've finished the exercise.

This is a journey. Each principle enables you to take more steps in the direction of wholeness. What you're learning and practising is vital to a life of integrity and meaning. This is important work. When you take responsibility for your own emotions you can be a better parent, partner, daughter, sister or friend. It also becomes easier to forgive others when they are unable to process their emotions because, in this simple exercise, you have come face to face with your human-ness and your vulnerability, and shown compassion to yourself.

When I'm having really strong feelings I sometimes remind myself that I've given birth to children and treat the feelings as I did labour pains. I breathe into the heart of whatever is hurting me. Trying to think my way out of the pain of a contraction would never have worked and it's the same for getting through difficult emotions. Thinking just puts off the feeling and stores up masses of synthetic and toxic pain. Of course, I still try to bargain with reality or enter into judgement about what should or shouldn't be happening, but increasingly I find myself remembering that there's no point – until I've released whatever feelings need to be felt, I'll be off centre, and my perspective will be distorted.

JN

....

DRAMA QUEEN

In feeling and releasing, your goal is not to prove to yourself, or to anyone else, how upset you are. It is to allow the feelings to pass through you, just as you would a fever or a bout of physical pain. As described earlier, getting too caught up in the drama of a situation is another way of avoiding real pain or the solutions to it.

When we witness friends doing this, it can sometimes feel disloyal not to join in and agree that, yes, things are really awful. But jumping into the maelstrom can destabilize your newfound process. Next time, take a deep breath and see what happens if you don't participate in feeding the fire of their distress. You can still be there as a calm, loving presence, but you don't need to take part in their production.

....

It may be the case that you can't actually work out what it is you're feeling. You try noticing and naming, but nothing recognizable comes up to feel and release. If you've spent a lot of time trying not to feel, it's completely natural to have difficulty working out what it is you do feel – all you know is that you feel bad. And if you're depressed, your feelings may be buried quite deeply.

Don't panic. If you create the space, they will start to surface when they are ready.

Remember that you'll find your feelings in your body, not in your head. Many of us have grown up thinking that thoughts and feelings are one and the same. Part of this process is learning to distinguish between them. Later on, in the Sixth Principle (p. 183), the focus will be on stilling your mind, but for now your concern is with feeling what needs to be felt so that you can move into acceptance.

In the meantime, if your head starts throwing in unhelpful or negative thoughts – that you'll never feel better, or you'll always be alone – try to ignore them as you would a noisy neighbour or a loud drill. It is, in fact, just noise.

....

SHAKE AND RELEASE

If you've ever watched two ducks fight on a lake, you'll notice that when it's over, the ducks shake their wings, and then swim away. The shaking serves a biological need: it releases the stress chemicals that built up during the fight.[13] Similarly, possums play dead when a predator is near and after the danger passes, they'll shudder to release the stress chemical.

Whenever we've had an argument or bad news, we too can experience the feeling and then shake our arms and legs to release the stress. We can go for a walk or a run. We can play music and dance. What we don't want is the trauma staying trapped in our system, so take your lead from the animal kingdom – shake, release and move on.

....

Changing what we can (accept and thrive)

'If you don't risk anything, you risk even more.'

ERICA JONG

When you move through your feelings and into acceptance you'll discover you have the space to focus on the things you have the power to change. Or as the Serenity Prayer puts it, you'll start to be able to 'change the things you can' (p. 93).

You can change your outlook, your attitude, your responses to life and your actions and reactions. You'll discover that when you practise acceptance, answers exist right alongside the problems you've been fixating on, you just haven't known where to look for them. You'll notice many doors that are open and available to you that you just didn't see before – often because you were so busy focusing on the one that had closed.

You may, of course, have to wait to see the answer or the open door before you take further action. Waiting is an action in its own right. As you wait, you get ready. You let go of what you can't change to make way for a life full of possibility.

Many of us have spent years wanting our lives to be different. When we release ourselves from that burden and accept ourselves and our lives as they really are, anything becomes possible. Before long, amazing things will come to pass.

....

ENJOY, CHANGE OR ACCEPT

Life is not an endurance test, although it can often feel like it – especially at the start of this journey. Over time we discover that there are three options in any situation: enjoy, change or accept. Notice that *endure* isn't one of them! The first choice is always enjoyment, but when that isn't possible we either change the situation or practise acceptance.

....

Many years ago, I was in so much emotional pain that I sought out a spiritual teacher to help me get to the other side of it. This teacher had written a book that, among other things, was about transmuting emotional pain. I discovered he was holding a retreat and, armed with his book, made my way towards it. It took two planes and a long car ride with many others heading to the same place, but I was so focused on my story of loss that I didn't lift my head out of the book for the entire journey. It was as if somehow the words alone were holding me together and the planes in the air. This 'stance' of mine continued for the first couple of days. I absorbed and was moved by the teacher's talks, but was so locked in my head and my pain that I barely managed to engage with anyone, struggled to make eye contact and definitely didn't acknowledge the beauty of the landscape around me. I was supposedly there to release, but I was completely unable to experience the joy that was manifesting for others before my eyes.

On the third day I received an invitation to a one-on-one meeting with the teacher. I was very excited, I had so many questions and was sure that he would be able to see the particular 'depth' of my story and help me towards understanding why it was so painful. I was led to the teacher's cabin and there he was – this little man with bright smiling eyes – the embodiment of pure love, pure joy and presence. I sat before him looking deeply into his eyes, gathering my questions, and there in the presence of what many agree is an embodiment of higher consciousness, I suddenly had nothing to say. All the questions melted away and meant nothing. They were all based in ego and my inability to let go and just be with what was.

In that moment there was nothing wrong. Nothing was happening to me. I was not ill or being tortured by anyone – except myself by perpetually hashing over and over the wrongs and the misunderstandings, the self-pity and the pain. I left that cabin with the broadest smile on my face and the deepest sense of joy I have ever experienced. Not a word had been spoken. More miraculously, I was then able to face the 'painful' circumstances in my life with nothing but love and acceptance. There was no more story left; it had been transformed.

GA

We will all notch up losses and heartaches as we walk through life, but when we allow ourselves to feel the necessary pain and learn the accompanying lessons, we grow in dignity, grace and wisdom. They become part of our journey and in time we discover that what we've suffered can be used to help someone else.

We come to understand that real pain can make us useful as a midwife for another woman's sorrow or fear. When this happens we start to regret less what we've lived through. Any residual feelings of hopelessness and victimization start to fade as we realize we are taking our place in a chain of women – stretching back through history – who have felt deeply and been there to hold a light for another walking in darkness.

Acceptance in the wider world

Politically, the idea of acceptance can bring up strong reactions. Because in many cultures and in many different ways we, as women, lack power and freedom, we are often forced to accept the unacceptable.

But this principle is not about accepting the unacceptable. It is about coming to terms with the problem, however ugly, so that we can begin to change it.

As the old saying goes: when it's raining, let it. Once you've stopped trying to prevent the raindrops from falling, you can put up an umbrella and take shelter while the storm passes. Or, better still, find a way of collecting and reusing the water!

Our goal as activists is simple: to reduce the amount of avoidable suffering that exists in the world. Practising acceptance in our own lives prepares us for the work ahead.

You can start right now by feeling what needs to be felt, avoiding self-made dramas and then making yourself available to walk with another as she does the same.

How different and more peaceful would the world be if we all took responsibility for feeling our sorrows? If we sought change from a position of wholeness and spent our energy on the issues where we can really make a difference?

Reflection

> *'The greatest illusion we have is that denial protects us. It's actually the biggest distortion and lie. In fact, staying asleep is what's killing us.'*
>
> EVE ENSLER

I used to think that accepting reality was giving up the fight. I didn't want anything to do with it – I wanted a world where pain and suffering didn't exist. Now I know that when I accept life on life's terms I can find peace no matter what.

Action: Today I will embrace life as it is and feel whatever emotions need to be felt.

Affirmation: My feelings guide me home.

Principle
3

COURAGE:
Ending the Victim Trap

'We don't develop courage by being happy every day. We develop it by surviving difficult times and challenging adversity.'

BARBARA DE ANGELIS

Courage is the principle that frees us from our past. It enables us to live fully in the present by shedding the stories and unresolved anger that can keep us trapped. It puts us firmly on the path to whole-hearted, authentic living.

This is not the courage of the stories we heard in childhood, which often focused on public (and almost exclusively male) acts of heroism – complete with dragons and angry crowds. The courage that's called for here is no less brave, but it's far more profound. It involves becoming the heroine of our own life and rescuing ourselves from the internal mechanisms that have held us captive.

Without courage we remain trapped by attitudes and habits that reinforce our sense of powerlessness and we risk being the victims rather than the heroines of our lives.

The story trap

'Life shrinks or expands in proportion to one's courage.'

ANAÏS NIN

The word 'courage' derives from the French word for 'heart' – *coeur*. In each of our hearts are stories that we think define and protect us, but in fact keep us trapped.

As we start to notice and name the emotions, masks and labels we've accumulated, we become more aware of the stories that lie beneath them.

Our stories are based on our experiences and our attitudes to them. They're the narratives through which we try to understand and make sense of our lives, and they're part of what makes us human. The problem is that they're rarely accurate. They're almost always distortions of the truth that can leave us feeling as if we're victims of events.

Your story is not who you are, but it is often who you *think* you are. It is one of the tricks the ego plays on us. And the stories each of us have about ourselves separate us from our real self, leaving us struggling to feel at ease in our own skin.

Plus, we don't have just one story. We have entire collections that we layer over each other, fundamentally distorting how we see ourselves.

Of course, not all our stories are bad. But it doesn't actually matter whether it is good or bad; if it's a story, it's not actually the truth. It's a racket – a subterfuge under which our real self hides.

It takes courage to step out from behind these yarns and own your reality. Even when our stories hurt us we can be reluctant to let go of them because we don't know who we'll be without them – our sense of identity has become so entangled with them.

'Who am I,' we might wonder, 'if I'm not the child who was neglected or the woman whose partner deceived her?' Who are we if we're not the mothers who gave up everything for their children and then were abandoned when they left home without a backward glance?

Who are we if we let go of everything that might have been or we believe should have been? Fundamentally, who are we if we shed our wounds and our defences? This path is about finding out. But before we can find out who we are, we have to summon the courage to let go of pretending to be who we are not.

....

EXERCISE 1: What's Your Story?
....

This exercise has two parts. The first will help you to identify and shed the stories that keep you trapped. The second gives you a wonderful tool to transform them.

Part I: Identify your story

Have your journal ready. Take five deep breaths to centre yourself. What is your dominant story? This isn't the story you'd give at a job interview or if you were speed dating. It's more likely what you'd say if you were having a heart-to-heart with a kindred spirit or a first session with a therapist.

117

Your story will have an emotional 'charge' to it – usually sadness, regret or anger. It will hurt.

It may centre on a childhood event, or a loss. Or it could be that you've been single for a long time, had an abusive marriage or have never been able to conceive.

Often it feels as if our stories about ourselves are hardwired. They are tattoos or brands burned into our souls – something that we'll never be able to change or erase.

Once you've identified a dominant story, sit down and write it out in your journal. Write it over and over, as if you were a child writing lines: 'I was abandoned as a girl', 'I'm a single mother', 'I'm long-term unemployed', 'I was left', 'I was betrayed'. Write it over and over again until it becomes as meaningless as any phrase does when it's repeated enough.

You may need to cry while you write it. But write through the tears, write through the pain, and write until you are out the other side and then still keep writing. Write until there is no emotional charge left to what you are writing and then, once it feels as if the pain has gone, write another full page's worth. Write until it is as meaningless as gibberish, because that is what it is.

You might think it's damaging to keep repeating a negative message, but the odds are you've been reinforcing it all along, countless times a day – to yourself and to everyone you meet – whether you were aware of it or not.

We tell our stories over and over again until they are worn out. We repeat them and repeat them, often until we die. Writing it out over and over again like this is an intervention. You drain the emotion out of it so that you are left with empty words on the page. But within those empty words, which feel like history, is hidden vital information that you can use to finally set yourself free.

Now it's time to mine the gold that lies at its heart.

Part II: Rewrite your story

Look closely at the sentence you wrote in the last exercise. It contains a message for you. What is the belief about yourself that lies within it? Not the detail, but the essence.

If your story is that you're alone, perhaps your underlying belief is that you are worthless or unlovable. Perhaps it's that you're just plain unlucky or doomed in some way. If you recognize the message as one you were given in childhood, that's a clue, because that's when most damaging messages are imprinted.

You'll know when you say it to yourself that it's true in the same way that you know you've got a splinter. The source is a sharp, clear pain.

Now write yourself an affirmation based on that sentence. You may have written one before, but if not, it should be short, simple, positive and stated in the present tense. It's not a statement of longing; it's a statement of fact. Here are some examples, but it's better to tailor one for yourself:

I exist.

I am loved.

I am resilient and strong.

I am perfect just the way I am.

I am enough.

Put it where you can see it – maybe on a Post-it note stuck to the edge of your computer screen, your bathroom mirror, your car dashboard or inside your journal or iPad cover. Say your affirmation whenever you start to wobble or revert to your story or the emotional reactivity or shut down that comes with it. Use it as a spiritual shield to protect yourself through-out your day.

Notice how many times a day you're tempted to draw on your story as a resource for defining yourself. Perhaps you're in a queue for lunch and someone pushes in front of you – 'I'm invisible' might pop into your head. Or perhaps you hear that you haven't been invited to a party that others you know will attend. You might automatically think, 'I'm unlovable'. Or 'I'm alone' might occur to you. Use your affirmation to neutralize and replace your story.

....

For many years, whenever I was doing a mundane task like cleaning or packing, there would be a constant argument in my head. I would be defending myself about something or telling somebody what I really wanted them to know about themselves – whatever it was, it was fraught and I was in attack mode. Fortunately, that is no longer my experience, but it reveals something about where my head was and what was essentially my default stance in the world.

Today what I notice more is my attachment to a particular story. It's more likely to be something that I want someone to feel sorry for me about. The refrain of 'poor me' or 'you don't understand'. Sometimes it heads into 'how dare you' territory. Much of it is an attachment to being right.

When I notice that this type of thinking has taken over, I need to interrupt it. It becomes important to get to the root of why I feel misunderstood. It's really easy to allow something like that to fester and to replay my side of events over and over in my head. Undoubtedly, that type of built-up emotion will in turn affect everything I do and get projected into my conversations with everyone I come into contact with. How can it not?

GA

Our stories keep us captive and mesmerized. We're like hostages who've become bonded to our captors. It takes courage to break the bond.

If you find yourself tempted to tell your story – good or bad – remind yourself: 'This is just a story, these are just words. The real truth is that I am [loved/worthy/beautiful/a regular human being]' and then carry on with your day. Your ego may put up a fight and want to revert to its version of you, but firmly and kindly use your affirmation to protect yourself from damaging narratives.

Be vigilant. Like weeds, stories can grow back, but if you're disciplined you'll start to see results. You'll experience a sense of possibility and expansiveness. You'll start to recognize your true nature, the essential self that doesn't change and isn't shaped by events or challenges. You'll start to see the truth.

Yet no matter how much awareness we practise, sooner or later we're likely to pick up another story, so use the previous exercise whenever you have a persistent negative thought or tale in your mind. Interrupt it and neutralize it with an affirmation. The only story that ultimately serves you is that you are enough just as you are.

The story I carried with me from growing up in an alcoholic home was that I was invisible. I told myself that nobody saw me and nobody cared, and I discounted any evidence to the contrary. I took the story into adulthood. No matter how many people watched me reporting on TV, no matter how many friends I had, deep down I felt as if I didn't exist. I was a leaky sieve – as soon as I was filled up with attention, it drained out again and I needed more. My childhood story drove me into a life of constant striving for more and more success and love that was doomed to fail.

My most recent Post-it says simply, 'I exist.' Every time I'm tempted to people-please or do too much, I remind myself, 'I exist.' I don't need to do, say or prove anything to justify my space in this life or to be worthy of love. I exist whether I do or do not clear a particular hurdle I've chosen for myself. I exist whether or not I'm told by anyone else that I'm wonderful or that I'm loved. Pure and simple, I exist.

JN

Having started the practice of freeing ourselves from our stories, we now turn to the courageous work of freeing ourselves from the resentments we've accumulated.

Expect resistance. As with our stories we often become attached to our resentments, despite the devastating harm they cause.

Releasing anger safely

'Holding on is believing that there's only a past; letting go is knowing that there's a future.'

DAPHNE ROSE KINGMA

When we don't process our anger properly at the time it arises, it can fester and has the potential to poison our outlook and our lives.

Anger is a vital and necessary emotion. It drives us to protect ourselves and others, to set boundaries, to say enough is enough. When harnessed properly, it can drive change in our own lives and in the wider world. But for a host of reasons, many of us have problems feeling and expressing anger in a healthy way. There have been social taboos against women being angry. We still risk being dismissed as hysterical, shrill or strident. For example, think of former prime minister David Cameron's dismissive 'Calm down, dear' to a female colleague in the House of Commons. Or the highly personalised criticisms levelled at Hillary Clinton that would never have been levelled at a male colleague.

Similarly, for many women it isn't safe to be visibly angry – either culturally or if confronted by an abusive partner.

Even if you're alone, it can be terrifying to experience your own anger – especially if you're not used to it. You can fear it'll overwhelm you or make you go crazy; that once you let the genie out of the bottle you'll never be able to get it back in again and return to your status quo.

So, for a whole panoply of reasons, many of us bury our anger, shelving it deep down inside where it becomes trapped inside us as resentment. Later you'll learn how to release long-held resentments, but first it's vital to understand how to process anger safely. It takes courage to release anger, especially when it has been trapped inside you for a long time – sometimes from early childhood. Anger, when properly felt and released, is the engine that will drive you to sanity. It will give you the power you need to move yourself out of destructive patterns and into emotional freedom.

So call on the tools you learned in the First and Second Principles (pp. 65–90 and pp. 91–113). Notice and name anger whenever you feel it and then, as soon as you can, feel and release it.

Of all the emotions we experience, anger contains the most energy. Different techniques to release it will work best at different times, so experiment. You can hit pillows, punch bean bags, go for a fast run, box, dance, stamp, kick and smash things that you don't mind breaking. Shout, write, talk – do whatever it takes to release the feeling. But stay in your body – stay in the feeling. It's an emotion, not a thought, so ignore any stories your mind is telling you.

Now is *not* the time to communicate directly with the person you feel caused your anger. If you speak in the heat of the moment, you risk causing harm. Better by far that you wait until you are calm, powerful and in your centre before you engage. Plus, by the end of this work your perspective will have undergone a radical change. Old certainties will crumble, and new ones will emerge. So for now keep the focus on yourself.

When your mood is low or you're depressed, you may not even be aware of your anger. Trying to connect with it can be like trying to untangle a ball of knotted wool. But if you find the loose end – the flicker of emotion – no matter how small or hidden it is, and then follow it, you will be able to unravel it.

....

ANGER BUCKET

Imagine that you have a bucket deep inside you in which your anger is stored. Over your lifetime you accumulate anger. If you empty your bucket regularly – by releasing your anger in healthy ways – it is a lot easier to handle. But if you leave it to get too full, even the smallest event can cause it to overflow. The result is unpredictable and volatile behaviour or depression. You want to be calm and gentle, but from nowhere you find yourself raging.

....

When you don't express your own anger you may find others doing it for you. You may wonder why you're locked in so many similar situations of conflict – not realizing that you are generating the angry responses you encounter. Or, if you're depressed, you may wonder why others are short-tempered with you when you're clearly suffering.

To avoid acting it out and causing harm to yourself or others, anger needs to be released safely.

At the height of my worst depression my son started getting very angry. We sought professional help. 'It's very simple,' the therapist said. 'He's expressing your anger for you.' Once I began to own my anger and find safe ways of releasing it, his behaviour returned to normal. Anger works similarly to personal power. If we don't own and harness it ourselves, someone else close by will use it – often against us!

JN

Connecting with and then releasing your anger can have a dramatic impact on depression, but supplement this process with professional help if you need it. It's extraordinary how reluctant many of us are to allow ourselves to access the support that's available. We'll go to the gym for our bodies, but we resist doing the same for our minds.

CLINICAL DEPRESSION

There's a world of difference between the feeling of depression, which is a normal part of most people's emotional range, and clinical depression, which is a medical illness.

A prolonged period of stress, a major loss, repressed childhood trauma or a genetic predisposition can leave you vulnerable to clinical depression. If you've felt a low mood for an extended period of time and can't seem to shift a negative mindset, check it out with a doctor. You wouldn't battle through a serious physical ailment without seeking medical help, so treat your mental health with the same respect.

Seeking help when we need it is an act of courage, not a sign of weakness. There aren't any medals for trying to tough it out. We're lucky to live in an age where there are excellent therapists and medications to treat clinical depression. Our grandmothers and even our mothers were not so fortunate, so make use of the help that is available for your sake and the sake of those around you.

After my first marriage ended I buried my anger and tried to behave as if what had happened hadn't affected me. I was proud and I told myself I was taking the spiritual high road by not getting angry. To me, feeling angry couldn't change what was happening, it was pointless. Two years later when I developed severe clinical depression I discovered that all the anger I thought I'd avoided lay trapped inside me. My route out of depression involved both medication and a lot of work connecting with and releasing the anger I'd been too 'spiritual' to feel at the time.

JN

Releasing resentment

'You wanna fly, you got to give up the shit that weighs you down.'

TONI MORRISON

If we don't process our anger properly at the time it arises it churns and becomes the most toxic of all emotions – resentment. The word 'resent' comes from the French *resentir* – meaning literally 'to refeel'. When we resent, we refeel events that have hurt and angered us again and again.

We think it's the events themselves that leave us feeling victimized, but actually our attitude to events often causes us far more pain and, in particular, the resentments that we hold onto. Resentments leave us trapped in the past, either depressed or simmering with rage, hurt and bitterness. They can fuel self-pity and make us act mean as we think about or actively try to even scores. Like stone boulders, resentments block acceptance and letting go.

Each person whom we believe has let us down or caused us anger stays with us. That makes the going heavy. When we work through our resentments we are like weary travellers who stop to unload their luggage to rid themselves of what has been weighing them down.

While real anger is felt in the body, resentment starts in the head. It begins with a 'they shouldn't have' or an 'it's not fair' or an 'if only'. It justifies itself by listing wrongs and spiralling deeper and deeper into us until we've been totally consumed by it.

Most of us are incredibly sensitive. We often hate admitting how much we're hurt by tiny things. Big things we somehow often know how to handle, but the little hurts can burrow their way into our psyche and skew our whole perspective.

Resentment is the most harmful form of the synthetic pain you read about in the previous chapter (p. 102). It doesn't matter whether your resentment is big or small, it can steal your peace of mind and leave you obsessing, weaving yet more stories in your head. Before long those stories, too, can start dictating your reality.

....

HONESTY REQUIRED

Each time you 'refeel' a hurt from your past you tell yourself the story of what happened to you (see Exercise 1: What's Your Story? pp. 117–20). Each time you tell it, as with repeating any story, the version is likely to shift, particularly if it involves resentment. Each time you retell it, even if only to yourself, you're likely to make what the other person did to you a little more wrong and how you behaved in response a little more right. So you have to really practise rigorous self-honesty.

....

There'll be signs if you're resentful. You might be passive-aggressive – an angry nice person who smiles and says yes while inside she's screaming 'No!', who is nice to everyone else in the hope that they'll be nice to her and carries within her a fury that people aren't treating her as she deserves.

You might be depressed, your life force blocked by layers of hurt and anger that have been compressed within you for so long that you can no longer 'feel' beneath their weight.

You might be volatile and emotionally super-reactive, bristling with real and imagined slights to the point where others walk on eggshells around you.

Or you may be a combination — an exploding doormat — who yo-yos between being passive and easy-going one moment and suddenly erupting into rage the next.

If you're dismayed at how angry or hurt you can get over something that seems relatively small, it's likely to be the back catalogue of incidents you've suppressed breaking through the surface of your 'niceness'. When we're resentful our past hijacks our present.

Being right or being happy

> 'Hanging onto resentment is letting someone you despise live rent-free in your head.'
>
> ANN LANDERS

The most damaging resentments of all are those that stem from events where your initial anger was justifiable. If you've been betrayed, assaulted or misjudged, it takes extraordinary courage to let go of that resentment.

Resentment creates the illusion that we can somehow right the wrong that has been done if we just hang onto it for long enough. But the reality is that it's like drinking poison and then waiting for the other person to get sick.

You may get a temporary high from your outrage, and a relief from your hurt, while you anticipate your revenge, but as you wait the poison starts to take effect and makes you, not them, sicker and sicker.

....

THE MONKEY TRAP

According to an ancient Indian fable, the easiest way to trap a monkey is to put a piece of fruit inside a container with a narrow hole in it. The monkey slides its hand into the container and grabs the fruit. But its fist is now too big to pull back through the hole. The monkey, reluctant to let go of its find, holds onto the fruit and so gets caught by the hunter. To survive, the monkey needed only to let go and move on.

....

You can't change the past, but having courage makes it possible to change your attitude to it.

You can't live a fulfilling and happy life and keep your victim status. The two are incompatible.

It's a really simple choice: do you want to be right or do you want to be happy?

If you want to be happy then it's time to clear out all the resentments that may be backed up and festering inside you.

Spiritual Surgery

Releasing resentments is akin to spiritual surgery. It's the most exacting of all WE's processes. It involves having the courage to step back into your past – not to blame but to fact-find. The process that is outlined follows the exercise which is adapted from a highly effective system used in most 12-step fellowships. It involves listing anyone or anything in your past that causes you pain and releasing yourself from it. This process can be used again and again whenever you realize you're resentful. It is an intense but very powerful and affective experience.

As with physical surgery you need to take really good care of yourself before, during and after this work. So make sure you're using the Essential Practices as well as scheduling in some extra 'you' time (see the Befriend Yourself exercise, pp. 36–7).

....

EXERCISE 2: Releasing Toxicity

....

This exercise is set out in three parts and will help you release any toxic resentments you may still be holding. You will need to pace yourself, as you may not be able to deal with all your resentments in one sitting. However, it will be worth the effort. Once you've finished you'll have turned a huge corner and gained newfound energy and optimism.

You can choose to work on a single, particular resentment to start with or on everything and anyone you have ever had negative feelings about. Just make sure you use a fresh page in your journal or notebook for each resentment. The more thorough and detailed you are in writing out the source of the resentment, the more paper you'll get through and the better it will work.

Part I: The source

Write the name of the person, organization or event that you have negative feelings about. Beside it write in a few words what they or it have done to hurt you.

It doesn't matter whether what happened is large or small. There doesn't have to be any logic or reasonableness as to why you were hurt. All that matters is that you were. Nobody else will read this, so you are free to be completely honest. It could be someone not picking you to be on their team at school or it could be a lover who was unfaithful.

Write quickly and don't dwell on or get stuck in the pain. Reliving the drama is a form of avoidance. Your task is not to re-experience the experiences that you write down but to list them. So, as the saying goes, glance back but don't stare.

If you find it particularly difficult not to get drawn into the past as you write, invite a friend – perhaps one who is also on the WE journey – to sit with you as you do the work. Alternatively, you can write in a café or public place so that you remain anchored in the present while making this excursion into the past.

If you start feeling overwhelmed, treat yourself as you would anyone else you love and pause to do something nurturing for yourself. But don't abandon the process altogether – just as you wouldn't walk away from an operation once an incision has been made.

When you've finished congratulate yourself and, if you need to, take some time out. You're about to start making the turnaround, to stop being the victim and to start reclaiming your life.

Part II: Your role

Now your focus is going to shift away from the other person, organization or event and onto yourself, leaving behind the (sometimes exhilarating) surges of anger, to turn your focus inwards.

This is not about blame. It's about identifying what you can change. If it helps, imagine that each resentment is like a thorn you've trodden on that needs removing. The flesh around it may be tender, but you'll feel so much better once it's out!

So take each resentment and note down what part you may have played in the wrong that was 'done' to you. It might be your actions, words or attitude. Ask yourself: Did I rely on someone I knew to be unreliable and then end up distressed when he or she let me down? Was I expecting someone to give me something they were never able to give? Was I looking to hang onto something or someone that wasn't really mine?

Have I behaved in a way that might have courted retaliation – for example, by being arrogant or judgemental? Did I do something that might have hurt the person who hurt me?

Was I dishonest in any way? Have I distorted the event so that I can look more blameless and someone else more culpable? Have I ever done what was done to me to someone else?

It may be that you were completely blameless because you were just a child. In this case, only look at your attitude now.

Am I hanging onto this injustice and keeping it alive with my attitude? Have I allowed that event to become my defining story?

What is making it impossible for me to move on? Am I unwilling to relinquish the fact that I've been wronged? Am I choosing to be right over being happy? Am I unwilling to accept that something unfair or unjust has happened to me?

Am I keeping myself a victim in the hope that someone else will make it better or that the person who wronged me will suddenly realize and make amends? And if so, why?

Am I tormenting myself further by pointing out how much better other people's lives seem to be?

As you do this work you will identify the ways in which you've stoked and fed your hurt and resentment, how you've compounded it through your thinking. You'll see how when you can let go of being right you can accept and move on.

You didn't choose the hand you were dealt, but thanks to the work you're doing now you'll have the power to choose how you play it.

When you have worked your way through every aspect of the resentment, you are nearly there. The spiritual surgery is complete, but your wound still needs to be stitched.

Part III: The release

The final part of this process provides the gateway to a new relationship with a part of your history and, through that, your life. You'll be identifying what you need to feel and release so that you can move into acceptance.

To do this, ask yourself: 'How do I wish it had been?'

In just a few words write down how you would have preferred things to turn out. Feel the feelings that come up and then release them. This takes courage. But as you allow yourself to release your sorrow, anger and disappointment, you let go of the past and truly start to move into your present with meaning and purpose.

Acknowledge the loss and say quietly and respectfully to yourself, 'This is how it is.'

If you want, you can add the page describing your resentment(s) that you wrote in Part II of this exercise to your Acceptance Cup (pp. 94–5). Once it is there, it is over.

Repeat this process with each resentment that you feel is holding you back. It may take a while or even a few days or weeks. Don't be afraid to pace yourself. Take breaks when you need them. Go for a walk or sit in a park. There is no rush, but the sooner you do the work, the sooner you'll be free.

When you have completed Part III, congratulate yourself for having the courage to confront and liberate yourself from an aspect of the past that wasn't serving you. You are now well on the road to freedom.

When we use the exercise above extraordinary shifts occur.

You will cease to see yourself as a victim. You will find that you're able to pick yourself up and get on with your life. You'll no longer carry the burden of others' actions.

Repeat this exercise whenever you feel hurt or angered. It allows you to have a centred emotional response to a situation and then move on. Use it regularly to prevent further pockets of resentment from building up. You can do it at any moment in the day when you notice a resentment starting to niggle away at you – on the bus, at the school gate, in a meeting, before bed. Once you've done it, write a mini-gratitude list to wash the traces of it away.

Like many of the tools you're learning here, this one has a magic multiplying effect. The more rigorous you are at spotting and then releasing your resentments, the fewer you'll start to have. It will change your outlook and your attitude. You'll start to recognize how you fed your sense of woundedness and outrage and how disempowering that was. You'll see how you took the unfairness that life inevitably entails and made it worse by hanging on to it.

The longer I walk this path, the more essential it has become to get to the crux of what those building resentments are. The only thing I can control is how I react to situations. If I can look at my own behaviour in this scenario, for instance, and see where I have impacted another human being then I can choose to apologize. I have no control over whether they accept my apology, but I do have control over how I choose to let go of any resentments I have towards them.

GA

....

EXPECTATIONS

When we expect that someone will behave in a certain way, we set ourselves up to resent them if they don't. As the saying goes, expectations are the mother of disappointment and the father of resentment.

They are like contracts that the other party hasn't had a chance to read or sign, and yet we expect people to abide by them. Then when they don't, we're upset. It's a set-up. What's more, people often sense the weight of our expectations and experience them as demands or attempts to control, which they naturally bridle against. Once we let go of expectations, we're amazed at how others respond.

....

While you can't change your history, when you change your attitude to it a whole new future opens up.

You'll find that as you let go of the hurts you've been carrying your journey becomes a lot easier. You'll have new responses to situations and feel hurt less often because what's happening in the present is no longer being inflamed by resentment seeping through from your past.

Having the courage to release yourself from the burden of your past frees you up. It creates internal space for your intuition and instinct to find solutions you couldn't have imagined previously.

You will also start feeling less alone. Resentment and false narratives distance us from others. They put a barrier between us and reality, which distorts what we see and blocks real connection.

When new hurts arise, deal with them quickly. Notice, name, feel and release your anger and use what you've learned to let go of any residual pain. As you do, hope and optimism will become your travelling companions.

Courage in the wider world

'Memories of our lives, of our works and our deeds will continue in others.'

ROSA PARKS

When our lives are dominated by resentment, we find ourselves lurching from one upset to the next.

Open any newspaper and you can see the consequences of unhealed and unconscious emotional responses playing out in the world at large. Brawls, murders and wars often waged in the name of self-defence, but which in reality are the result of emotional wounds accumulating in intolerable feelings of umbrage and impotency.

Hurt people hurt people. When we're not healed we do to others what has been done to us. We react with rage, rather than compassion and insight.

How much more peaceful would the world be if we each took responsibility for processing our hurt feelings so that we didn't act them out on others?

How many more solutions would be found if we let go of our personal need to be right?

How much more powerful would we be in our engagement with others if we harnessed our anger rather than raged about our suffering?

When we have the courage to let go of our rage and resentment we discover we are powerful beyond measure.

Reflection

'Above all, be the heroine of your life, not the victim.'

NORA EPHRON

If I'm upset by someone or something, I have to be diligent and process the anger or hurt it provokes. If I don't, I'll be in danger of acting out my resentment on those I come into contact with. That could be my child who is nagging me to play while I'm busy or it could be the shop-assistant whom I snap at because I'm preoccupied.

Action: I will take responsibility for feeling and releasing my anger safely.

Affirmation: Today I let go of being right so that I can be happy.

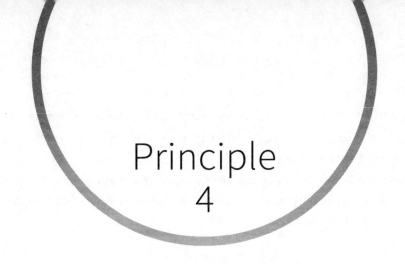

Principle
4

TRUST:
Living Without Fear

'You can never leave footprints that last if you are always walking on tiptoe.'

LEYMAH GBOWEE

Trust is our antidote to fear. It aligns us with the flow of life –
a magnificent energy that guides and directs us so that we
can live expansive, happy and fulfilling lives.

With trust, life starts to open up. We're able to embrace opportunities, have fun and make the most of our time on this earth. Trust fosters cooperation and compassion, rather than competition.

Without trust we live in fear and anxiety. We doubt ourselves, we doubt others, we worry, we compete and we try to control outcomes. We live small when we could be living big.

A miracle is sometimes defined as a change in perspective, a moment when suddenly everything shifts. That's what trust leads us to – a completely new perspective on our life.

Choosing trust over fear

'The most difficult thing is the decision to act, the rest is merely tenacity.'

AMELIA EARHART

Trust offers us freedom from fear. But as with all WE's principles, there is just one thing that is required from us if we want to experience its magic: willingness.

To start with, choosing to trust can feel foolish, giddy and maybe even ridiculous. Trust can seem irrational, illogical and irresponsible. We want to know what we're trusting and how it's going to work.

But the truth is you already know how to trust – you've been trusting for many years. It isn't new to you, it's just that you have been trusting the wrong thing – you've been trusting in the negative outcomes that fear tells you are just round the corner.

When we adopt trust as a spiritual principle we do the opposite. Instead of assuming negative outcomes, we assume the best. And, crucially, we accept that we don't necessarily know what the best looks like.

Often it is only with the value of hindsight that we get to see that what we thought would be disastrous has actually turned out for the best.

EXERCISE 1: Living Proof

This exercise will strengthen your capacity to trust by showing you that — despite your worst fears — you have been taken care of in the past.

Close your eyes and breathe in and out deeply at least five times. When you are centred, scan back through your life. Look for situations when you were absolutely sure something terrible was going to happen but things actually turned out OK.

Maybe you were in an accident that could have killed you; maybe you had a brush with a serious illness that you survived; maybe you thought you'd be alone forever but met someone and fell in love; maybe you took risks with alcohol or drugs and lived to tell the tale.

Write down in your journal as many unexpectedly good outcomes as you can remember. It's your proof — when you need it — that things don't always turn out as you feared. And that even events that seemed catastrophic at the time can still lead to positive outcomes.

When I wound up in treatment, I thought it was the worst thing that could ever happen to me. I thought my life was over. Now, more than two decades later, I can see that it was actually the best thing that could have happened to me. It was where I was introduced to a spiritual way of living and began the journey back to my true self. Without it I'm not sure that I would be alive today. So now, when something upsetting happens, I try to replace my instinctive response of 'how terrible' with one of 'how interesting', and then trust that, somehow, it will all work out.

JN

I feel like I have so many examples throughout my life where my assumption was that things were undoubtedly going to go wrong. There used to be, and on the rare occasion still is, a bit of catastrophizing. The relationship was going to fall apart, I was going to be fired, the desired event wasn't going to take place. And yet more often than not I have looked back and thought, 'Actually, thank God that didn't happen! How things have turned out is so much better for everybody.' What has gradually changed over time as I've become more trusting is not that more things have gone the way I've wanted them to but that I've come to trust that, no matter what happens, even if the relationship does fall apart or the job goes away, I will be OK. More than OK.

GA

Unmasking fear

'Fear has always been the driving force behind all dictators' repression.'
MARJANE SATRAPI

Fear is an interloper. It pretends to be our friend but, in fact, it plays a highly destructive role in most of our lives, inhibiting us and preventing us from reaching our full potential.

Of course, fear has a healthy biological function – to keep us safe. It stops us sticking our hand into a fire and reminds us not to have unprotected sex or walk in front of fast-moving traffic. The problem is that for many of us it has ceased to be a tool we use to help us assess real risk and has instead taken control.

Fear often comes disguised as common sense. It focuses on the future – on what could happen or, more specifically, what could go wrong. When we try to make changes or move outside our comfort zones fear pipes up with advice like, 'What if it doesn't work out?' or 'What if you never meet anyone better?' or 'What if you're not good enough?' It tells us that if we just live a little smaller now, we'll be a little safer further down the line.

You might think worrying keeps you safe, but it's an illusion. It's like sitting in a rocking chair – it gives constant motion that doesn't actually get you anywhere. In reality, fear robs us of our sleep, our perspective and our self-belief.

None of us can know the future and yet fear has us in anguish over what it might be like. It can sound convincing, but it peddles lies. Think of it as an acronym for:

False

Evidence

Appearing

Real

When we rely on fear, we undermine ourselves and inflame any under-lying self-esteem issues. Fear has us worrying about what other people think. It calls our abilities and decisions into question and has us doubt ourselves.

It tries to protect us by preparing us to be disappointed and keeps us stalled when we could be moving forward. It persuades us to say no when we should say yes and steals our peace of mind.

There are plenty of valid reasons for our levels of fear. Many of us have learned to live fearfully from an early age. Perhaps bad things happened and we now cling to fear to try to prevent them happening again.

Or maybe we see the suffering that exists in the world and try vigorously to avoid it for ourselves. Fear can offer the illusion of control – convincing us that if we live small enough we can avoid bad things happening.

The problem is that allowing fear to govern our lives doesn't work. We can't control the uncontrollable – no matter how hard we try. Even if we lock ourselves away like modern-day Sleeping Beauties in our apartments instead of towers, there'll always be a metaphorical spinning wheel some-where that pricks us.

....

THE BODY-MIND CONNECTION

Fear produces a stress reaction in the body – the fight-or-flight response, designed to get us out of immediate physical danger. We can have a similar response when we watch a TV drama or the news or browse the Internet; if what we're seeing makes us fearful, our body becomes flooded by the stress hormone cortisol, even though we are not in any danger at all. Unfortunately, chronic or prolonged circulating cortisol can give rise to health problems such as raised blood pressure and insomnia. The body–mind connection and its implications to our health is now well-established,[14] so while it's important to be an informed citizen where current events are concerned, you also have a responsibility to monitor the diet you feed your mind carefully.

....

What we focus on grows. The more we focus on possible negative outcomes, the more fearful we become and ironically the more likely they are to happen. Instead of protecting us our fear often seems to become self-fulfilling. We stay in relationships we should have left for fear nothing better would come along and then the relationship falls apart anyway. We overwork and neglect nourishing our personal lives to keep our job and then get made redundant. We play it safe and turn down opportunities, and wonder why we're lonely, unfulfilled, anxious and afraid.

As you saw with WE's Second Principle, Acceptance (see pp. 91–113), we can manufacture unnecessary pain by being attached to how we *think* things ought to be. When we fear, we similarly generate unnecessary suffering. As the expression goes – we 'borrow' trouble. We imagine bad outcomes that might never happen. We think we're protecting ourselves while we are actually trapping ourselves in a place of negativity and fear.

Of course bad things do happen, but living in constant preparation for them is like keeping an umbrella above your head to be ready for the day it will rain. All that time we spend sheltering beneath it we're unable to enjoy the blue skies that exist between the storms.

There is another way to live and it involves replacing fear with trust.

EXERCISE 2: An Upgraded Operating System

This exercise will help you reprogram your fear-based response system.

Find a sheet of paper and a pen. You're going to create a new map for your life. Centre yourself by taking at least five deep breaths in and out.

On one side of the paper write the word 'fear' in the middle. Scan your mind for situations that you have a lot of fear around. It could be that you're scared of public speaking, asking your boss for a raise, being honest with someone you're close to or being alone. Perhaps you have bigger fears, like dying or getting sick. Jot each one down in a circle around the central word 'fear' so that you create a mind map of what your life looks like when it's governed by fear. Add in any feelings that those situations evoke: anxiety, hopelessness, despair, indecisiveness.

How does it look? Not pleasant! OK, now you're going to look at upgrading your operating software.

Use coloured pens if you have them. Turn the page over and write the word 'trust' in the middle.

Ask yourself, 'How would my life look if I wasn't afraid? How would I feel? What would I do differently?' Jot down keywords about how each situation would be transformed if you weren't afraid.

What would you do if you weren't scared to say how you felt? How would you live if you weren't scared of losing your job? What would you try if you weren't scared of failing? If you didn't tell yourself you were too young or too old, what would you be doing? Really get honest.

Visualize what your life would look like if you weren't afraid. Make those visions more vivid and real than the lies fear has given you. Enjoy them. Write down words that sum up how your life looks without fear: free, big, adventurous, bold, safe, courageous, happy. Enjoy these feelings.

Congratulations! You've just mapped out a new direction for your life. The map marked 'trust' is how your life is going to become. Look at it each morning to set your direction for the day and give your subconscious a goal to aim for.

Notice that when you're looking at the side of the page marked 'trust' you can't see the one marked 'fear'. The choice is as straightforward as that – you can either live by fear or by trust. Flip between the two images and decide which one you prefer!

....

A new direction

'I am learning to trust the journey even when I don't understand it.'

MILA BRON

When you face a choice, picture yourself standing at a crossroads with two roads pointing in opposite directions. You can either choose the one marked fear, which will lead you straight back to where you've come from, or you can choose to trust and head towards your vision and a courageous, rich, fulfilling life.

Any time during your day when you face a choice simply ask yourself, 'What would I do if I weren't afraid?' And then do it. Take the leap and the net will appear.

This new way of life takes practice. The chances are that you've been ruled by fear for most of your life. So don't be surprised when you encounter resistance. Fear won't necessarily go, but your response to it will change dramatically.

....

THE THREE-SECOND RULE

You can't stop fearful thoughts arising, but you can choose what to do with them. You have roughly three seconds to interrupt a negative thought. Allow it to rest in your mind any longer and it starts to take hold. The faster you decline its invitation to engage, the less likely it'll be to take up permanent residence. So when you have a fearful thought don't invite it in and offer it tea and sympathy!

....

Happy talk

When you're feeling fearful allow the adult part of yourself to talk to the frightened part of yourself, as you would talk to a scared child. Connect with your inner girl (pp. 84–7). Notice and name what's happening to her. Encourage her, praise her and coach her through situations. When she doubts she can succeed, remind her of all her successes so far and encourage her to trust her instincts. Tell her when she's doing a good job or when you think she's being brave. Celebrate her achievements and console her with love when she's disappointed. And when you have, congratulate yourself for trusting enough to try something new even though it makes you uncomfortable.

Growing up, the rule at home was that children should be silent. I wanted to please my father and so was virtually mute in the company of adults. In school, I'd freeze with fear whenever the teacher asked me a question. I was so scared of speaking out loud that I'd answer in whispers. Nobody would be able to hear me and the whole class would erupt in laughter. Now, of course, I'm no longer that terrified, silent child, but occasionally, when I'm in a particularly challenging situation I can find myself becoming mute again and I have to work extra hard not to slip back into that early role of being a silent player in my life. The fear can be enormous and I have to take a real leap of faith, open my mouth and trust that I won't be humiliated in the way that I was as a girl.

JN

I'm not sure exactly when low-grade anxiety started in my life. I do recall that waking up with a sense of panic became an everyday occurrence in college and the fully-fledged attacks started when pregnant with my first child. It's safe to say that getting a handle on this is what initially strengthened my faith in spiritual solutions. But despite the fact that I have lived my adult life with some form of it either in the periphery or front and centre, the only way I have been able to step into my life as a student, a parent or an actor who does live stage performances is to feel the fear and do it anyway. To say yes to life in all its complexities and terrifying twists and turns, despite potential paralysis around every corner.

GA

Trust in what?

Trust in exactly the opposite of what you fear. Trust in the flow of life. Trust that you're glorious, that you're enough, that you're lovable. Trust that life will unfold as it should. Trust that the lessons others need to learn will be taught without you needing to intervene.

Remember fear's acronym – False Evidence Appearing Real? Well, trust has a much better one:

To
Rely
Upon
Spiritual
Truth[15]

Trusting is really a commitment to believing that love has more power than fear.

If you're not convinced, experiment. Try trusting for a week and see how it plays out. Each day choose to do what you would do if you had no fear. Refer to your mind map. Assume the best in every situation, even though you can't fathom how anything good will emerge. Say yes when previously you'd have said no. Take risks. Know that you're capable. Take knockbacks as information – signs that a better opportunity awaits. Be aware of how it makes you feel. Notice how much more resilient and enthusiastic about life you become.

Trust allows you to live in the present. The future will unfold as it needs to. The space you previously spent worrying and strategizing becomes available to enjoy. When you wake up each day think of your mind as a garden. See how many wonderful, fine-smelling plants you can put in it. If fearful thoughts reappear, uproot them as if they were weeds before they can choke out the blossoms you're nurturing.

If you lapse back into fear, be gentle with yourself. Learning a new behaviour is not always smooth. You'd never have learned how to walk if you hadn't fallen down many times.

....

THE SUBSTITUTION RULE

Every thought and behavioural pattern you have creates a neural pathway in your brain. That's why breaking a habit can be so hard – you are literally wired to keep repeating your past behaviour. With the Substitution Rule you don't just try to stop doing something negative, you actively substitute a positive behaviour or thought to take its place. By doing this you actually create a new neural pathway.

Recent research suggests that it takes on average just over 60 days to create a new behaviour,[16] so each time you replace a fearful thought or action with a trusting thought or action, picture the neural pathways in your brain changing.

When you catch yourself saying something fear-based like, 'I'll never be fit,' substitute it with a positive thought, such as, 'I am getting fitter and healthier each day.' And remember, what you focus on grows, so focus on what you are choosing, not what you're giving up!

....

When my long-term relationship broke down other long-term single friends seemed to pounce on me. 'There's nobody out there,' they told me. 'It's a jungle. All the good ones have gone.' Of course, everything they said reinforced my deepest fear – that I'd be alone forever. I became desperate. I was a single mother with two kids and in poor health – who was ever going to want me? I started making some bad choices, which reinforced my fear that I was unlovable. Then someone told me to start doing the opposite of what fear wanted me to do. So I took six months out of dating to give myself time to recover and to prove to myself that I could be happy on my own. Each time someone asked me about how I felt about being single I repeated my new affirmation – I trust that the right person will come when the time is right – and the more I repeated it the more I started to believe it. What I discovered in that time was life-changing – a source of happiness within me that wasn't dependent on another person, and when I stopped trying to run the show it somehow – magically – gave room for something more powerful to work its magic.

JN

What if?

Once you decide to start practising trust, be prepared for fear to launch a tirade of 'what ifs'. 'What ifs' are the fear-based questions that your mind will pose once you start to even think about making positive changes.[17]

Maybe you ask your boss for a raise or you ask out the girl or guy in the coffee shop, or you enrol in the dance class full of people who look like they know all the moves perfectly. Well, those are exactly the moments when a 'what if' might come thundering into your head: 'What if she fires me?' 'What if he rejects me?' 'What if I make a fool of myself in front of the whole class?'

The moment you hear a thought that starts with 'what if', interrupt it. Halt it right in its tracks and answer it head on with this short phrase: 'I'll handle it.'[18] Whatever the 'what if', use 'I'll handle it' to neutralize it. Remember, you only have three seconds to stop the 'what if' taking hold (p. 147), so be vigilant.

....

TYING UP YOUR CAMEL

Trusting doesn't mean we stop taking action. We still have to take responsibility for our own well-being and do the footwork – put the stamp on the envelope, have the breast examination, check out someone's online profile before agreeing to meet them.

What shifts is that our decisions are made on the basis of a right-sized assessment of risk – not the exaggerated versions we've often lived by. Fear had us trying to control outcomes. Trust asks that we let go of that control and simply do whatever needs doing. Then we let go of the outcome. As the old saying goes, we trust in God, but we still tie up our camel.

....

Resistance

Some of us experience huge resistance to trust. If that's you, ask yourself whether it benefits you in any way. How does not trusting serve you? What's the hidden payoff?

Many of us discover that we use fear as a form of avoidance. We cling to fear because if we let go we'll have to feel emotions we're trying to avoid. Maybe we don't want to trust that we'll meet someone more appropriate because we want to avoid the pain of saying goodbye to someone who's not treating us right. Maybe we don't want to trust that we'll get a better job because that will mean admitting that where we are is actually harming us.

If you find yourself getting stuck, talk to a trusted friend or therapist. Sometimes we can take a perverse comfort in clinging to fear. It might be corrosive, but at least it's familiar. We can trap ourselves in a better-the-devil-you-know mentality. Feeling that you're a victim of life is painful, but fear, with its twisted logic, can convince you it's safer than daring to believe things could be better.

The problem is that refusing to trust puts you in a catch-22 situation. You won't know how much better life will be until you try. The net only appears once we've leaped. So if you need support from others before taking the leap, ask for it.

....

FAKING IT

It takes time and repetition to establish those new neural pathways in the brain, so while they're still under construction there's nothing wrong with 'faking' a new behaviour until it becomes authentic. Try acting as if you're not afraid. It sounds improbable, but it works!

....

There was a time when I didn't know how I would pay all my bills and was pretty close to losing everything. The fear was crippling; I couldn't sleep and the stress was affecting every area of my life. Finally, I called a good friend and asked her for advice. 'Your job is not to worry about the bills later this month,' she told me. 'You have this debt and it is your responsibility to pay it. If you pay them what you can today, the money will be in your account when you need it for the next payment and for your future bills. Take responsibility now and then let go and trust.'

Those words changed everything for me. Each month, for many months, there was the same situation, and each time I paid what was in front of me or negotiated to pay in parts, and every month, somehow, there were sufficient funds. The fear wasn't gone entirely, and some days I still found it hard to smile, but taking responsibility and seeing that I was taken care of changed my understanding of letting go and trusting. And I've since found that this works in so many areas of my life. So often I want to hold on tight to an idea or a plan, and every time I fight against the change it causes pain. And every time I let go and trust there is a greater plan that is out of my hands and my only job is to show up and do the footwork, it takes the stress out, the fight out, and my life flows more smoothly.

GA

EXERCISE 3: Moving from Fear to Trust

This exercise will give you a taste of the freedom trust brings. You'll need your journal and to be undisturbed for about 20 minutes for this visualization. Take at least five deep breaths to centre yourself, read through the following instructions and then close your eyes.

Imagine you are walking up a mountain. Try to make the scene as vivid as possible. Breathe into it. Think about what you might be smelling and hearing as well as seeing.

You started your climb in good time. The sky is clear, the air is fresh and the sun is warm but not too hot. The path curves round and you discover you are higher than you thought. You sit down for a moment to savour the view and to think about how your life looks now that you're learning to trust.

Take out your journal and write a list of things you trust. They can be things you already trust or things you'd like to trust, if only you could make the leap. (Remember, you're allowed to fake it to make it!) Our subconscious listens to the messages we give it – whether they're true or not. So you can plant trusting thoughts here, even if you don't yet believe them. Make your list as uplifting and beautiful as you can.

Remember as you write your list that you are not alone; there are women everywhere right now making the same journey from fear to trust.

Here are some examples. I trust that …

I am in the right place at the right time.

Things happen for a reason.

I will be able to handle whatever life throws at me.

I am lovable just as I am.

I am worthy of respect and dignity.

I can live without active addiction.

I am trusted.

I am honest.

I am safe.

I am powerful.

I can make a difference.

I have a voice.

If you get stuck, look for where you have fear and then choose to substitute its opposite.

Here on the side of the mountain, as you look out across the beautiful view, give yourself permission to really believe each affirmation and allow yourself to experience the relief that brings.

Your list can also include those fears that you might want to dismiss as petty but can nevertheless steal your peace of mind. For example, I trust that …

If I'm not invited, I'm not meant to be there.

If I'm rejected, I am being protected.

When one door has closed another will open.

My kids are learning exactly what they need to.

My body is perfect just as it is.

I am glorious and deserve to experience joy.

Make your list really positive. Allow your spirit to soar.

Transfer the statements that give you the most joy onto Post-it notes. Stick them places where you'll see them frequently to remind you that today your beliefs are shifting, thanks to having trust as your guide.

People often tell me how brave I am because I seem to fearlessly jump into challenging and sometimes terrifying situations. But there are certain areas of my life where I am not brave at all – usually in the more personal zones. It has taken a lot of work, concerted effort, trial and error, and awkwardness to actively do things differently and face things head-on despite my deep-rooted reluctance, pessimism and desire for anything uncomfortable to just go away. And it is still a work in progress. It is hard to say 'I'm sorry' or 'I was wrong' or 'can we please make time to talk about something difficult'. Or 'when you say that to me I feel shamed/uncomfortable and I don't want you to say it anymore'. Or 'thank you so much for doing that today, next time it would be really great if you could do it this way'. Or 'I'm sorry, I don't think I was clear in my description. What I meant was …' Each requires a deep breath and a degree of humility, which certainly doesn't come easily to me. But it is transformative. Trusting the process and putting fear aside to take responsibility for one's own communication and quality of relationships is truly miraculous in its power and scope. It will change your life.

GA

It takes time, but slowly, if you use WE's tools, trusting can become your automatic response. When something unexpected happens you'll be curious rather than frightened. The fear that used to paralyze becomes transmuted into excitement. You'll wonder how situations will turn out, rather than your old habit of presuming a disaster.

The more you leap, the more you'll learn that life really does catch you and take you to exactly where you need to be.

When we trust we discover how limited our vision has been and how much more there is to look forward to when we allow life to flow through us, rather than constantly trying to control and contain it.

Trust in the wider world

'Every time you replace a fearful thought with a loving thought, you make the world a better place.'

DENISE LINN

From early on most of us have been taught to compare and compete with each other, feeding our fear that we're not enough. We've been culturally encouraged to view each other as rivals – to try to work out who is prettier, who is smarter, who is more likely to win love or to succeed. Fear leads to a binary system of winners and losers, of haves and have-nots.

Trust liberates us from that scarcity mentality. It tells us that we're enough and that there is enough. We no longer need to fear or be jealous of another's success because we no longer see happiness as a finite resource whose stock is diminished by other peoples' gains.

It gives us permission to substitute cooperation and compassion for competition and to see each other as allies rather than rivals. Before long the magic multiplying effect that attaches to all spiritual principles kicks in and we discover that the more trusting and open we are with others, the more they respond in kind.

What's true for us as individuals is also true for the world. Trusting that there is enough, for us all, is a political as well as a spiritual act. It's also factually true.

For example, we could feed every person on the planet if we just chose to. There is more than enough of all that is essential to life to go round. The problem is that when fear governs our decision-making, we believe the lie that there isn't enough and so we hoard and grab and leave those who are less able to fend for themselves to go without.

Trust gives us a new approach to life. Instead of competing we can now cooperate – it's a much more efficient way to allocate our planet's resources.

It's also a much more peaceful and sustainable way to live. When fear drives our choices it creates conflict, fuels overconsumption and generates avoidable pain. So next time you're making a choice, whether it's about how to vote, how to live or what to do with your evening, ask yourself, 'What would I choose if I was able to trust?' And then allow love rather than fear to be your guide.

Reflection

'Nothing in life is to be feared, it is only to be understood.'

MARIE CURIE

When I'm frightened I live smaller than I am. I clutch and I cling because I fear that I will get hurt or I will fail, or that there won't be enough to go around. This creates a circle of negativity as others become wary and distance themselves from me. Today I live a different way. I hold my face to the light and trust that my needs will be met, and if they aren't I will have the courage to ask for them to be met. I no longer need to worry about the future; it is being taken care of and that leaves me free to enjoy my day.

Action: When I feel fear I will ask myself what I would do if I weren't afraid and then do it.

Affirmation: Today I am safe and I am happy.

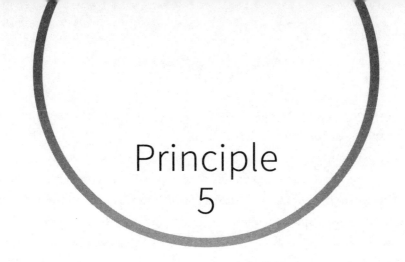

Principle 5

HUMILITY:
Unmasking Our Ego

'Humility is freedom from your own driven ego.'

MARTHA KILPATRICK

Humility allows us to be one of many, to know that we are wondrous and enough just as we are. When we practise humility, we have a strong sense of our own intrinsic worth that isn't dependent on anything we do, have or own.

With humility we are able to look for what joins us rather than what sets us apart – our common humanity, our wounds, our longings, our joys and our frailty. Instead of pursuing bleak self-interest we foster connection. We work to heal division. And as hard as it is sometimes, we choose to assume that everyone is doing the best they can.

Without humility we are at the mercy of our egos. We compare, control and compete. We worry about status, success and what we do or don't have.

WE's principles lead us down the road less travelled – and humility provides us with a spiritual defence against our egos. Humility right-sizes us – we're not the worst, we're not the best; we're just who we are and that is wonderful.

The previous principles will have helped you to start clearing away the emotional scar tissue and fear that may have blocked your path. Now with WE's Fifth Principle our focus begins the shift from our relationship with ourselves to how we relate to the world.

EGO: Edging Goodness Out

'The human ego's motto is "Seek but do not find".'

MIRANDA MACPHERSON

We live in a world dominated by the ego – one that holds material status and accomplishments as paramount. One that loves pecking orders and lists of who's who and judges by external appearance, not decency or depth.

Our ego cares deeply about how we look in relation to others. It wants us to be better than others but it's scared that we're actually worse. One moment it tells us we're fantastic, the next that we're a failure. Like the critical parent we can never please, it makes us feel as though nothing we do or have is ever quite enough.

Our ego's goal is ultimately to keep us safe. But it's pre-occupation with worldly concerns means that it doesn't take into account our emotional and spiritual needs. It drives us to abandon our values in the pursuit of our goals and has us living a roller-coaster ride of 'I won' or 'I got' highs followed by the inevitable 'now what?' lows.

Most of us are so used to the voice of our ego that we have become oblivious to the impact it has on our thinking. That thinking then influences how we see ourselves, how we see others and how we experience the world.

A mental high

'The origin of all demons is in mind itself.'

MACHIG LABDRÖN

Like a drug, your thoughts can change how you feel.

Close your eyes and think of something that really upsets you – perhaps a disagreement with a friend or a difficult situation you can't resolve. Observe what happens to your mood and energy. Notice the emotional jolt you experience as you think about it, as if the hurt or offence was happening again.

Now think of something or someone who really makes you excited – someone you're attracted to, a child's embrace, an amazing job opportunity or a holiday. Feel what happens to your energy levels. This positive thought lifts you up.

Thinking certain thoughts can give you a high – whether it's imagining yourself in the arms of someone you really desire or browsing the Internet for things you want to buy. But, like eating sugar, it's a temporary lift, a fantasy, and sooner or later you will come back down to reality. The scariest thing about the drug of fantasy is that we don't need to go anywhere to buy it – it's just there, available 24 hours a day, inside our heads.

....

A NEGATIVE BIAS

We have roughly 60,000 thoughts a day, and as many as 87 per cent of them are estimated to be negative.[19] No wonder we find it so hard to maintain our equilibrium!

....

Thinking in and of itself isn't, of course, bad – it enables us to navigate our way through life – but only a small portion of our thinking is helpful. The rest is driven by our ego and keeps us locked into patterns of conflict and dissatisfaction.

Attack thoughts

An attack thought is a kind of egoic thinking. It's quite easy to spot and starts with phrases like 'How dare she ...?' or 'Couldn't he have just ...?'

It doesn't matter whether your attack thought is aimed outwards at someone else or inwards at yourself, the outcome is always the same – you are the one who gets hurt by the thought. If you consciously take your mind off the negative assault on yourself or someone else, you will feel better. You will be let off the hook of negativity that you placed yourself on.

It's not possible to think an aggressive or violent thought and maintain your peace of mind. So the moment you notice yourself mentally criticizing someone – stop! Use the Three-Second Rule you learned in the previous chapter (p. 147). Interrupt the thought by telling yourself very simply, 'I could have peace of mind instead of this.'

Of course, you might not want peace of mind. You might want to keep thinking about how wrong someone else is. But you now know that you can't be both right and happy. So the choice is yours: righteous indignation or peace?

Self-blame

When our attack thoughts are pointed inwards, we tell ourselves we're the worst parent/friend/worker/boss/daughter/person. We get stuck in the awfulness of distorted thoughts about who we are.

Beating ourselves up is subtly addictive. Some of us started doing it in childhood as a defence against situations we had no control over. It gave us an explanation for the bad things that happened. It was less scary to blame ourselves than our caregivers because if our caregivers weren't to be trusted, then surely we couldn't survive.

> 'It's time we start writing a new narrative that doesn't focus on the struggle but on progression.'
>
> NANCY KACUNGIRA

Thinking we're bad protects us from disappointment – if we're not good, we don't deserve anything good to happen, so we won't mind when it doesn't (only we still do!).

None of us is as bad as we think we are. It's another one of those lies our ego tells us. Pretending to be worse than we really are is just an inverted form of boasting – it's pride in reverse. Sorry to break the news but you're not actually the worst anything – you're just you!

Compare and despair

We may believe that everyone is born equal, but how often do we actually act on that belief? Most of us spend a lot of our lives thinking we are superior or inferior to others. We're constantly reading situations and trying to work out how we fit in. Who has the power? Who's the smartest, the most attractive? Who's the loser, or the one who'll make us look like one?

Society, of course, actively encourages us to compare and compete with others. We are conditioned to see ourselves as objects that have to be made worthy of selection — educated, groomed and honed to the max. We're trained to rake over each other's appearances and told how to get someone else's look, wardrobe or lifestyle, feeding the lie that who we are isn't enough. The woman on the magazine cover has always got the body or the job or the relationship that would complete our lives.

It's all too easy to end up feeling as if other women are our rivals and that we're all in competition with each other. That's the work of our ego.

When we compare ourselves with others sooner or later we end up in despair. Our ego loves to make comparisons, but most of the time it doesn't even compare like with like. It usually contrasts how we *feel on the inside* with how other people *look on the outside*, and it makes no allowance for the fact that most people put on a front.

Thanks to social media the opportunity to compare and despair is only ever a click away. We can instantly see what we haven't got and the places we haven't been invited to. We live with our faces pressed up against the virtual lives of friends and colleagues who seem to have exciting careers, luxurious holidays, immaculate children and so on, and wonder why our lives don't match up. We forget that most people only post the good-news stories, the successes and sunrises, not the day-after-day struggles or the slog to pay the bills.

When I was offered my first pupillage at the Bar by a chambers of more than 20 barristers I was told, 'We're happy to have you as a trainee, but we won't have a permanent place for you because we already have a woman.' It wasn't said with malice, more a statement of fact – they had their token female. It affirmed what many of us already know: that our sex is the first thing many employers see when interviewing us. That can make it hard not to feel as if our only real competitors for any job are the other women. Now if I'm in that situation I make a special effort to connect with the other female candidates and build a bond of solidarity to replace the competition and the comparisons that my ego (and often society) wants me to make.

JN

The Toxic Cs

There's a handy technique for spotting when you're in egoic thinking. Generally, our ego has five really bad habits – all of which are culturally encouraged and all of which handily begin with the letter 'C':

- Comparing
- Criticizing
- Complaining
- Controlling
- Competing

These attack thoughts are defence mechanisms, only they don't work. They rob us of our peace of mind and set us apart from others. Each time we pick up one of the Toxic Cs we cloud our minds and our outlook.

Humility provides us with a spiritual alternative.

Humility – the path less travelled

'The thing that is really hard, and really amazing, is giving up on being perfect and beginning the work of becoming yourself.'

ANNA QUINDLEN

WE's principles provide us with an alternative way of living and relating to each other. It's a path less travelled but much gentler. In exchange for the five Toxic Cs, humility gives us three more powerful ones:

· Compassion
· Cooperation
· Connection

These three Constructive Cs are important not just for your own well-being, but also for the planet as a whole. They give us a new template of how to be in the world and they help us to stop replicating a system that has caused so many of us to suffer for so long. The fact is, if we gain power and influence and then use the old system we've inherited from men, nothing will change.

Instead of seeing each other as rivals competing for scarce resources, humility asks that we treat each woman we encounter as a potential ally and friend. Where once we might have compared and criticized, humility enables us to practise compassion, cooperation and connection.

Many of us have suffered discrimination – direct or indirect. We can be hungry for our chance of success. Humility doesn't mean we can't still pursue our goals, but it does ask that we don't pursue them in a way that causes others (or ourselves) harm. When we find ourselves drawn into any of the Toxic Cs we reach for our spiritual antidotes – the Constructive Cs.

Remember WE's acronym for trust: **To Rely Upon Spiritual Truth.**

The 'spiritual truth' that humility gives us is that our worth doesn't depend upon externals. When we truly comprehend this fact, we free ourselves to focus on the journey and our experience of it rather than the ultimate outcome. Our sense of identity is no longer wrapped up in obtaining goals. Instead, we judge ourselves by our values.

One of my biggest lessons in humility wasn't voluntary. I loved my working life as a television correspondent. I loved being able to call politicians to account, to be part of the events as they unfolded, to have a voice and a platform. I always had an interesting story to tell over dinner or a cause to galvanize support for. Then overnight I burned out and lost the ability to work. That was it, gone.

For the next decade I was too ill to work or do much else. I no longer had stories to wow people with. I no longer had the inside track on what was happening in Westminster. I was long-term sick – that wasn't quite so glamorous! But that period gave me freedom from my egoic self. There was nothing I could do to feed my ego – on many days I couldn't even get dressed. To start with, when people asked me what I did, I'd tell them about what I used to do, but it made me feel ill again. I'd become allergic to my egoic self.

Then I discovered the freedom of saying 'I don't do anything' – the truth. I'd watch the look of panic spread across strangers' faces – perhaps worried about what there'd be to talk about – but I was no longer scared of not having an external identity because I'd found who I really was inside.

JN

The rewards of the spiritual journey you're now on are enormous, but the work isn't always easy. It requires honesty, willingness and commitment. But remember that nothing has to be done perfectly. Perfectionism is banned, but there are other Ps you can use – like persistence and practice. The more you practise, the more spiritually fit you will become and the easier it will get.

EXERCISE 1: Spiritual Gym

This exercise is in two parts. In its entirety, it will help you build your spiritual muscles to tackle some of the ego's worst habits. You'll start to recognize when your ego is in charge and doing the talking.

In the warm-up, you'll need your journal and a dictionary. Using a dictionary, even an online version, may make you feel like you're back in school, but the beauty of working this way is that it harnesses your intellect for spiritual purposes.

Part I: The warm-up

Look up the definition of the following words and write them down in your journal: arrogance, dishonesty, envy, greed, impatience, intolerance, jealousy, lust, pride, self-centeredness, selfishness, self-pity.[20]

Some of the definitions may appear to be contradictory. For example, pride can refer both to satisfaction in a job well done and an inflated sense of one's own importance. For this exercise concentrate on the aspects that the ego likes to harness – the negative ones.

Each one of these characteristics has the power to distort your thinking and your response to life events. They can make you feel deeply uncomfortable.

Have a look at this list and see how many of these responses are familiar:

Arrogance – 'Why can't they just do things my way?'

Dishonesty – 'I'd never behave like that.'

Envy – 'I want what they've got, it's not fair.'

Greed – 'I want more (than my fair share).'

Impatience – 'It needs to happen now.'

Intolerance – 'I can't stand x, y or z.'

Jealousy – 'I'm going to be replaced by this person or left out.'

Lust – 'I don't care, I really want him/her.'

Pride – 'How dare they?' or 'Don't they know who I am?'

Self-centeredness – 'How can they do this to me?'

Selfishness – 'What about me?'

Self-pity – 'Poor me, doesn't anyone understand how difficult this is for me?'

These often-habitual responses to what life throws at us cause discomfort and pain. They lead us straight into a destructive cycle of attack thoughts and one or more of the Toxic Cs.

Note down which ones you resort to most often. We all have some that are our go-to responses. 'Poor me' (self-pity) or 'how could they?' (pride) are usually favourites.

Notice and name them as you go through your day. There is a spiritual cure for them, which we'll look at in Part II of this exercise.

Our ego focuses on externals. It complains that life isn't fair and looks for someone to blame. But as we do this work we discover that whether we're happy or miserable is more likely to depend on our *responses* to the hand life deals us, rather than the actual hand.

With humility we learn to replace our habitual ego-driven responses with spiritual ones.

Part II: The workout

Each of the negative characteristics we examined in Part I of this exercise has a spiritual opposite. When you notice yourself struggling with one, you can defuse it by focusing on its counterpart. It's like a gym, only spiritual. Just as when you have a bad back you're told to strengthen your stomach muscles, you want to work with the spiritual opposite of a problem.

Take up your journal and dictionary again. Write down in colour the definitions of the following words: humility, gratitude, acceptance, courage, compassion, generosity, honesty, kindness, tolerance, patience, love. These are your defences against the ego's attacks.

As you write them out, focus on where they reside in your body. Ego-centred feelings are experienced as thoughts in the mind, but their spiritual opposites exist in your heart and in your core. As you develop these new muscle groups, the ego will begin to relinquish its hold.

Below is a rough guide to which spiritual principle to exercise to counterbalance each egoic trait. Adjust it according to your needs. The moment you spot a negative characteristic, replace it with its spiritual opposite.

Arrogance – Humility, Acceptance

Dishonesty – Honesty

Envy or Jealousy – Gratitude, Acceptance, Joy

Greed – Gratitude, Humility

Impatience or Intolerance – Humility, Kindness, Peace

Lust – Gratitude

Pride – Humility, Acceptance

Self-centeredness – Humility, Kindness

Selfishness – Generosity, Joy, Kindness

Self-pity – Gratitude, Courage, Joy

You might notice that we left one principle off this list: Love. That's because you can use love in every single instance. So if you're struggling to remember which principle to use to diffuse a particular ego attack, choose love and you'll always have a healthy defence.

Try practising a different spiritual principle every day, or every few days. Developing these new muscles and behaviours will take time and patience. This is not a race – we're in it for the long haul.

....

Increasingly you will find that the gap between your values and your actions starts to close. Your life starts to become more congruent. And this in turn creates another of WE's magic multiplying effects: the better you feel about yourself, the better you're able to act on your beliefs. As you do, so you become.

....

IDLE MINDS

A healthy habit that will distract your ego from its destructive tendencies is to give yourself intellectual stimulation each day. Read something educational, do a puzzle or learn a new skill. Otherwise, sooner or later, like a bored puppy, it will start roaming around looking for trouble and something inappropriate to gnaw on.

....

Forgiveness

'Forgiveness is the key to action and freedom.'

HANNAH ARENDT

Humility frees us from the need to pretend we're better or more perfect than we are. That means we can apologize more easily when we've acted in ways that have hurt others or failed to reflect our values.

Humility also provides us with a spiritual skeleton key: forgiveness. Of course, our ego doesn't want us to forgive – ever. It feeds on having enemies and on being right. From its Neanderthal perspective, forgiving is letting the other person win. It stokes both our longing for vengeance and our need for the other person to realize just how much he or she hurt us and to make it better. Our ego – if we don't neutralize it with humility – can lead us to rekindle the resentments and stories we processed in the Third Principle – Courage (pp. 115–137).

....

A WISH THAT WORKS

If you find yourself craving vengeance, here's a remedy that really can help.

Every time the person who wronged you comes into your head, wish or pray for him or her to have every good thing you want for yourself: happiness, fulfilment, love, peace of mind. Wish for the other person to have it all.

Your ego will naturally try hard to resist it. You may be happier praying for the other person to suffer, but that will just keep you trapped. Your desire for vengeance makes you a prisoner.

174

If you can manage to do this every time you think of that person for as long as two weeks, amazing shifts will take place. After three weeks, you'll feel free.

....

'All too often we sanitize and simplify forgiveness, when in fact it's an arduous, exhausting task — messy, risky and unpredictable.'

MARINA CANTACUZINO

Forgiving doesn't mean forgetting and it doesn't mean that what happened was acceptable. It just means you want freedom. Without forgiveness, you remain bonded to those who've hurt you.

It isn't enough that others want to be forgiven, although that can sometimes help. Forgiveness isn't something you can force or deliver on demand. Be kind to yourself if you are struggling with it.

At its core, forgiveness involves experiencing loss. Letting go of the hope that things can be otherwise or the belief that the other person deserves your anger. Anger can feel like the only way you have to show that you're not totally powerless. But so often we cling to that anger in order to avoid the grief or disappointment that comes with loss. Only in forgiving can you give it up.

Ask yourself, 'How is this anger continuing to serve me?'

Listen carefully to the answer that comes up, and if you're still struggling to forgive, use the following exercise to help you let go of the hurt.

....

EXERCISE 2: Emotional Archaeology

....

This exercise is to help you release your attachment to past hurts. You will need two pieces of paper, a pen, a candle and a pair of scissors.

Write down in one sentence the crux of what wrong was done to you. Not the detail (hopefully you will have attended to that as you worked through your resentments on page 130), but what lies at its heart – were you betrayed, abandoned or left out? Or maybe you were exploited. What is the nature of your hurt, shorn of all detail and story?

Now ask yourself when else in your life you've experienced a similar feeling. List all the times you can remember. Trace the moments backward and forward until you have a timeline of similar experiences.

It's unlikely that the wrong you're unable to forgive has only happened once at the hands of one person. It's likely to be part of a pattern – the details and magnitude may not be the same, but that core wound is likely to have been activated more than this one time. Some of the instances you find may be more extreme than others, but there will almost always be a connection through time that is keeping you tied to it.

When you realize that you've experienced this wound before, some of its power is instantly released. No wonder you've struggled so much. The pain has been repeated and compacted over time.

On another piece of paper draw a large figure of eight. Put the name of the person you're struggling to forgive in the top half of the loop, along with the nature of the core wound. Write your name in the bottom loop. See how you're separate but also tied together.

Now light your candle. Take the scissors and cut the figure of eight right down the middle. Burn the half that has the name of the core wound on it. It's over, consigned to your past. You can now start to live fully in your present. If it floats back into your mind, remember that you have cut the cord.

....

....

AN EYE FOR AN EYE

Our jails are overflowing, but many of the people within them don't need to be there. In the US, 50 per cent of prisoners are serving time for non-violent crimes,[21] while two-thirds of prisoners held in custody awaiting trial in the UK are likely never to receive a custodial sentence.[22] It's been proven time and again that for the majority of offences prison neither deters nor reduces the likelihood of future offences. Yet instead of finding more effective ways of rehabilitation and crime prevention, we waste billions and contribute to future offences[23] in order to meet our culture's hunger for vengeance.

Imagine all the good that could be done with that money if we found more effective options – such as tackling poverty or providing lessons on conflict resolution in schools.

....

Living in the day

'Surely the world we live in is but the world that lives in us.'

DAISY BATES

The thoughts that cause us the most pain, courtesy of our ego, generally concern events that have already happened or ones that we fear might occur. As we're thinking about yesterday's slights or how we'll get ahead tomorrow, we rob ourselves of the chance to experience the day we're actually living through. Crazy, isn't it?

Humility brings you into the present. When we're genuinely in the present, the chatter in our head subsides. We feel at peace – for that moment we're a *human being* rather than a *human thinking*.

In the next chapter you'll learn some powerful meditation techniques to help you connect more deeply with the present, but for now start with an incredibly effective tool – one that's used to help beat heroin addiction and alcoholism. Try to live just one day at a time. In other words, only let yourself think about the 24 hours ahead.

The minute I engage in worry about one thing or another outside of this moment I become paralyzed. Seriously start spinning in circles in my head. Out of necessity, over time, I've learned to adapt to thinking only of the day that I'm presently in and sometimes, literally, just this minute. That isn't to say I don't plan and think ahead – I can tell you what I'm doing on any given day for the next seven months – but I've trained myself not to worry. The future event exists in time, but I won't think about it until it's upon me. In any day when I get an uneasy feeling in my stomach, which signals that I am afraid or nervous about something, after naming it it's important to determine if there is anything I can actually do about it in this moment. If there is, I do my best to address it now, even if it's just scheduling a time in the future to deal with it – that in itself is action. Taking care of myself in this way takes commitment and discipline because it's also about showing that I'm trustworthy and that when I say – even if just to myself – I will deal with something at a certain time, I actually do.

GA

....

TODAY OR TOMORROW?

To help you stay focused on the present, imagine your mind is your desktop and it has two folders on it. One is marked 'today' and one is marked 'tomorrow'. Each time a thought intrudes, glance at it and see whether it's about today or tomorrow. If it's about today, you can think it. Otherwise just pop the thought into the folder marked 'tomorrow'. If they continue to intrude, use the Three-Second Rule (p. 147) so that you don't let unnecessary thoughts about the future distract you from the business of living in the now.

....

Living in the day sets a no-excuses perimeter. If things are tough, tell yourself you only have to get through this one day. If things are good, remind yourself that it may only last for this day, so make the most of it instead of worrying about when it'll end. Nothing — neither good nor bad — lasts. Attend to what has to be done and then set yourself the goal of making the most of the day you have — not the future that hasn't arrived yet.

When you give yourself permission to reduce the time you spend thinking about the past and future, you create the space for joy, grace and wonder to emerge.

Right-sizing

'I love who I am, and I encourage other people to love and embrace who they are. But it definitely wasn't easy — it took me a while.'

SERENA WILLIAMS

With humility we become right-sized — in other words the same size as everyone we encounter. You don't need to be intimidated by someone who has more success or power, and you don't need to be deferred to by those who have less. There is no pecking order in the spiritual world. We are all exactly the same.

Often it's those with the biggest egos who have the lowest levels of self-esteem. They overcompensate with material accomplishments and possessions to make up for their lack of internal worth. Like the Wizard of Oz, their ego hides behind levers and screens, hoping to intimidate us.

Observe your own ego rise and reach for the Toxic Cs. Then remember the magical Constructive Cs – compassion, cooperation and connection (p. 168). By replacing one with the other you prove to yourself and others that you can actively become an equal part of a whole.

> My experience of success is that it's like candyfloss. It makes me feel good for a moment and then I have a post-sugar crash and crave more. I remember how great I felt when I had my first book published. Becoming a published author was something I'd dreamt of since I was a child. But then I went to the bookshop and saw how many other books there were – thousands of titles sat like tombstones on the shelves – and I suddenly 'got' it. There was nothing I could do that would satisfy the calling of my ego and make me feel special enough. There was no material achievement that would fill the God-shaped hole inside of me. Now I'm grateful for the satisfaction I get from doing a piece of work well, but I no longer take it as any kind of measure of my real worth.
>
> *JN*

If you find yourself hungering for more 'ego-food' – more success, more recognition, more things to make you feel better about yourself – make sure you're still using the Essential Practices from the beginning of the book (pp. 19–56). When we take care of what our real self needs, the needs of our ego will diminish and ultimately fade into the background.

There's no taking our trophies with us at the end of this life. Everything we hunger for now will turn to dust. So keep your focus on the good you can do and the lives you can touch today and then enjoy the freedom and love that practising humility brings.

Humility in the wider world

'It is a most certain truth that the richer we see ourselves to be, confessing at the same time our poverty, the greater will be our progress, and the more real our humility.'

SAINT TERESA OF ÁVILA

Humility allows us to take our rightful place on this wonderful and extraordinary planet. It frees our thoughts and vision from the ego's petty concerns. To the ego, enough is never enough, and it demands that we possess and accumulate more and more. It always chooses short-term gain, no matter the long-term pain it causes the world around it.

A prime example is how we humans treat our precious planet. Overconsumption drives climate change and harmful emissions. The poorest half of the world is already paying the price in droughts and rising sea levels. At least 10,000 species become extinct each year[24] and we are ploughing through the earth's resources as if it were a planet three times its size.

Humility enables us to challenge that head-on. If we can see ourselves as one of many rather than as an individual who has to make her mark at any cost, we will change how we consume and how we live.

Together we can demonstrate that there is a different way of being in the world that puts compassion and cooperation ahead of competition and status. We can acknowledge that we're here as custodians of our exquisite world and need to preserve it for those who come after.

Imagine what would happen if we each said, 'This is enough. I don't need more'.

What would happen if we said, 'They don't have enough and so they can have some of ours'?

What would happen if we all asked, 'How can I help?' rather than 'How can I win?' Your ego may not like it, but your soul will start to soar.

Reflection

'It's never about how little we have. It is about what our little has the potential to become.'

CHRISTINE CAINE

Today I know that when I feed my jealousy and envy by competing or comparing they grow. So instead, today I will turn my gaze inwards and work on their spiritual opposite – generosity, gratitude and love. Before long I will be back in balance and glad to be me.

Action: I treat every woman I meet as a friend.

Affirmation: My worth comes from within.

Principle 6

PEACE:
Ending the Conflict Within

'There is no need to go to India or anywhere else to find peace. You will find that deep place of silence right in your room, your garden or even your bathtub.'

ELISABETH KÜBLER-ROSS

Peace resides in the stillness beneath the chatter of our thinking minds. In that state of serenity, we experience freedom from inner conflict and a sense of wholeness. We feel connected to the world in which we live and loneliness begins to evaporate.

Peace leads us to a safe space within ourselves that we can return to whenever we are feeling distressed or unsettled. Over time we discover that when we rest in peace our levels of emotional reactivity are reduced and our capacity to experience joy is increased.

Without peace we are restless, searching and stuck in a state of almost constant *dis*-ease and dissatisfaction.

And yet, being still in the moment has become so foreign to many of us that it can feel uncomfortable. With our hectic schedules and the demands of modern 24/7 living many of us have lost the habit. We spend our time *doing* rather than *being*.

In the last chapter we saw the damage our ego-driven thinking can cause. WE's Sixth Principle takes us a step further – to a place that lies beyond our thoughts. It is there that we get to soak up the healing energy that peace brings.

Beyond our thinking minds

'We've known about the transcendent power of solitude for centuries; it's only recently that we've forgotten it.'

SUSAN CAIN

Most of us have spent so long listening to our thoughts that we are now completely identified with them. We have become like computer operators who think they are the computer.

We also believe that thinking can bring us peace, but actually the opposite is true. It's by detaching from our thoughts that we find peace. Meditation is our gateway to the extraordinary realm that exists beyond our thinking selves – the part of us that *knows* we're thinking.

EXERCISE 1: Our Internal Landscape

This exercise will give you a glimpse of the peace that exists within us all.

Set a timer for five minutes. Take a few deep breaths. Imagine your mind is a clear blue sky. Now watch and wait to see how soon thoughts start swarming in. Observe them. How many of them make sense? How many of them really need to be thought? How many of them instigate pain, anger or fear? How many of them repeat themselves? We live amid that swarm day in and day out.

Now close your eyes again and imagine your mind is a clear blue sky. This time when the thoughts appear try not to focus on them. Try to let them fly by as you would a wasp. Gently say to yourself 'thinking' every time you find yourself trying to grab onto one and instead return to the gentle rise and fall of your breath. Keep your focus on the blue sky rather than the wasps, and soon they'll find it harder to get your attention.

'You are the sky. Everything else — it's just the weather.'

PEMA CHÖDRÖN

PROOF POSITIVE

Scientific studies show that meditation creates a whole raft of physical and mental benefits: increased energy, reduced blood pressure and depression, better sleep, improved immune system, decreased inflammation and pain, increased attention and memory, enhanced self-control and emotional regulation, and higher emotional intelligence.[25] In addition, a University of California study found that daily meditation for just two weeks helped improve focus and memory: overall, the students who meditated had a 16 per cent higher score than others.[26]

....

Meditation

'Breathe. Let go. And remind yourself that this very moment is the only one you know you have for sure.'

OPRAH WINFREY

The West is finally waking up to the wonders of meditation. Doctors now recommend it. A growing number of businesses provide training for employees to reduce stress levels and increase efficiency. But its benefits go way beyond the physical and mental.

When we meditate on a daily basis we reconnect with our core – the authentic part of ourselves that lies beneath the defences and scar tissue we accumulate through life. And with that comes a sense of belonging. We start to feel connected at a deep level to the world of which we are a part.

When we meditate we reach a higher state of understanding and perception. As a result, what we have in common with others becomes more important than what separates us. Our intuition strengthens and leads us to a sense of purpose and fulfilment.

If you've been using the meditation technique you learnt at the start of this journey (pp. 53–4) and sitting for a couple of minutes each morning, you'll have already started something wonderful for yourself. You'll have established a meditation routine.

The length of time you've been sitting is less important than the habit. But now that your habit is in place, you can start to lengthen the time you sit. Notice your resistance to this idea. You may already be listing in your head how little time you have. So take a moment here to analyse how you spend the time you do have.

···

TIME AUDIT

For one day, make a record of how you spend your time. Note down the times you spend working and doing necessary tasks, but also pay particular attention to the time you waste. Maybe you repeatedly check your phone or lose hours checking out people you barely know online or daydreaming about the distant future. Maybe you fritter away time talking to people you have no desire to speak to, or doing chores that don't matter at all, or watching TV programmes you don't really enjoy. Whatever you notice, write it down.

Identify what you could do differently to free up 20 minutes each day to devote to your meditation practice. Your peace of mind will be well worth the adjustment.

···

Many of us are addicted to our gadgets. The average smartphone user checks their phone 150 times a day – that's every six and a half minutes.[27]

Our ego likes to pretend that we're so important that we have to keep this connected, but for many of us there are other factors at play. We use gadgets to stave off an inner emptiness or fill an awkward pause, or perhaps as an emotional buffer to avoid difficult feelings like sadness, grief, loneliness, guilt and fear. And who wouldn't rather be watching the world's funniest cat videos on YouTube than feeling those emotions?

But when we turn to our gadgets to change how we feel we feed rather than soothe our inner restlessness.

Pathways to peace

'Inside myself is a place where I live all alone, and that's where you renew your springs that never dry up.'

PEARL S. BUCK

There are many ways to meditate. None of them are right or wrong. They are merely different routes to the same place. There aren't any rules other than to find a practice that works for you.

Experiment to see which method you find most effective. Maybe you're a member of a church, have a yoga practice or attend a synagogue or mosque where meditation is taught. Perhaps you love movement or chanting, or would prefer a technique with strict guidelines. You may want a religious component or something entirely secular. Keep seeking until you find a method that resonates with you.

Be open. Be curious. But don't let seeking become a form of avoidance. This is not about perfection. It's about action. Whichever path you choose will work if you commit to it.

....

EXERCISE 2: Mantra Meditation

....

This exercise introduces you to a simple and very powerful technique that is used by millions of people around the world. It uses a mantra which is a word or a sound that gives the mind a focus during meditation, and will make it easier to switch off your usual merry-go-round of thoughts.

You may already have a mantra you like or, if not, try using the Sanskrit word *Om*. Alternatively, a word like 'Love' or 'Peace' – that has a positive meaning – will do, or you can find mantras online.

Settle yourself, set your timer for five minutes, close your eyes and take five deep breaths. Allow the mantra or word to appear in your mind. Repeat it to yourself silently.

Imagine the sound is a magic carpet and watch it rise and fall on your breath. Now climb onto it.

Feel the magic carpet beneath you as you breathe and allow yourself to rest on it. You don't have to concentrate on it. You are safe and supported. This is not about focus, but about softness and ease. So just let yourself rest on the carpet as you repeat the mantra silently to yourself. It doesn't matter whether you repeat it several times a breath or once per exhalation. Just do it with ease. Let it establish its own rhythm. You'll find that the pace at which it comes to you tends to quicken and slow naturally. As you repeat your mantra you may also notice that at some point it ceases to be a word that you are repeating and becomes something you are experiencing.

If you find yourself drifting into thought (and you will), gently shift your focus back to the mantra. Do it gently. You may have to do this many times. Thoughts are persistent. Don't strain, stress or judge what's happening. Just gently return your focus to your mantra.

Be loving with your mind's antics. Think of your mind as a puppy you are training to 'stay'. You may have to put it back on its mat numerous times before it learns, and even then it will sometimes stray.[28]

There is no rush and there is no destination. When your timer goes don't open your eyes right away. Respect your practice. Allow yourself to slowly and gently come back to your physical surroundings. Then say thank you to yourself and to your mantra for the experience.

When I started meditating I was in so much emotional pain I couldn't sit for longer than a couple of minutes. So I used a walking meditation. I'd walk for 20 minutes and the movement soothed me. After that I used to meditate during morning prayers in a nearby chapel. I couldn't sit by myself, but I could sit when others were around. Then I went through a period of spiritual tourism – trying every technique that was going until someone suggested it was time to stop searching and start doing. I decided to commit to a mantra-based technique and it works. I now sit for 20 minutes on my own each morning. In fact, it's the part of the day I look forward to most. I make my coffee, read a portion of a spiritual text, and then set my timer.

Some days it's easier than others to find peace, but I try not to judge myself – what matters is that I've shown up and made myself available to the process. Often my six-year-old will come and sit with me. He rarely lasts the full 20 minutes, but he finds the stillness comforting and is instinctively drawn to it.

JN

Deepening your practice

'Surrender to what is, let go of what was, have faith in what will be.'
SONIA RICOTTI

To start with, developing your meditation practice takes discipline. As with any form of training, you have to show up if you want to see results. But while it may feel like a chore at the beginning, it will soon become a source of joy and you'll wonder how you ever lived without it.

If you liked using the mantra meditation then try it again tomorrow in the regular time you've set aside. If not, use whatever technique works for you.

Each day set your timer for three minutes longer until you get up to 20 minutes. Then allow an extra minute at the start of the session to settle into your breathing and an extra two at the end to come back into the world. Using your timer frees your mind from needing to monitor the time, making it easier to let go.

If you can, find the time before your day gets under way. Set your alarm to go off early to enable you to get up before your other commitments start.

Some people add an additional meditation time at the end of their day, but for now see if you can commit to the morning.

All you need to bring about extraordinary changes in your life is 20 minutes a day. You'll find yourself becoming calmer, less reactive, less easily hurt. Meditation creates the emotional equivalent of a moat. It's harder for life's arrows to penetrate when you have a spiritual buffer protecting you.

As your practice becomes more ingrained in your daily life, you'll find that activities and people that alienate you from your inner equilibrium become less attractive. Why would we want to do things that make us feel worse rather than better?

Once you've started to taste that sense of peace, you're likely to want more. You'll start to prioritize it. And that will mean making different choices about how you spend your time.

....

EXERCISE 3: Your Inner Circle

....

This is an exercise to help you make choices that will prioritize your inner peace.

Draw three large circles, one inside the other, on a piece of paper.

In the outer circle write down all activities that almost always make you feel bad. Perhaps it's looking at photos of an ex's new partner on their social media page. Maybe it's checking out a gossip column, going on a crash diet or binge drinking. These activities manufacture pain.

In the middle circle write down behaviours that sometimes make you feel good and sometimes bad. For example, speaking to a close friend who is also close to your ex, surfing shopping sites, being in touch with a member of your family who causes you concern.

In the inner circle jot down behaviours that make you feel great. For example, spending time with a good friend, meditating, exercising, laughing, playing with a child, walking in nature, playing a sport, painting, writing, dancing, creating, sculpting or singing. Write down as many as you can.

Take a look at your map. That inner circle is where you're happiest, safest and most fulfilled. It's firm ground. Your aim is to spend as much time there as possible.

Now look at the middle circle. You can do these activities when you're feeling emotionally robust, but they carry risks and could lead you to lose your centre. When you feel emotionally vulnerable try to avoid them as much as possible and return to the inner circle as soon as you can.

Your goal is to stay out of the outer circle altogether.

Your peace of mind is precious, so use this tool to foster it and keep it safe.

MENTAL DETOX

Most religious traditions insist on a day of rest from worldly engagement for good reason. The idea is that it enables us to return to centre and remember what really matters in our lives. You don't have to have a faith to benefit from the practice. Try giving yourself a day of rest each week when you decline to shop or actively consume, where you prioritize being in the life you have rather than getting or having more.

If you enjoy it, how about taking a complete mental detox by not reading or listening to the news? Think of your mind as a glass of clear water. Every time you listen to or read a fear-driven or shocking report, it's like injecting ink straight into it. So why not make disengagement from it a regular part of your week?

....

Letting go of knowing

As you learn to detach from your thoughts, you'll begin to notice how your mind likes to categorize your experiences as either good or bad. Whether it's the fact that it's raining again or that a friend failed to show up, you'll probably discover you have a running commentary assigning value to it.

You'll almost certainly do the same with people – sorting them into goodies and baddies, and making all sorts of assumptions about their motives and intentions.

The problem is that we think we know what's going on, but actually we have no idea. We don't have a crystal ball, nor can we read minds. Instead, our assessments are based largely on our past experiences and fear. We project what has already happened onto our present and then wonder why the same experiences keep happening to us again and again.

....

NEITHER GOOD NOR BAD

Once upon a time, the fable goes, there was a farmer who had no ox with which to plough his field. One day he woke up and saw a horse grazing in his pasture. He was ecstatic and rushed to the wise man in the village.

193

'Wise man, wise man, I thought we were all going to starve as we had no ox to plough our field, but now we have a horse. This is the best thing that's ever happened to me.'

The wise man replied, 'It is neither good nor bad, it just is.'

The farmer left, shaking his head. 'What an idiot that wise man is,' he thought. 'He understands nothing of value.' Then he and his only son set about ploughing the field.

Suddenly the horse reared up, injuring the son, who broke his leg.

The farmer rushed back to the wise man. 'Wise man, wise man,' he said. 'You are so wise. You were totally right. The horse was not a good thing. It has broken the leg of my only son and now I have nobody to help me bring in the harvest.'

The wise man shook his head and repeated, 'It is neither good nor bad, it just is.'

Exasperated, the farmer returned to care for his son and do what he could with his crop before the rain came.

The next day an army marched into the village and rounded up every able-bodied young man to help fight in the war. They were taken off to the front and before long word came back that they had all died.[29]

How often do we, like the old farmer, think we know what is good and bad in our lives? And how much time do we waste trying to puzzle it out? While we're busy trying to get more of what we think is good and avoid what we think of as bad, we miss out on what happens in between – which is actually the vast majority of our lives.

Living consciously, mindfully

What would happen if instead of waiting for the 'good' moments to arrive, we remained present for all of life – including the parts we often dismiss as boring and unimportant?

The peace we can find when we meditate at the start of each morning is actually available throughout our day if we open ourselves to it.

EXERCISE 4: The Miraculous Mundane

This exercise will help you transform your present – no matter what is going on.

Pick one of the activities listed below that you find really boring, perhaps something you barely notice yourself doing:

- Brushing your teeth
- Putting on your clothes
- Getting to or from work/school
- Eating lunch
- Making your bed
- Washing your face
- Doing the dishes

Now, for the next week do that activity mindfully – in other words, be really conscious and aware of every aspect of it.

Be aware how extraordinary the mundane action you've chosen really is, and how amazing it is that you, with the unique make-up and gene pool that you have, came into existence and are using the instruments that you're using. How many hands have been involved in gathering the raw materials, manufacturing, selling and delivering them? How many different sensations can you feel in your body as you use them?

Imagine how you'd feel and how your life would change if you lost the physical ability to do these things again. If you are eating, take time to be aware of every single taste and sensation. Chew your food properly. Marvel at the miracle of how the body digests sustenance and converts it into energy.

Say a silent thank-you for the experience, for the growers and the harvesters and the distributors and the makers; thank them for nourishing your body so that you may be alive today. Try to imagine that you're from another land or universe and see everything anew, as if for the first time. Connect with the awe and wonder you'd feel if you'd never tasted food or drunk a glass of water before.

These 'normal' tasks can be stress busters. They can be like a church bell or a call to prayer that reminds us to return to the present so that we can encounter the sacred.

When you bring attention to the wonder of the small things in your life, the details of the bigger issues start to assume less importance. And miraculously, when you loosen your focus on them, they often somehow start to slip into place.

I don't know how many times a week I arrive at my destination on autopilot with little or no memory of my journey. The days of my life that I remember the most, even though side by side they appear the same – same bus, train, route to work and home – are the days I was present in my life. When I chose not to multitask – not to be on my phone, listen to music, read a book, think about the weekend – but instead was there on that train and looked around, noticed the woman next to me who was heavily pregnant and the man with the handlebar moustache and the saxophonist busking in front of the coffee shop. When I've stopped and was grateful for the moment; for the gift of his music, her smile, my life. That, I've learned, is peace.

GA

The more practised you become at switching your focus from your thoughts to where you actually are, the greater the sense of freedom and joy you experience. You no longer rush to get things done. Instead, you get lost in the detail and the glory of them and wonder how you could have missed out for so long.

Consciousness transforms life. Whatever you're doing – making a cup of tea, waiting for a bus, or getting dressed – use it as an opportunity to connect with what is. Decline your mind's invitation to worry and instead focus on the task at hand.

Presence of mind is peace of mind.

The power of pausing

'Give your morning to God and he will give you your day.'
CARMEL MURPHY

Life will present countless challenges to your practice of peace. They'll come in the form of relationships, traffic, supermarket checkout lines and so on. You'll be triggered because you're human. Any strong emotion like jealousy, anger or fear can catapult you back into anxiety and negative projection.

When this happens, see it as an opportunity to practise – hit the pause button, fast. Focus on your breath. You have one goal: to preserve your peace of mind while not robbing someone else of theirs.

Your mind may tell you you've been offended. It will almost certainly want you to dive into the future or rake through the past. Refuse its pull to rope you into a story and instead stay present.

Notice what you're experiencing and then name, feel and release it. If you're struggling to stay in the moment, excuse yourself from the room or even go to the nearest loo to realign yourself and calm down.

Pausing buys you vital time. It enables you to respond with kindness and curiosity rather than fear. As you do so, how others respond to you will, in turn, miraculously shift.

If you feel your mind flooding with attack thoughts, pause for longer. Wait until you're centred and then wait some more.

Have some useful phrases ready such as, 'I'll need to get back to you about that', or 'I'm sorry you feel that way'. Stay soft and stay open and remind yourself that whatever the problem is, love, in one form or another, is the answer.

One hasty word or reaction can alter a friendship for a lifetime. I often struggle with inserting a pause. I'm too worried that I won't get my way unless I respond straight away. But over time I've come to see that my way doesn't necessarily help me or anyone else. I think I know what's best, but often I'm just trying to control outcomes to avoid my own anxiety. On a daily basis I try to observe before I respond – and things always turn out better when I manage to insert a pause.

JN

....

MOVE A MUSCLE TO SHIFT A THOUGHT

If your thoughts are particularly persistent, try using movement to dislodge them. Remember, Action Changes Things.

Shrug your shoulders, wiggle your toes or even try balancing on one leg. Singing and dancing are great too – anything that allows you to get out of your head and focus on the moment.

Again, watch out for your mind. It is going to use every opportunity to try to persuade you to return to living in your head. It may even tell you this new way of life is lazy and irresponsible. But just remember how many moments you lost as the result of being caught up in loops of obsessive thoughts.

....

Indecision

Pausing is also great for indecision. When you're not sure about something, instead of forcing a resolution, try to put the dilemma in the back of your mind. If necessary, write it on a piece of paper and put it in your Acceptance Cup (pp. 94–5).

Accepting that you 'don't know' is one of the fastest routes to allowing an answer to emerge. And be careful not to short-circuit the process. It's like baking bread: each time you prematurely open the oven door you jeopardize the outcome.

Using the pause button for decision-making gives you space to hear your inner voice, your intuition, your inner knowing. It usually has answers that the conscious mind can't deliver. Sometimes it will take the form of a hunch, at other times a coincidence. The more regularly you meditate, the easier it becomes to hear – learn to trust it when it comes.

When I'm suffering from indecision – which has happened a lot in my life – it's generally because there's a conflict between my overly educated brain and my inner knowing. My father was an academic, so I came from a home where the intellect was prized above all else and talk of intuition was dismissed as airy-fairy. Meditation has proven to me beyond all doubt that there's another form of knowing that has nothing to do with education. It comes in the form of an inner nudge. To start with, it was so gentle that I often overrode it. It would say turn left rather than right, or call this person or wait a while. Now, whenever I can discern it, I listen – it always leads to something more wonderful than my limited mind could have predicted. It's as if through meditation I've tapped into a collective pool of wisdom that makes itself known through my heart rather than my head. Just as in the Bible it was eating from the tree of knowledge that led to Eve and Adam being cast out of paradise, I can see how I exile myself from a state of peace when I give my thoughts too great a priority.

JN

Uncertainty

Living with uncertainty – a pause that's inflicted on us rather than one we've chosen – can be incredibly uncomfortable. It can send us into a tornado of antics trying to force a resolution. Be it a job loss, a medical diagnosis or just the absence of a phone call, sitting with uncertainty takes courage.

When one door closes it can be tough to trust that another really will open. Notice when your ego tries to persuade you to close the gap between what was and what will be by obsessing about possible outcomes. Watch it generate fearful attack thoughts. Do your very best to not engage with any of it. When you allow yourself to rest in the uncertainty of what is, space opens up for answers to emerge.

There is a great deal of uncertainty in the line of work I am in. There have been times when I have scheduled months of childcare and schooling and travel only for the job to fall through, or other times when there are three jobs that might go around the same time, but none can be counted on or let go of, yet all will impact the other aspects of my life and my relationships. I have by necessity come to a place of acceptance that uncertainty is just part and parcel of what I do. I try to make sure that, no matter what, my time with my children is protected, but beyond that I have no control and simply have to let go and trust that whichever job is right for me will stick. When I hold on too tight to the end result, I only get disappointed and resentful. As provocative as it can be to not know what the next six months will look like work-wise, it's so much better for my peace of mind if I let go into the unknown and let the cards fall as they may.

GA

'If you take care of your mind, you take care of the world.'
ARIANNA HUFFINGTON

....

COINCIDENCES

Some people call them coincidences, others synchronicity. Start looking out for them in your day-to-day life. The time you spend meditating brings you into alignment with whatever it is that orders our universe, so you're likely to notice them occurring with increasing frequency.

You may think of someone you haven't seen for ages and suddenly they'll call. You'll finally pluck up the courage to leave the job that was making you miserable and a fantastic opportunity that you'd never imagined presents itself. Or you'll trust your instinct to take time off work to care for a loved one and you're offered extra pay for work you can do at home.

Make sure to add these moments to the list you started in the Living Proof exercise (p. 141). They're further proof that this new way of life yields tangible results.

....

Transforming difficulty

As you get used to pausing when you're disturbed or upset, you'll find it gets easier and easier to contain your responses and not react inappropriately.

If you find yourself struggling, take the more difficult feelings into your formal meditation practice.

As you sit down to meditate, hold a gentle awareness of what's upsetting you. Don't seek to repress it or puzzle it out, just offer it up to your practice and see what happens.

The secret is not to struggle. It's like learning to float — we think we'll sink unless we do something. In fact, the opposite is true. When you allow yourself to rest in your own consciousness you discover you can float and the weight of your worries is taken away.

When you are present to your difficulties and pain in this way, meditation becomes like a magical composter. You actively nourish the parts of your life and yourself that you find difficult and, over time, miraculously transform them.

Being human

'Ultimately, we have just one moral duty: to reclaim large areas of peace in ourselves, more and more peace, and to reflect it towards others. And the more peace there is in us, the more peace there will also be in our troubled world.'

ETTY HILLESUM

As your meditation practice develops, when you lose your balance you'll find that you have a place to come home to. A place that doesn't depend on your accomplishments or possessions. A place where you can feel safe and be at peace.

You'll still lose your emotional footing from time to time. When it happens it doesn't mean you're failing. It's a sign that you're not shut down or anaesthetized but open and sensitive and truly alive to life.

When we shift from a state of internal war to one of peace, the change is reflected externally. It's as if meditation helps us chart a course that keeps the wind in our sails.

Life will begin to feel less complicated and problematic. You will start to feel lighter and you'll laugh more. You'll be less confused by situations and notice a new ease in your relationships with others. The stronger the connection you feel with your inner self, the more connected you'll feel to all humans. Prejudices and judgements will start to fall away as you sense the interconnectedness that lies beneath what divides us.

I used to be addicted to the drama of life. To the rights and wrongs, the 'he said/she said'. I'd want to get straight into the middle of whatever was happening and try to sort it out. But often, when I do that, I'm really just pouring paraffin onto someone else's emotional bonfire. Now, when I remember, I try not to stoke the embers of any conflict. Instead of fanning outrage I try to just listen and be a peaceful presence. A port in the storm is more useful than someone fanning the flames.

JN

Peace in the wider world

Peace is contagious and, now that you have it, you can help to spread it.

As you take your thinking mind less seriously you'll find you have the capacity to be present for others in a new way. You might not be able to salve another's pain, but you can sit with them while he or she processes it.

When you allow your inner peace to light another's way you'll find that their pain starts to dissipate and solutions start to emerge.

When we make peace our priority we can be of real service in the world. If all we do to help change the world is meditate, we will still make a difference. We'll be less likely to react with anger and rob others of their peace of mind.

'One of the advantages of being born in an affluent society is that if one has any intelligence at all, one will realize that having more and more won't solve the problem.'

JETSUNMA TENZIN PALMO

We all know the power of an unkind or harsh word. Remember; hurt people hurt other people. So if we reduce the harm we do, we will instantly create a ripple effect.

Try – one day at a time – not to cause harm to yourself or others. When you're uncertain, hit pause. Remember that you don't have a crystal ball – none of us knows what will ultimately be for the best, but if we do the next right thing then the right consequences will follow.

If everyone in the world took responsibility for their own mental well-being, think how much more peaceful the world would be instantaneously!

Reflection

'No matter who causes you grief, take your complaints to the meditation room, where your real friend is.'

AMMA

When I find myself getting too caught up with or too hurt by the drama of my life, I can take a moment to pause. I can remember that while the surface of my life may be like a choppy sea on which I get tossed and turned, deep below the surface there is a part of me that remains constant and unaffected by what is happening above. I picture myself as a stone dropping down beneath the surface of the waves, falling deeper and deeper into my own internal ocean until I find a place of peace to rest. When I reside there, I know that everything is actually all right.

Action: Today, if I feel overwhelmed I will pause and remind myself that underneath the surface, my true self resides.

Affirmation: Whatever else is happening, deep down I know I am absolutely OK.

Principle
7

LOVE:
Transforming Relationships

'The cure for all the ills and wrongs, the cares, the sorrows and the crimes of humanity, all lie in the one word "love". It is the divine vitality that everywhere produces and restores life.'

LYDIA M. CHILD

Love knows no bounds. It wants the best for everyone and doesn't discriminate or judge. Love is our authentic nature and is always present but, like the sun, can be temporarily obscured.

Love transforms us. It dissolves our prejudices and opens our hearts. It connects us to ourselves, to each other and to all humanity.

Without love we feel alone, we erect barriers and divisions, often without realizing it. We may long for connection but we cut ourselves off from it.

This is a path of love, and love is woven through every step of the journey. The essentials and the principles you've learnt so far have been preparing you to be able to experience true love in its most powerful, spiritual sense.

The key to love

'I am happier when I love than when I am loved. I adore my husband, my son and my grandchildren, my mother, my dog and, frankly, I don't know if they even like me. But who cares? Loving them is my joy.'

ISABEL ALLENDE

Many of us come to this journey looking for love. In Western cultures, romantic love has become almost a religion – something we're encouraged to devote ourselves to seeking, in the belief that it will bring a perfect union and meaning to our lives. We're raised on fairy tales of girls transformed by the kiss of their handsome prince and bombarded by images of happy couples. Movie after movie ends with a happy couple who, after overcoming the requisite obstacles, look certain to live happily ever after.

It's not surprising that many of us have come to see love as a Holy Grail, something to be sought, found and won. Something we have to look for in the arms of others or in our worldly endeavours. Often our hearts take a battering. Some of us may shut down and turn our back on the very idea of love, others just try harder. But no matter how deeply we bury our desire, all of us ache for love to transform and make good our lives.

The good news is that you don't need to search for it any longer; it is available right here, right now, in every one of our lives. If you use the principles in this book to clear the fear and emotional scars that can block love's flow, you'll experience an extraordinary truth: love isn't something you have to seek or win. There's an infinite supply of it – enough for each and every one of us. All we need to know is how to gain access to it.

Love isn't something that we either do or don't have according to what we feel. It's something we can experience at any time. That's because the key to unlocking love's flow is very simple, it comes from realizing that love isn't a *feeling* but an *action*.

It is loving action that connects us to the constant supply of love that exists within each of us. Every time we act with love we generate more. It's like a muscle – love may be hidden behind years of righteous anger, fear or hurt, but we all have it and can choose to use it.

Like gratitude, it has a magic multiplying effect: the more loving you are, the more loved and loving you'll feel.

What's more, it doesn't matter whether you're giving or getting it; you'll experience love either way. It's the flow that counts.

Be prepared for your ego to object. To the ego, love is a two-way street, something to be traded, a transactional relationship. 'What about me?' it'll want to know. Your ego will tell you to ration love, to save it up for the special or deserving people in your life. But, of course, when you withhold love you deprive yourself.

Love – in the spiritual sense – has no limits, it's unconditional. It has nothing to do with how anyone else behaves. Giving in order to get back isn't love – it's a form of manipulation. And giving love only to those you judge to be worthy is a subtle form of discrimination.

With practice, it becomes possible to choose to respond with love no matter how somebody else behaves.

Love begins with you

The preceding principles have been getting you ready to love. You can't love if you're a bouncing ball of emotional reactivity or a jumble of unmet needs. Nor can you experience love if you're walled into a fortress of self-protection or wearing boxing gloves.

You can't give away something you haven't got. If you fail to meet your own needs you risk slipping into co-dependency and hoping that others will make good your own internal sense of lack. Your home can't be made in anyone else's arms or company. Your true home is right where you are, within you.

Every relationship – whether with a friend or a partner – is like an arch: if each of you stands tall and strong in your own space, love can be the keystone. But if one of you leans, it can topple.

....

LOVING VS CO-DEPENDENCY

Compulsive helping or co-dependency is now recognized as a serious, and sometimes life-threatening, addiction. People who are co-dependent attempt to get their self-esteem from taking care of others; often thinking they are just being kind or helpful. They obsess about others and try to control, help or guilt them into doing what they think is best. Other symptoms include saying yes when they mean no, accepting unacceptable behaviour, staying in a harmful relationship to please another, giving unsolicited advice and trying to save someone who doesn't want to be saved.

It can be hard to say no when we can see that someone needs help, but saying yes when we want to say no or giving what we haven't got is a form of dishonesty, not love. It sets us up as victims and martyrs who then resent the people we've helped or become angry when our 'love' isn't reciprocated. It also puts us at risk of depression, anxiety and chemical addiction.

Encouraging others to rely on us to meet *their* needs can make us feel needed and less immediately vulnerable, but it's the flipside of the same coin. Dependency in either direction doesn't work long term.

....

Hopefully the work you've been doing since you opened this book will have given you a sense of self-connection. Love will never ask you to abandon yourself. As women we're encouraged to be selfless, but the meaning has become misunderstood. It does not mean to override our needs, but rather to love without ego. The very same obstacles that block us from connecting with our authentic selves can block us from experiencing love. Our ego-based thinking, emotional wounds and fear can all get in the way.

WE's principles enable you to heal and foster in yourself the sense of oneness that you've longed for in your connection with others. It's from that position of wholeness that we're able to really experience love's flow in our relationships with others.

Loving others

Love asks that we don't discriminate. That we love those we know and those we don't, those we like and those we'd rather avoid. Our neighbour is abso-lutely anyone – friend, stranger or foe.

As women we're all familiar with what it feels like to be on the receiving end of discriminatory or abusive behaviour. But without realizing it most of us also discriminate against and judge others.

Think about it. In your friendships do you always go for the cool, popu-lar people? Do you only want to be with the people you judge as being like you? Do you justify avoiding those who come from a different background or socio-economic strata by saying you're not likely to have as much in common?

Do you let your own agenda and needs influence your engagement? Do you automatically critique the people you encounter – their dress, their class, their race, their appearance? Are you one-upping and one-downing without even being aware? Are you impatient or intolerant with those who aren't as smart as you? How do you treat those you have power over – i.e. dependent family members, newcomers to any social group or anyone you employ? How do you treat the strangers you pass in the street, the newspaper vendor, the shop assistant, the waitress?

Every one of your encounters gives you the choice to either set yourself apart or to practise love.

The further down this path you travel, the less you will find yourself able to engage in behaviours that were once second nature. How often have you bonded with others by gossiping? Or pretended (even to yourself) that you weren't gossiping at all but assessing a situation to work things out for everyone's benefit? Perhaps you use it as a way of making yourself look insightful. All gossip is a form of attack – no matter how good it might make you feel.

In each encounter ask yourself: 'What would love do?' Apply the Golden Rule (pp. 5–6) and treat others as you'd like to be treated yourself.

....

THE SHAME GAME

When examining our own actions it can be easy to slip into shame, guilt or self-blame. Resist the temptation. Beating yourself up is just another racket. This is fact-finding. It's about becoming aware, because without awareness we can't change. The behaviours you're noticing and naming were developed to protect you and get your needs met. They may not be desirable, but they're understandable. Now that you're aware of them you've got a choice. So use your energy to change rather than blame or shame. Remember, love isn't just for others – it's for you as well.

....

Our template

All of us are in relationships all the time. And whether they're romantic or not we can find ourselves slipping into old, harmful patterns. With frightening speed we can recreate our childhood patterns of relating: in the workplace, at the school gates or in the bedroom.

The template for how you love others lies in your family and upbringing. What you grow up with you learn. If you lived with abuse, you'll carry within you the knowledge and capacity to abuse.

If you grew up with compassion, you'll find it easier to have compassion for others. But no matter how wonderful our parents or early caregivers, most of us carry wounds that affect our ability to love.

....

ABANDONED OR ENGULFED BY LOVE

Two of the most frequent ways we can be wounded in childhood is by receiving too little or too much love. Both significantly affect how we conduct ourselves in adult relationships.

Emotional or physical neglect can reveal itself in adulthood as excessive neediness. Whereas being smothered by love, due to our primary caregiver's own neediness or anxiety, can lead to a paradoxical fear of intimacy and a pattern of avoiding the connection that's craved.

Most of us can swing between feeling needy or feeling smothered, depending upon whom we are with and their pattern of relating. Extreme states of neediness and avoidance can be signs of an underlying addiction. The medical profession now accepts that love can be an addiction in its own right and there are specific 12-step fellowships one can go to for help with it.[30]

....

If we don't take responsibility for those early childhood wounds, we can stay stuck in a lifelong standoff. We can find ourselves repeatedly recreating the same dynamics that we experienced as a child in the hope that the ending will be different.

But when we try to make someone else – a parent, friend, partner or even boss – heal our early wounds by giving us what we lacked in childhood, we end up getting what we got first time round: a mountain of pain.

Others can't change our template, but we can. So when you find yourself struggling, look back to see if a childhood wound is being reopened and then use the spiritual tools you've learnt to bring about change.

Keep your focus on what you can change – yourself (NOT your past or your family).

It was many years into my working life before I realized that I was carrying my childhood template for relating into my adult workplace. It was not a good look! My boss (who, this being a newsroom, was typically male) always became my father. I'd seek his attention at every opportunity. Those I worked with became my siblings and I'd feel rivalry whenever they, too, sought his praise. I'd regress to being the jealous but good girl who overperformed to win her emotionally distant father's attention. I often did win my boss's approval (and became a workaholic in the process), but it didn't do anything to heal my inner girl's broken heart. No matter how much acclaim she got, she wanted more. Because, of course, what she really longed for was to be loved for who she was, not for what she did. Thanks to these principles I learned to give her the love she needed, but if I skimp on my self-care I can easily slip into that pattern of relating when I'm in the presence of a powerful, competent male.

JN

The stronger the connection we feel with someone, the greater the triggers into our past will be. You may be amazed at how quickly you can regress into child-like feelings. So take time out to connect with the wounded part, your inner girl (pp. 84–7). Ask her what she wants and needs. Usually it will be to feel seen and heard and safe. You can provide that for her.

....

INSTANT RELIEF

If you're overwhelmed in the moment by an emotion, try this simple but effective tool. Make your hand into a fist and then place it over your heart. Press it gently into your chest as you breathe in and out deeply, telling yourself (silently if you're in public), 'Although I'm sad/angry/upset about _____, I am safe and I'm OK.'

It's a great way to self-soothe when you're feeling triggered.

And don't forget the tools you've learnt so far: notice, name, feel and release your emotions; use affirmations and meditation to help you return to centre; look for your part in your resentments and then bring yourself into the present and ask what love would do.

....

I owe a large chunk of my spiritual growth to my first husband. We had an incredibly messy and painful divorce with lots of horrible conflict, which it took many years to recover from. If it hadn't been for all that pain, I wouldn't be on the path that I am on now. Looking back, I can see how it led to transformation. I had to learn to love in the face of anger and what felt like hatred – otherwise I wouldn't have survived. I am no longer the wounded child who entered that marriage demanding to be loved. I am an adult woman who is happy in her own skin – with or without a partner. I now refer to my first husband as my greatest teacher and, extraordinarily, I feel genuine gratitude and love, despite the pain we put each other through.

JN

Understanding

'And the day came when the risk to remain tight in a bud was more painful than the risk it took to blossom.'

ELIZABETH APPELL

While much of your life may have been spent wanting to be understood, love turns the tables and asks that you make trying to understand others your priority. With understanding comes compassion and the realization that deep down we are all the same, have the same needs, wants and fears.

When we truly understand others and our awareness of differences evaporates, love becomes easy. We see beyond our personal story, prejudices and preferences, and can become truly present and available. We realize that our similarities matter most and we can start to be able to practise love in every situation.

EXERCISE 1: Our Enemy's Shoes

This exercise can help you gain more insight, and therefore more compassion, for those who have hurt you.

Pick someone you feel animosity towards. They can be someone from your own life or even a public figure.

Imagine you're an actor and you are to play their part. To do that effectively you need to understand his or her motivation. You're a professional, so take the time you need to find out as much as possible about the person's early life and influences. What was their childhood like? Why do they think and act as they do? What has hurt them? What has nurtured them? How have they become who they are today? If you want, you can write it out or, if they are someone in the public eye, use the library or Internet to do your research.

If the person is a political figure, try to understand their cause and why they fight for it. What does it mean to them? You are not seeking to excuse or condone anything they've done but to understand, so that you can play your part as effectively as possible.

When you've gathered as much information as you can, centre yourself and close your eyes.

Imagine sitting opposite the person. If they are truly someone who makes you feel unsafe, you might prefer to imagine that you are visiting them in prison or perhaps under the protection of a bodyguard or guardian angel.

Hold this person in your mind's eye. Notice and name the strength of your feeling. Is it hate? Is it hurt? Is it a combination of both? Whatever it is, try to allow yourself to connect with the feeling and then to release it. Remember, you are not here to judge but to understand. They are sitting in front of you, just a few feet away. If you both reached out your arms, your hands would touch. Look straight into his or her eyes. Hold their gaze and then hold it some more. Keep staring straight ahead and hold this imaginary focus for the rest of the exercise.

Now, as you look into their eyes, ask yourself why they've done what they've done. Start your questioning in the present and then move back in time. Keep asking why. Was it because they were abused themselves? Because they were abandoned or their father died when they were young or they grew up in poverty? Let the question lead you further and further back in time. Keep looking into their eyes. What do you notice about their eyes? How different are they from your eyes? How different are they from the eyes of someone you are close to? Now cross the divide between you and imagine you are that person. See and feel what it's like to be in their skin.

This may make you very uncomfortable. It may bring up all kinds of difficult emotions. But it may also bring you one step closer to feeling compassion for this other human being. When you feel you have learned all you can, take your time returning to centre. Breathe in and out as many times as you need to. Say your name out loud and maybe shake your arms and legs to return to being you.

Think of your 'character' and their motivation. Now try to reconnect with the animosity you felt for them. Notice how much it has diminished. The more we educate ourselves about another, the harder it is to judge. Next time you feel the desire to condemn, try to defuse that natural impulse through understanding.

....

Those who hurt us can become our greatest teachers. Love – in the form of compassion – shows us that they're usually caught up in their own wound-edness, grievances or fear. Hurt people hurt people. So set the boundaries you need to set (p. 252) and instead of retaliating, try to trust that they are doing their best – however that looks.

Looking for romantic love

The crucible of romantic love will stress-test your spiritual growth more than any other challenge. If you don't feel happy and complete on your own, you're not yet ready for someone else. So ironically, we know we're ready for romantic love when we no longer feel a desperate *need* for it.

There's no rush, practising the principles in this book will bring you the sense of comfort you long for in someone else's arms.

....

SINGLE BY CHOICE

If you find yourself obsessing about when you're going to meet the perfect person, try doing the opposite of what you feel. Step back, take time out and see what's lying underneath the urgency.

It can also be liberating to set ourselves a specific time period during which we're not going to look for a partner. Try setting a commitment to yourself of three to six months. During that period, put down the habits that feed your neediness. Stop scanning and stop flirting. No more placing yourself in locations that might possibly bear results. Give up trying to make yourself lovable and you'll discover that you already are.

Use this opportunity to seek out friendships with women who are comfortable with themselves and their singledom. But also use this time to really enjoy your relationship with yourself. Take yourself on dates, buy yourself treats and really enjoy the only person whom you can guarantee will be with you until death does you part. You'll then be in much better shape when you start dating again.

Then, after your self-designated time is up, test your readiness by seeing how reactive you are around your family. This may feel like it's beside the point, but if you're still red-hot with hurt and resentment then there's more work to be done. You want your adult woman, not your wounded inner girl, to be in charge of whom you choose to be with.

....

Dating

'We are not what other people say we are. We are who we know ourselves to be, and we are what we love. That's OK.'

LAVERNE COX

Dating is the process of looking for someone who is worthy and able to fill an incredibly important and intimate role. It's an information-gathering process that takes time. Do first interviews and then second, third, fourth and fifth. As many as you think you need. Use it to find out who the person is and whether they might be able to meet your requirements. Treat dates as opportunities to research whether you want what's on offer. Don't try to close that anxious gap between liking someone and not knowing whether it's going to work by pushing things along too fast.

From now on you're the chooser, not the chosen.

If you find yourself focusing on what your date is thinking about you and whether or not they like you, hit the pause button. The moment you're trying to work out what they're thinking you're abandoning yourself. What others think of you is their business. What matters is what you think of you – and, in this instance, of them.

....

HISTORICAL BAGGAGE

It's not surprising that dating can be fraught. Historically, as women, how our lives unfolded depended upon whether or not we were taken on by a man through marriage or as a dependent. When women finally got the vote in the UK in 1918, it was only given to married women over 30. Even today the tax system rewards marriage for both heterosexual and same-sex couples. Add to that the economic and social benefits of sharing a home, the ticking of our biological clocks (if we want children) and the societal stigma that can accompany being single, and it's easy to see how a natural longing for a mate can morph into something less healthy.

....

In the past, you may have worried about whether the person you've just met liked or fancied you more than whether you actually liked and wanted them. But now, if you are really practising WE's principles, your attitude will have shifted. You'll have come to see yourself as a precious and unique being. So instead of worrying about *being* chosen, actively work out what you do and don't want.

....

EXERCISE 2: Drawing Up a Partner Spec

....

This exercise will help you get clear on who exactly is the right partner for you. This is a great exercise to do, whether or not you're actively seeking love. If you're in a relationship, it can remind you to stay honest. If you're looking for a relationship, it gives you a job spec. And if you're taking time out, you can shelve this exercise for when you are ready to start looking.

Take a blank piece of paper and draw a line down the middle from top to bottom. Head the left-hand side 'Needs' and the right-hand side 'Wants'. In your 'Needs' column write down the qualities of a relationship and attributes of a partner that are non-negotiable. So you might put 'mutual attraction' in 'Needs' but 'good looks' in the 'Wants' column. 'solvent' may go in the 'Needs' column, but 'wealthy' should go in the 'Wants'. The reason to be rigorous about this is that it's likely you have adopted attitudes that reflect your conditioning, rather than your authentic values, without even realizing it.

Fill out both columns with as much detail as you like. Then take a look at what you've written. Is there anything that you really long for that isn't on your list? Add it to the 'Wants' column.

If you want, share what you've written with someone you trust to make sure you haven't confused your wants with your needs.

All lists will differ, but there are two qualities that should be on everyone's 'Needs' column: 'available' and 'kind'. If you didn't write these down, please add them now. 'Available' means that the person is not with someone else and is also emotionally available. That, of course, rules out anyone who is in active addiction. Using addicts, of whatever kind, are not emotionally available. Their primary relationship will always be with their drug of choice.

Everything that is in your 'Needs' column is non-negotiable. You must get your legitimate needs met 100 per cent. Your 'Wants' are less important. They are the icing on the cake, but without the cake they're meaningless.

Keep a copy of your 'Needs' column in your journal or phone. Remind yourself that you're not settling for anything less. Then fold up the original list and place it in your Acceptance Cup (pp. 94–5).

You've charted your course and sooner or later the universe will respond. How will you know when that time has come? You'll meet someone who meets your needs. Your side of the bargain is that you must decline to settle for anything less.

....

THE GOLDEN RULE FOR DATING

The Golden Rule gives us a simple code of conduct. We treat others as we'd want to be treated ourselves. That means not flirting with anyone else's partner. If they're with someone else, they're out of bounds, period. If that person is flirting with you, check in with yourself to see if you're reciprocating. Ask yourself how that person's partner would feel if she saw you and you'll know instantly. Simple, perhaps, but easy to forget.

For years society has pitted women against each other. The time for this to stop is now! We need to start treating each other as if we are important, precious and worthy of respect if we want society to do the same.

....

Staying honest

'It's not your job to like me — it's mine.'

BYRON KATIE

No matter how powerful we may feel in other aspects of our lives, many of us adapt ourselves to fit into relationships that can never meet our needs. We do it out of fear that nothing better will come along. We hide the parts of ourselves we are afraid aren't lovable and alter ourselves to fit into the space we think a current or future partner might want.

Of course, we want to be liked. We want to be chosen. We want to fit in. But if we allow parts of our real selves to be invisible, we eventually erase ourselves and before long are back at the start of this journey — lost and in pain.

Remember your commitment from the First Principle to being honest about who you really are? If you catch yourself pretending to be something you're not to please a partner, or saying you like something that you don't, or professing that something is OK when it isn't, immediately notice and name it. Then check in with yourself to see if you're fearful or need to feel and release emotions (p. 105). If you are fearful, take time out to reassure the scared part of yourself. Remind yourself that you're loved and lovable as you are. Nobody else matters enough to abandon yourself again.

So many of my relationships during my high-school and college years went the same route – I met someone, instantly fell in love and spent every possible waking hour with them, but stopped doing the things I enjoyed doing, stopped taking care of myself. I adopted their interests, friends, music, tastes and ended up immersing myself so much that the old me was no longer recognizable. Before long I'd start to resent them, even though it was me who actively let myself go. I've since learned that one of the biggest gifts we can give ourselves, the person we love, and the relationship on the whole, is our commitment to remain who we really are and to purposefully carve time and space for ourselves to be able to do so.

GA

When I've met someone I like I do three things. I make sure they see me without my make-up on; I make sure I sing out loud (I love to sing but am virtually tone deaf, so they need to be able to handle that). And I disclose my vulnerability. I don't do this to push someone away but to make sure that they want me for who I really am, with all my so-called imperfections. Like everyone else, I long to be loved and I try to keep myself honest by being real.

JN

....

BEING PERFECTLY IMPERFECT

If we don't embrace our so-called imperfections then how can we expect anyone else to? If you feel yourself starting to become afraid that you're not measuring up to contemporary notions of what women are expected to be, remind yourself that they are unrealistic and instead of trying harder, do the opposite.

If you're ashamed of your singing voice, sing out loud. If you worry about your weight, wear something tight. If you wear foundation because you fear your skin tone is too uneven, try not wearing it at all.

Do whatever it takes to remind yourself and those around you that you are real and three-dimensional. You're not a cut-out from a magazine, so don't erase those parts of yourself that don't fit the image. Show the world that you are perfect just the way you are.

....

Sexual love

Sexual attraction is all too easily confused with love. It's often tempting to mistake being wanted sexually for being loved or liked for who we are. And if we're feeling insecure, it can be tempting to use sex to foster a feeling of closeness and bridge the gap.

But sex — and the feelings it releases — can mask underlying issues and blind us to the reality of a situation. By the time we realize our needs aren't going to be met we can find it hard to leave because we've become invested and/or attached.

So, really get to know them first and try waiting for a period of time before having sex. Set yourself a time frame. A month? Two? A particular number of dates? It may seem impossible, but anyone really interested in you will be happy to wait.

....

THE NO-HARM RULE

Once you're sure you want to be sexually involved with someone, use the No-Harm Rule to protect your emotional, psychological and spiritual well-being. Whatever you want goes, as long as you don't harm yourself or another. That means taking responsibility for your sexual and reproductive health. It also means not saying yes when you want to say no and not pretending to like something you don't in order to please another. Lying to someone else to make him or her happy does both parties a big disservice.

The No-Harm Rule means you don't objectify yourself either. Society encourages us to mistake self-objectification for freedom. But if you're contorting yourself into a sexual paradigm that is designed to please the male gaze then, however powerful it might make you feel, at some level you're still abandoning and therefore harming yourself.

....

Sexting or having anonymous sex with someone you've just met online can similarly feel like an act of freedom, but if you're risking your sexual and emotional health, it's really a form of self-harm. So roll the tape forward. Ask yourself how you'll feel the day after. Treat yourself as you'd treat anyone else you love – gently, kindly and with respect.

Healthy sex is fun and can be a fantastic release, but it shouldn't be the emotional glue to fix a faltering relationship. And, of course, you don't need a partner to have a healthy sex life. You can learn to self-pleasure so that your unmet sexual longings don't drive you into the arms of someone you wouldn't otherwise want to be with.

....

OMG YES!

Our need for sexual release is no different from any of our other physical needs. It's healthy and natural, but as women we've often been taught to fear and conceal it.

Whereas for men masturbation is taken as a given, for women there is still a stigma. Getting to know your own sexual needs and how to meet them will make you feel more of an agent and less of an object. Plus you'll know what brings you pleasure. It's hard to have an equal and reciprocal sexual relationship if you're not aware of how your own body works.

You can find techniques online at websites such as www.OMGyes. com. Your clitoris has 8,000 nerve endings – double the nerve endings in the glans of a penis – and exists solely to give you pleasure.

There are also health benefits. Masturbation is associated with improved cervical and cardiovascular health, increased pelvic floor strength and better sleep.[31] Remarkably it can also even lower the risk of type 2 diabetes.

So shed any lingering shame and acknowledge and meet your natural needs.

....

Love or infatuation?

Infatuation and falling in love can both feel like a kind of glorious madness. At first it can be hard to distinguish between the two. But if it's the real thing, it'll be congruent with who you are. You won't be ashamed of introducing your partner to your friends, and you won't make excuses for him or her. You'll genuinely like the person for who he or she is. And you'll find that sexual chemistry will be less important than soul connection. You may discover that attraction comes *after* rather than before you get close.

Infatuation, on the other hand, relies on fantasy. Its bubble will burst if it comes into contact with reality. Sometimes intense sexual chemistry is an indicator of infatuation – you need the sexual high to feel OK about yourself or who you're with. There's a fantastic saying in 12-step meetings: if your eyes meet across a crowded room, run like hell. That instant chemistry can be a sign that you've met someone who fits your childhood template, rather than someone who feels 'right' for healthy reasons. If you find yourself having to stay 'high' to keep the fantasy alive, you're probably denying aspects of your partner or yourself. Sooner or later the giddy phase will wear off, and when it does you'll find out whether it's real or not.

If it is real, you'll like the person you're dating. You'll have a real friendship and want the best for him or her. It's at that point the journey really begins.

The three stages of romantic love

All relationships go through phases – most especially those that last long term. First comes the honeymoon, which usually lasts between 6 and 18 months. For that period, we're on a natural high and our partner can do little wrong.

Next comes the power struggle, where most relationships get stuck. The qualities we fell in love with are now often the ones we find most intolerable. We once loved them for being so outgoing, now we resent them for not being around. We loved them for being sensitive, now they appear weak or needy. We can feel shocked at how our loved ones have morphed before our very eyes. Of course they haven't — reality has just punctured the projections we thrust onto them.

> 'True love is not a strong, fiery, impetuous passion. It is, on the contrary, an element calm and deep.'
>
> ELLEN G. WHITE

Many couples remain in this power-struggle stage for the rest of their lives or for as long as the relationship lasts. Each tries to get his or her needs met, often dancing to the same emotional tune learned in childhood. Even if one partner gives in, the tension bubbles away beneath the surface.

....

THE INTIMACY DANCE

Most of us will have issues with intimacy and will dance the intimacy tango: one partner stepping back as the other steps forward. If you find yourself caught in this dance, notice and name what you're frightened of – it'll likely be fear of abandonment or engulfment. Use the Essential Practices (pp. 19–56) to anchor yourself so that you needn't retreat or encroach.

....

If you're lucky and do the work, you can reach the third stage where the power struggle is over, a sacred space is created and the issues that emerge within the relationship are seen as opportunities for each to support the other in healing and spiritual growth.

The magic of listening

'Listening is love in action.'

KATHERINE WOODWARD THOMAS

Listening is an act of love that we can practise in all our relationships. But ironically the closer the relationship, the harder it can be to really hear what the other person is saying.

A lot of the time what we call listening is actually just waiting for our turn to speak. And while we wait we're working out what we're going to say rather than really hearing what is being said to us.

It is only through listening that we get to the truth — otherwise we just react to what we *think* the other person is asking or doing. And that's how conflict starts.

EXERCISE 3: Magic Listening

This exercise will teach you a style of listening that will transform your interactions, not just with partners but with children, friends and work colleagues as well.

Sit opposite your listening partner, near enough to hold hands but not so close that you're invading each other's personal space — ideally a few inches apart from knee-to-knee if you're facing. Both of you take five deep breaths in and out. Then set a timer for an agreed length of time so that you can each have the same amount of uninterrupted magic listening.

You will each have an opportunity to say whatever is on your mind. There's just one rule – keep everything you say to 'I' statements. Start each statement with 'I feel …' or 'I understood …' Don't accuse the other person – this isn't an argument. It's an opportunity to talk about your thoughts and feelings without blame.

At intervals the listener repeats back to the person what he or she has said, using that person's own words. It's important that you use the other person's words. If you substitute your own, you're likely to give them your own spin and the other person won't feel heard. You might start by saying, 'What I heard you say was …' and when the other person confirms that you heard correctly, say, 'I hear you.'

When we don't like what the other person is saying or are hurt, it can be especially hard to listen. You may need to park your feelings – that means not allowing them to overtake you; this isn't the time. When the other person has had his or her say you'll get your chance to have yours and express your feelings. Remember to stick with 'I' statements and stay out of blame.

Be bold. Take the risk. Give up the desire to control through silence, bully through ranting, or wound by sniping, and give yourself and your relationships the gift of open, loving communication.

....

Empathy

Hearing another person's truth helps us to understand and to feel empathy. You might not agree with what you're hearing – you may think the other person is completely wrong – but understanding their reality will help you both.

Set aside your idea of what he or she should be thinking or feeling and imagine how you would feel if you were in their shoes and had that particular interpretation of events.

Allow yourself to truly see things from the other's point of view. You'll see the other person visibly relax when you show that you've not just heard but understood.

I know I've said hurtful things in past relationships. I know I've reacted instead of paused. And I feel huge shame. In some cases I've apologized. In others I am not ready yet, but I feel confident in the knowledge that I'm working my way towards it.

GA

Appreciation

Often we take people for granted once we've known them for a while. It's easy to spend more time focused on what's wrong with them rather than celebrating what's right.

Try telling someone you love – this can be a partner, a sibling, a child or a friend – something you appreciate about them every day for a week. Make it specific, just as you would a criticism, and include how the quality or action you appreciate makes you feel.

The harder we find it to think of an appreciation, the more we need to do it. If you're finding it particularly tough, write a gratitude list specifically about that person every evening. What you focus on grows, so the more you look for someone's good qualities, the more you'll find.

A spiritual advisor encouraged me to start thinking of an ex-partner as my 'beloved'. That regardless of our separateness we will for the rest of our lives be raising two children together and that makes him one of the most important people in my life, whether I like it or not. As you can imagine this is not easy, but the times I am able to do it genuinely and instigate my relations with him from a place of love and appreciation rather than resentment, hardness or, as he says, 'againstness', the more my actual perception shifts. When I practice this actively, my casual thoughts about him have a tendency towards, at the least, neutrality, which is something in and of itself, but sometimes even fondness and, miraculously, deep appreciation and gratitude.

GA

A non-verbal solution

When words fail, try hugging. When we squabble most of us end up regressing – and toddlers are never good at resolving their disputes. So set aside words if they're not working and hold each other until the emotional storm passes. Hugging may be the last thing you feel like doing, but just as an angry toddler can be soothed through holding, so can most adults.

You can even agree in advance that, if you can't resolve things within 30 minutes of starting to talk, you'll stop talking and hug. Hug until you both feel completely relaxed and then resist the temptation to start talking again. Soothe each other and yourselves by acting kindly. You can also pre-agree that you won't bring up the subject again for 24 hours, and by that time you might not even remember what you were fighting about.

Abuse

Research shows that once someone has crossed the line into behaving abusively they are likely to continue, and the longer women tolerate abuse, the harder they find it to leave.

Research also shows that although most women think they'd never tolerate abuse, it takes an average of 35 incidents of violence before a woman reports a partner to the police.[32]

If you experience abuse, tell someone immediately. The action of saying it out loud places you one step further away from slipping into denial. If you're unsure whether or not what has transpired constitutes abuse, check it out with someone else or call a specialist helpline for advice. You are responsible for your own self-care and that includes, as a priority, not allowing someone else to hurt you.

If you were abused as a child then this may be especially hard. If the relationship you're in now fits the template of 'love' you experienced back then, that wounded part of yourself may convince you that the relationship is 'right' even if the behaviour is 'wrong'. Now that you are an adult, you can tell yourself that it doesn't matter what you feel; the facts speak for themselves. Nobody is allowed to abuse you. Nobody. There may have been no one around when you were young to protect you, but now there is someone who's got your back 24/7. That someone is YOU.

When I found myself in an abusive relationship I blamed myself. It catapulted me straight back into being a terrified little girl who wasn't good enough. I needed to try harder, to jump higher, to please. Despite having qualified as a lawyer and written a book on domestic violence, I was so side-swiped that I didn't even recognize it when it happened. It took a therapist to point out that the situation was abusive. I wanted to understand my partner, but she was firm. Abuse is unacceptable: full stop. She told me to tell the younger, traumatized part of myself very clearly: 'This isn't OK. Nobody is allowed to treat you like this.' And it was only then that I found the ability to leave.

JN

....

PROTECTED BY LAW?

Until ridiculously recently the right of men to abuse women was preserved in culture and in law. Marital rape only became a crime in the UK in 1991 and in the US in all states in 1993, so legal protection is only a recent reality in the West and is still absent in a staggering 127 other countries across the globe.[33]

....

Stay or go?

'The key to happiness is freedom. The key to freedom is courage. The key to courage is love.'

KATE TRAFFORD

Pride masquerading as self-esteem can tell us to quit when the going gets tough. The thing is — and this is a big one — what you don't heal in this relationship you are likely to repeat in the next. So provided you're not in an emotionally or physically abusive relationship, you can use every relationship as an opportunity to learn.

If your relationship is going through a difficult phase, it can feel like a relief to move on and start afresh with someone new. But if you haven't done the work, you'll be like a guest at the Mad Hatter's tea party: you'll move to a nice clean place setting, but before long it'll look as messy as the last.

As the saying goes: you can either have the same relationship with lots of different people or lots of different relationships with the same person. If you keep the focus on your part, you'll grow and heal whether or not your partner changes. When you get to a place where you're no longer triggered by your partner's behaviour, you'll know what is right for you in the long term.

As you engage more in your life, with clarity and integrity, the right solutions follow.

Love goes on

'With every goodbye you learn.'

JOY WHITMAN

When a relationship or close friendship ends we're often so heartbroken that we feel as if love itself has disappeared. But as hard as it is to remember during those painful times, there is in fact an infinite supply of love all around us.

Every encounter we have – romantic or not – has the potential for true love and connection. Be open to experiencing it in all its many and often unexpected guises. It doesn't reside in any one person. While we're yearning for the 'special' relationship or wondering how it could have gone wrong, we're missing out on the love that is readily available.

Love is always there – just like the sun on a cloudy day – waiting for you. It's an action. It's a choice. And when you allow love to flow through you by taking loving action, not only will you connect to the never-ending source of love that resides within us all, but also you won't ever need to feel its absence again.

Love in the wider world

'Give light and people will find the way.'

ELLA BAKER

The lessons we learn in our close relationships are easily carried into the world. When we listen, empathize and appreciate other people, we become peacemakers in our daily interactions.

From early on in our lives we learn to divide ourselves into groups: genders, families, classes, teams, towns, countries, nationalities and ethnicities. We work out who is on our side and who is not. But we can't foster a sense of solidarity with one group without fostering a sense of 'other' towards another. When we focus on our differences, judgement and intolerance follow not too far behind. Then comes hate. That is how feuds, fights, wars and genocides begin – by focusing on how we differ. Intolerance breeds intolerance. Violence breeds violence and ultimately entrenchment and terror.

Love asks that we realize it is our similarities, not our differences, that matter most. Through each one of us is sewn a thread of humanity that connects us, one to the other. As human beings, aren't we, in fact, all on the same side?

Love does not discriminate – whatever our colour, sex, sexual preference, gender identification, religion, class, disability, cultural background. Love is love is love.

We don't have to know or even like someone to show love. We can act with love even when we don't feel it – the bigger the stretch, the greater the gain. The more you give love, the more love you'll receive.

Think what would happen if we all started to allow ourselves to feel love for everyone – not just for those in our own special tribe of family and friends, but for everyone we encountered.

Try starting with strangers. Look for the common humanity that connects you and do your very best to act with love. Then think of those you actively dislike, park your judgement and look for the tender, wounded part that is present, often hidden, inside every human – the part that is crying out for love. Ignore the outer casing and seek to connect to their hearts.

Each of us needs and deserves love. You have tools that enable you to process your hurts, rather than act them out.

Refuse to hurt yourself or anybody else. In every situation – small or large – ask yourself: 'What would love do?' And do your best to follow the answer.

Reflection

'Keep your face to the sunshine and you cannot see a shadow.'

HELEN KELLER

It's often much easier to feel anger, fear and hate as I focus on the pain and struggles around me. But when I allow myself to settle I discover that deep beneath my negative emotions, love exists. It's like the sun behind the clouds on a rainy day. I don't have to see it to know that it's still there. If I allow the clouds of judgement and fear to part and I turn my face up towards it, I will feel love's warmth.

Action: Today I will meet the gaze of all those I encounter with love.

Affirmation: I am love.

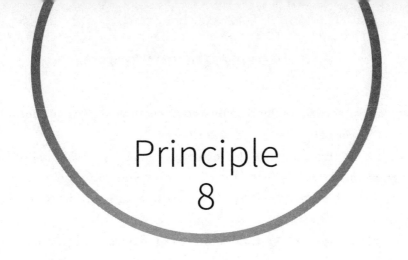

Principle
8

JOY:
Living Fully

'Let us dance in the sun, wearing wild flowers in our hair.'

SUSAN POLIS SCHUTZ

Joy feels like happiness, only better. It's generated from
within and doesn't depend on what we have or haven't got –
it's vital for our well-being and arises in the moment.
Joy connects us with a sense of the divine.

With so much suffering in the world around us, joy can seem like a luxury,
an indulgence, but in fact it's the opposite — it's a necessity. When we cut
ourselves off from joy we jeopardize our emotional health by leaving

ourselves vulnerable to depression and burnout as well as our ability to connect and be of use in the wider world.

So far on this journey WE's principles have given us tools to heal our emotional wounds, care for our bodies and calm our chattering minds. WE's Eighth Principle teaches us how to tend to the needs of our souls.

Joy replenishes our spiritual reserves so that we can be of maximum effectiveness. When we are joyful, we are resilient and able to relish our lives.

The necessity of joy

'The majority of patients I see admitted for inpatient psychiatric care are there in part because they've cared too much. They've given more than they've got to give.'

HELEN BACKHOUSE

Inside each of us is a pilot light – a life force. It's our job to tend that flame.

When we're depressed our internal light diminishes. If we allow ourselves to become too fearful, it will flicker precariously. Resentment, jealousy and ambition can smother it; so can overwork or compulsive caretaking.

But when we feed that flame with joy it burns gloriously and brightly. Joy is the oxygen we need to keep our inner light aglow. When we find ourselves fatigued, flat or flagging, turning to joy boosts our energy and our spirit.

Most of us struggle to live in balance. Often we end up living in a boom-or-bust cycle where we're either over-functioning or overwhelmed. We may be fantastic at dealing with crises, but afterwards we're on the floor because we've given all we've got and more.

There's no virtue in running on empty, no matter how worthy it can make us feel – it risks our emotional, spiritual and physical health. Life is to be enjoyed, not endured.

Joy nourishes us. It gives us reserves of spiritual strength to meet life's challenges by connecting us to a source that is stronger than any of the battles we face.

Joy is always with us

'I'm singing, oh I'm singing in my soul, when the troubles roll, I sing from morn' till night, it makes my burdens light.'

SISTER ROSETTA THARPE

No matter how difficult life is, joy is always available.

Our job is to be open, to be curious and to commit to noticing the extraordinary nature of the ordinary. To make sure we're not too busy to hear joy's call.

Perhaps the roses in the garden you walk past on your way home from work invite you to enjoy their fragrance, or the girl singing by the bus stop makes you stop and listen, or the old set of paints on the shelf above the pile of laundry beckons or a song thrush calls when you wake in the middle of the night.

Take care to respond to joy's call – each moment will never come again and every ounce you allow yourself to experience will give you resilience for the road ahead.

'It is those who have a deep and real inner life who are best able to deal with the irritating details of outer life.'

EVELYN UNDERHILL

One of the main things that brings me joy in my life aside from my children – who also bring other stuff with them – is meditation. I often access a state of joy when I am meditating and the chances are that some of that leaks into the rest of my day and therefore my interactions with the world. There is also a good chance that if I have meditated, my experience of my children will feel more joyful, and I will take that away from the interaction rather than the other stuff.

GA

Creativity

'When we open ourselves to our creativity, we open ourselves to the creator's creativity within us and our lives.'

JULIA CAMERON

Creativity fosters joy.

All of us need to create to feel fully alive. We don't have to do it formally or be 'good' at it, whatever that means. Creativity isn't about being good or bad or skilled or amateur. It's *not* about what you produce – it's about the process of creating. It's about connecting to the creative flow that pulses through us all.

Every activity contains within it the opportunity to create. It doesn't have to fall into the categories that are traditionally thought of as 'artistic' to count. Whether you're tidying a drawer, cooking a meal or chairing a board meeting, if you tap into your creative flow you'll find it restores, nourishes and rejuvenates you.

Creating – in whatever form – brings us into the present moment. It gives us a single point of concentration, which, like meditation, takes us out of the normal passage of time. And in that creative zone our concerns about past and future slip away.

··

FLOW

Psychologists researching happiness discovered that when we are completely absorbed in an activity we enter a state of flow.[34] In that state we feel joyful, positive, aligned and full of energy.

For artists and writers, flow is the place where inspiration comes from and ideas arise effortlessly; for athletes, it's the zone where peak performance is achieved. Flow feels like the 'state of being at one with things' described by Eastern religions. All of us can access it if we allow ourselves to use our hands, eyes, ears, voice and bodies to play and create. Regularly entering into a state of flow is a key component to happiness.

··

All of us are artists, but many of us have forgotten how to be. Think of those early drawings you did as a girl, before you learned to label them as 'good' or 'bad'. We often have to strip away layers of conditioning to allow ourselves to create. We have to learn to override the criticisms we received from the art teachers who told us we couldn't paint and singing teachers who told us we were off-key. We have to rediscover what we once knew and loved as children and then allow ourselves to do it.

'Your voice is simply your voice, like your nose is your nose. It's nothing to worry over.'

SHIVON ROBINSON

At one time creativity was simply part of daily life – whether it was painting, letter writing or sewing. Pre-television and radio, families and communities used to sing together, irrespective of whether individual voices fitted into formal musical categories.

The voice that may now be dismissed as off-key would once have had a place and a use. But now we're so used to hearing commercially recorded voices that we can be dismayed at and judgemental of our own and others. Auto-tune provides the audio equivalent of airbrushing. It gives us a distorted idea of what's normal. So reclaiming your voice through singing is a political as well as a joy-filled act. It says that we can be active participants in art rather than just passive consumers.

When I was seven my music teacher announced to the class that I was tone-deaf. From then on she'd leave me out when she went round the room getting the other pupils to sing. I didn't sing out loud from that day onward. In church or at school concerts I'd lip-sync – I knew all the words and could feel the music flowing through me, but I didn't dare to utter a sound. When I had my first child I discovered that the only way to soothe him was to sing to him. I was flabbergasted that my tone-deaf, tuneless renditions of the songs I'd mimed to as a child could stop him from crying. To begin with I was too ashamed to let anyone else hear me sing to him, but eventually I realized that if my voice could comfort my son it couldn't be all that bad. Now I sing at every opportunity. I sometimes see my friends who have 'perfect' voices wince when I fail to hit the correct notes, but I don't let that stop me. Now that I've found my voice I'm never going to let anyone else ever shame me out of using it.

JN

Nature and beauty

*'People from a planet without flowers would think we must be mad with
joy the whole time to have such things about us.'*

IRIS MURDOCH

Awe and wonder generate joy.

Connecting with nature and allowing yourself to be uplifted by beauty
can give you the same experience that the process of creating provides – a
moment out of time. There is joy in finding wonder in the delicacy of each
leaf, the trillions of atoms joined to make each one of us, the infinite lapping
of waves against the shore.

Every second spent in nature is an opportunity to encounter joy. It is
never a waste of time to take the slightly longer route home through the park
and to allow the leaves dancing in the wind to distract you from your worries.

Next time you are tangled up in a problem look at the sky – see what the
clouds are doing. Or check out the sunset and take in how extraordinary it
is that no two are ever the same. Wherever you are and whatever you are
doing, find a moment to connect with nature each day. Let the life-force in
each growing thing inspire and nourish you.

'What a wonderful life I've had! I only wish I'd realized it sooner.'

COLETTE

Think of each day as a blank canvas and try to fill it with things that uplift
you. Look for beauty, because joy is never far behind it – whether it's in a
spider's web, an art gallery or the rhythm of falling rain, it is always there,
waiting to be noticed.

Be curious about yourself. Notice and name the things that lift your
spirits and make you laugh. Give yourself permission to have more of what
enthuses and impassions you in your life.

Commit to joy and then open all your senses to the unusual or unexpected. The daisy that insists on growing where it shouldn't, the tattoo on a stranger's arm, the lyric of a song you've listened to a thousand times but never really heard before. These are simple moments we don't notice in our rush, or notice but don't appreciate for the gifts they are. Committing to joy means you make a commitment to yourself that you will start to pay attention to those gifts.

EXERCISE 1: The Artist's Life

This exercise will help you connect with the opportunities of joy that are all around you. Find or make yourself a notebook – one that you can easily carry with you. Use it to record what you find beautiful or uplifting each day. This can be anything you see, hear or experience – or even something you taste or smell. Describe it in as much detail as you can: sketch or doodle it, take a photo, jot down the name of the piece of music or quotation that made you laugh or weep, paste in tickets to events that you attend.

There's no right or wrong way of doing this.

Artists and writers rely on their sketchbooks and notepads to store inspiration, observations and ideas. If you already practise this habit, use this as an opportunity to collect examples from beyond your regular areas of interest.

Just as your regular gratitude lists leave you feeling more grateful, so connecting with what inspires and enthuses you makes you feel more inspired and enthusiastic.

When your notebook is full, review it. See whether it reveals any areas of interest you didn't know you had – ceramics? Music? Architecture? Drawing? If you can, take a class, go to a free concert, find a way of developing that interest further.

How extraordinary is the world we live in? We are all creative and the more we allow ourselves to connect with our creativity, the more joy we'll feel.

························

My mother tells me that as a child I was happiest when I was painting – apparently I whistled, which, if you knew my usual adolescent demeanour, might startle you as well. But something in me knows that if I were willing to give up what I think I 'should' be doing with my life and do what I know would make me the happiest, I would be … happy. But there are so many 'buts' in the way! So now I carry a simple sketchpad and a fine-tipped pen and once in a while I endeavour to sketch something – a corner of a room, a table, a face. Not only does this feel like I'm honouring a long-standing desire within me, but it's also honouring my creative self, honouring moments in my life that so often whizz by, and honouring that part of me that has always wanted to be – were I not so attached to my phone and its camera – one of those people who did things like write letters and drew things in notebooks.

GA

Creating space for joy

'It's a helluva start, being able to recognize what makes you happy.'
LUCILLE BALL

Joy requires space, which in our 24/7 lives can be hard to make. When our days are full of the noise of the world – be it radio, TV, work or online chat – we can starve joy of the space it needs to grow.

Children generate joy effortlessly through play, and so can we. Use your mental detox day (pp. 192–3) to open up the space to play, create, explore and tap into joy.

....

EXERCISE 2: Joy in Practice
....

This exercise is to help you brainstorm activities that bring you joy. Think of things that you enjoy doing – that aren't about consumption or end results but about the process of doing them. Ice skating, rollerblading, dancing, making pottery or collaging? Maybe you like gardening, listening to music, sharing a meal with friends, painting, reading or going to the cinema. Or is it travel, table tennis or rock climbing?

Think of as many as you can – at least ten. Now, beside each item on your list write the date when you last did it. How many of your passions are in your life right now?

If it's been a while, you may feel a pang of sadness at the time you've lost. Often there are good reasons why we've had to stop doing something – perhaps children, work or financial constraints have got in the way. But living in deficit doesn't work. It fosters envy, resentment and sadness. It makes us cling to others to fill the void in the centre of our own lives.

Without thinking about any practical limitations, ask yourself which joyful activity you most long to do. Try to pick something you haven't done for a while and that you especially used to enjoy. Put a star beside it. Now find a way of doing it, and do it on your own. Having a companion will distract you and dilute your experience.

If there are practical problems in doing the activity you've selected then brainstorm a way of getting round them – you just need to honour the spirit of what you've chosen. Perhaps you long to walk on a beach but live miles from the coast. Instead, find a lake or even a pond and take yourself there.

Perhaps you've selected dancing but don't have childcare or the money to go out. Instead you could set aside half an hour, put on some of your favourite music, close your eyes and dance around your room. Try your best to really let yourself go. Leave your mind and all your worldly concerns aside and let your body be absorbed in rhythm and movement.

It doesn't have to cost anything to have a good time or to awaken the joy inside you.

....

The word enthusiasm has its roots in Greek and means 'possessed by God's essence'. If you feel enthusiastic, go with it. Similarly, the word 'inspire' derives from the Latin *inspirare* – to breathe in. So seek out inspiration and breathe it in!

Once you've created space for joy, protect it.

Seek out the company of people who radiate love and warmth. It's infectious, and increasingly you'll find that you want and need to be around it.

Misery loves company, but you don't have to provide it. You don't need to abandon old friends, but you can choose not to collude with their negative thinking. Set boundaries and protect yourself from situations that rob you of your love for life. Negativity, like positivity, is catching.

Now that the principles are generating huge shifts in your life, you'll find it harder to be around friends who are resistant to or cynical about the possibility of change.

I used to think that anyone who wasn't a pessimist was fooling themselves. I prided myself on my ability to see the possible negative outcome of any course of action. But my experiences on this path have transformed me. I'm now an evangelical optimist, because I know that wonderful things can and regularly do happen.

JN

....

SETTING BOUNDARIES – LEARNING TO SAY NO AND YES

'No' is an essential part of our vocabulary. Setting boundaries is one of the ways we define ourselves. It lets others know where we begin and end and is particularly important to use if we're given to people-pleasing (p. 81).

Saying 'no' when someone wants you to say 'yes' can feel brutal – particularly if you're not used to saying it. So apply the Golden Rule (pp. 5–6) – speak to others in the same way that you'd like them to speak to you: kindly. Let people know what is and isn't OK for you. We can't expect others to read our mind. There's always a way to say what you mean without being mean and without levelling accusations.

Of course, others won't necessarily want to hear your 'no'. People want you to do what they want you to do. But capitulating won't serve anyone and it will leave you feeling angry, resentful and overwhelmed.

Saying 'no' to what isn't good for you frees up the space to say 'yes' to activities and opportunities that bring you joy.

....

When you aren't meeting your innate need for joy you leave yourself spiritually hungry. No matter how good your life is, you end up feeling restless and discontented, and before long start looking for answers in the wrong places.

Just as when you're physically hungry you might pick up junk food to replace the meal you've missed, if you're spiritually hungry you may end up grazing on unhealthy relationships or pointless activities that leave you feeling empty and more restless still. As you do this, your chances for internal freedom and peace diminish.

Watch out for feelings of restlessness and dissatisfaction. They are signs that your soul is hungry and needs to be fed with joy.

I have to really work hard to create space for joy in my life. Self-imposed misery and sadness and irritability come much more naturally to me. I find it so hard to do something that I know from experience will bring me greater happiness and a sense of contentment. When I know that there is a solution, why do I choose to stay in the struggle? I've learned over the years that being in synthetic pain is so familiar to me that I have become comfortable in the discomfort. That often I don't feel like 'me' without it. That part of me feels alive when I have something to complain about or fight against. And there is a small part of me that enjoys the rebellion of not doing something that I know is good for me. The longer I push against that rebellious self and allow myself the gift of happiness without judging it or feeling like I don't deserve it or that it's sappy somehow, the more space I naturally make for joy to be a part of my life.

GA

Soul food

'Happiness is not a station you arrive at, but a manner of travelling.'

MARGARET LEE RUNBECK

Joy feeds our soul and connects us with a sense of the divine. Everyone has an inner sense of the divine and, when we use the principles to bring us into alignment, we become increasingly aware of it.

Many of us equate the divine with religion. That can cause problems for those who don't have a formal faith, as it is all too easy to point to the harm that's been done in religion's name: wars, persecution, abuse of power – sexual and material. Not to mention the legacies of guilt and shame that it has left so many of us burdened with.

But, WE's path is spiritual rather than religious. It connects us to a source of power that is stronger than any of the difficulties we face and helps us to weather life's storms.

Your sense of that source of power will grow as you walk this path. Your knowing will develop experientially rather than intellectually and it will resonate with the same part of you that recognizes love, authenticity and truth.

You can think of that power as God, but if you don't feel comfortable with that term, try thinking of the power as simply 'Love'. Or add an extra 'o' to God and think of it as the 'Good' that exists in all of us. Reclaim that power for yourself and think of it as you choose.

....

THE G-WORD

If you're someone who has a strong reaction against the G-word – 'God' – you may find it helpful to make a list of why you object to it so much. See how many of those objections still apply if you substitute the word 'Love' instead. Or how about 'Goddess'? Religion is man-made, but God is divine, so don't let your experience of it be limited by those who've historically laid claim to it.

....

Many atheists experience the divine but call it awe and wonder. Recovering addicts may find the divine in the power of a group, others in beauty or nature. Still others may return to the God of their childhood but update it as a loving God rather than one to be feared.

Keep an open mind. Instead of reasoning about God and Love, experience it in your soul.

Wisdom can be found in traditional faiths and in the many spiritual teachers who are alive today (pp. 316–8). We're lucky to live at a time when there are so many different routes to developing our faith. They all lead to the same place, so it is simply a matter of finding a path that speaks to you and then following it. Almost all faiths and teachers share common truths – and the principles in this book are distilled from them.

....

MORE UNITY THAN DIVIDE

While the world's great religions make war against each other in the name of dogma, cultural difference, morals and ethics, enter any mosque, synagogue, church, temple or place of religious worship and you might be surprised by the similarities you find.

The same guiding principles lie at the heart of most religious teaching: kindness, humility, peace. The names and language may be different, the doctrine and ritual unique to each, but wherever we choose to worship we are reminded to turn towards joy and seek out transcendence and love.

....

It's easy to get caught up in definitions, but they're fodder for our intellects and egos. Spiritual truth is beyond the comprehension of the human mind, but not the experience of the soul. It doesn't matter what we do or don't call the source of power, how we do or fail to define it; what matters is our experience of it.

I had faith as a child, but when my father became ill with Parkinson's disease it evaporated. As far as I was concerned God either didn't exist or was so cruelly indifferent to suffering that I wanted nothing to do with Him. I became an evangelical atheist and dismissed anyone who had faith as either deluded or intellectually dishonest. And then one day – 20 years later – I found myself in treatment and we were taken on an outing to a small country church. I was in my usual cynical mode, ready to lampoon the worshippers who'd fallen for a made-up story. But halfway through the service I was suddenly transfused with the most powerful feeling of love I've ever experienced. I knew in that moment that God did exist and that s/he was love. It was a knowing that had nothing to do with my intellect – it came from deep within me and has never left. Instead of blaming God for the suffering that exists in the world, I now turn to God for help in negotiating my way through it. I've discovered that I can access that feeling of love any time I pray or am of service to someone who is struggling.

JN

Asking for help

'Why must people kneel down to pray? If I really wanted to pray ... I'd go out into a great big field all alone or in the deep, deep woods and I'd look up into the sky – up – up – up – into that lovely blue sky that looks as if there was no end to its blueness. And then I'd just feel a prayer.'

L. M. MONTGOMERY, *ANNE OF GREEN GABLES*

Wherever you are and whatever is happening, asking for help is a necessary part of being human. You can't, and don't have to, go it alone.

There are so many paradoxes on this journey. And one of them is that the stronger we become the more vulnerable we can find ourselves. As we come to know ourselves and connect with our true centre we find that we can no longer bury feelings or slip into denial. We need to reach out and connect. Isolating yourself from others does not work, nor does pretending to be OK when you're not.

When we're operating from a place of authenticity, there's a shift in the way we relate to others. We discover that we need people, but we need them in a healthy way. We can ask for help from a whole range of people: friends, other women who are on a spiritual path, professionals.

But there's also another way we can ask for help, which is available any time we need it.

We can ask for help by praying. Prayer is a tool that works for all of us – atheists as well as the devout.

Asking a power greater than ourselves – whether that's the sky, God, good, nature, love – for help, for a return to joy, involves a surrender. It involves admitting that we don't have the power to sort everything out. The moment we surrender, we move towards acceptance and the possibility of peace.

There's no set format for how to pray. If you have a formal path, you might choose to turn to some of the beautiful formal prayers that exist. Anyone, of course, can use them, or you can make up your own.

If we're blown off course by disappointment and we pray, it can help to bring us back to centre.

We can pray if we're furious. Things haven't gone our way. What we wanted hasn't happened. We can rant and rage at the universe or our god. We can tell it why things aren't fair or how we've been let down.

At other times we can just gently confide – we can chat to the power that's always there and tell it how we're feeling: good, bad or middling. As we talk we start to feel a connection. We come back to centre as we disclose our truth – even when we're doing it to a God we don't believe in. It's amazing.

A word of warning: prayer works

'Whenever I'm confused about something, I ask God to reveal the answers to my questions, and he does.'

BEYONCÉ KNOWLES

Some prayers are answered after a humble request in the midst of our busy lives. Others are dramatically answered after messy, miserable pleadings shouted with snot and tears running down our faces.

We don't always know what answers prayer will bring. Sometimes it's 'yes', other times it's 'no', and often it's 'wait'. Whatever the answer, when we look back we find we've been guided in ways that have led to outcomes that surpass our limited vision.

Each morning when you meditate, add a prayer to your ritual. Rather than asking for things or specific outcomes – as you may have been taught to do as a child – try simply asking to be aligned with what is good and right. If you are able to do the next right thing in any situation then the right things will unfold.

One straightforward prayer – which can bring us into alignment at any moment – is simply to say, 'Thy will, not mine, be done.'

Gratitude – saying thank you – can also be a prayer. Try saying it at night before you go to sleep. Try saying it when you're struggling with your reality. When we connect with gratitude we free ourselves from the burden of unhappiness. Prepare to be amazed. Prayer works. It's an action, and Action Changes Things. So try it.

If you hold your head up to the sky, sooner or later you will start to feel the warmth of the sun. And so it is with the light of the spirit.

Keeping an open mind

'And then in a nano-second JOY swoops in and in a humungous way clears it all away, just like that.'

MONI VANGOLEN

Some of us come to the spiritual path with an active faith, others with a faith that has been broken, and yet others with no faith at all or with an active antagonism against faith.

It doesn't matter what you think you know. If you keep an open mind and seek out joy, you will start to have a spiritual experience.

Spiritual experiences take many different forms. They might be a dramatic, life-changing moment of spiritual awakening in which your whole attitude and view of life changes forever. But for most people the process is gradual. It starts as a result of using the principles to heal the wounds and attitudes that have blocked you from seeing your own and the world's true nature.

As you nourish yourself with joy, you will notice that you are lighter in spirit. You will begin to feel a sense of ease and confidence where before you felt awkward and insecure. You will find it easier to enjoy time alone and will start to seek it out.

Increasingly you'll find yourself grateful but not surprised when life meets your yearnings and needs in return for you nourishing your soul with joy and stepping forward into your own spiritual truth.

You'll become aware of coincidences and opportunities that are increasingly difficult to dismiss as happenstance.

You'll notice that the trust you once found hard to practise has crystallized into a faith that you are being taken care of.

You'll notice that others who are walking a spiritual path will be drawn to you and you will find companions to aid and accompany you on your way.

Then you'll realize that you are experiencing joy and an internal sense of freedom and happiness.

The process may sound magical, but it comes about as a direct result of you applying the principles to your life. And the more joy you allow into your life, the brighter the spark of the divine burning within you will shine.

Joy in the wider world

'When you shine your unique light, bit by bit, you light up the world of those around you. And, one by one, you inspire them to light up too.'

REBECCA CAMPBELL

When we attend to the needs of our soul, we prepare ourselves to be of real use in the wider world. The brighter we shine, the greater the light we'll cast for others.

Joy prepares us for the work to come. WE's final principle – kindness – leads us out into the world of activism, where we will be called to have emotional resilience, and it's joy that will sustain us.

The more urgent and necessary the work we undertake in this life, the more important it is that we make space for joy. It will prevent us from slipping into adrenalin-driven or ego-based ways of working. It doesn't matter if we're engaged on a micro or macro level, joy makes our work sustainable.

Whether we're battling climate change, volunteering in a hospital or trying to help a friend deal with her divorce, we have to connect to something stronger and bigger than the challenge we're facing if we are to be effective. That means taking time to connect with the energy that pulses through life and allowing it to nourish and nurture us.

But joy does more than just sustain, it also informs how we work as activists. It allows us to play and laugh along the way. We don't need to be serious all the time. We can scatter joy as we go.

We're told that angels fly because they take themselves lightly. But it is joy that puts the wind beneath their wings. So create, pray and look for moments to enjoy beauty, and you will not only find yourself soaring high, you'll also beam light into the darkness for others.

Reflection

'Lighthouses don't go running all over an island looking for boats to save; they just stand there shining.'

ANNE LAMOTT

When others are suffering and I'm trying to help, I can get so caught up in the urgency of the situation that I can forget to make space for joy. When that happens I take a moment to connect with nature, beauty or the wonder of a beating human heart, and that reminds me that there is a much bigger picture. And that joy can shine a light to brighten any darkness if I let it.

Action: Today I will seek out joy and let it fill my heart.

Affirmation: I am resilient and filled with joy.

Principle
9

KINDNESS:
Love in Action

'Even the briefest touch of kindness can lighten a heavy heart. Kindness can change the lives of people.'

AUNG SAN SUU KYI

Kindness is what love looks like when we take it out into the world. It pierces our hearts as keenly as any arrow, and in so doing it allows love to flow in and out. Through gentle, loving actions kindness transforms us into spiritual activists.

Kindness brings a sense of meaning and purpose. As we apply this principle to our lives we discover that love starts to flow through us with increasing velocity and that we now feel truly part of the extraordinary world in which we all live.

Without kindness, no matter how much we do, have or achieve, there's a hollowness at our core. A yearning that persists.

Most of us have spent our days pursuing goals that don't ultimately bring meaning. What we're conditioned to think matters most often ends up mattering least. As we shift from a state of self-concern to one of inner freedom we acquire a new perspective.

We see that our ego's quest for 'more' will ultimately always make us unhappy. We realize there is no 'enough'. We have been suffering – individually and culturally – from the disease of more. And each time we've scratched the itch, it has only got worse.

The journey has shown us that no amount of material achievements or possessions can assuage our spiritual longing. But the good news is that where self-seeking has failed, kindness steps in to bring meaning and happiness. It is the final step on our journey from *me* to *WE*.

What really matters?

'Happiness is not a goal, it's a by-product.'

ELEANOR ROOSEVELT

At the centre of all our lives is a quest for meaning. When times are tough all our energy may be absorbed in trying to get by. But when the pressure eases we find the question there, lurking beneath our daily struggles, calling for our attention. Is this it?

How should we spend the time we've been given, the uncertain number of days between birth and death? What will bring fulfilment and a sense that there is a point to our existence?

EXERCISE 1: Gaining Perspective

This exercise will connect you to that which really gives your life meaning.

Have your journal ready and then centre yourself by taking five deep breaths in and five slightly longer breaths out. Close your eyes and imagine you are a much older version of yourself, coming to the end of your life. Look back at your time on Earth and ask this older you what has really mattered. What are you glad to have experienced, and what do you care about most?

Open your eyes and write down what the older you has to say. Stay in this future state with your wiser self until you feel she has given you all you need to know.

Now close your eyes again and allow yourself to time travel back to today. Centre yourself in the present. Take a look at what you wrote down and think about how you spend your time now.

How much of your energy is focused on the things on your list? How many of the items on your list have to do with looks, achievements and material possessions? How many are about relationships and love?

If you keep this list in mind as you go about your days you'll find that the awareness it gives you will gently result in your priorities starting to shift.

'How wonderful it is that nobody need wait a single moment before starting to improve the world.'

ANNE FRANK

Like love, kindness is an action. It allows love to flow through us so that we become channels for a greater purpose than our own limited wants and needs.

It's the neighbour that keeps an eye on the elderly lady next door. It's the woman who passes a homeless person sitting in the street and stops to offer them help. It's the mother who offers a home to a stranger's child. It's the student who sets up a stall to collect food for a local soup kitchen. It's the friend who noticed you were looking sad and calls to make sure you're OK.

Before we started this journey, kindness was easy to overlook. It felt limp, small, not quite up to the job, but increasingly we come to understand that if it were to govern our interactions, the world could be a very different place, and our own quota of happiness would increase as a natural result.

Kindness carries within it the potential to overthrow orthodoxies, hierarchies and regimes. What if we care for those whom we are told are our enemies? What if we give to those we are told are not deserving? Kindness busts the myth that there is nothing we can do to change things.

The previous principles have prepared you. Now kindness plants you firmly on a path of spiritual activism. Through four simple practices: Choosing, Acting, Joining and Giving we discover how to unlock kindness' transformative power.

Choosing

'If not me, who? If not now, when?'

EMMA WATSON

Every day life involves making choices. Often we feel small and powerless as if there's nothing we can do to change our world, but there is.

With every choice you make, you have power.

All decisions have some impact. When you use kindness to guide your decisions you will begin choosing the options that represent your values and beliefs. Your goal is congruence and the inner freedom and outer influence it brings.

Start small. Start where you are. Remember that mustard seeds can shift paving stones. You choose how you spend your time and your money – no matter how much or how little you have of each – so start using those choices.

'Our actions – and inaction – touch people we may never know and never meet across the globe.'

JACQUELINE NOVOGRATZ

Women in the US control 80 per cent of all consumer purchases.[35] Imagine if we used that power to demand ethically and sustainably produced goods, at affordable prices.

....

AN UNTAPPED POWER

In the United States alone, about 50 million plastic water bottles are used every year.[36] The plastics used can take over 500 years to decompose.[37] Scientists predict that by 2050 there'll be more plastic than fish in the sea.[38] Plus, it takes 17 million barrels of oil each year just to produce them – enough oil to fuel a million cars for a whole year.[39] Some American cities like Concord and San Francisco have banned the sale of small plastic water bottles, as have a number of university campuses like Leeds in the UK. How great would it be if we got their use banned altogether, first nationally and then globally?

....

Kindness can guide all sorts of choices: who you bank with, who you shop with, who you do business with, who you invite into your home. But don't beat yourself up with it. Change comes incrementally – your job is not to force it but to allow it.

Notice and name when you discover a gap between your beliefs and your actions. Over time, if you create the space and awareness through using WE's principles, you'll find you're making new choices across the board.

....

EXERCISE 2: One Choice a Day

....

This exercise helps identify the choices you make on a daily basis that you could make differently. How often do you notice something that upsets you and do nothing about it? We can get so used to living with situations or avoiding things that are unpleasant or unacceptable that we stop noticing.

For the next week notice the small, everyday decisions that you make from habit, necessity or haste that don't reflect your true values and note them down in your journal.

Perhaps you are passionate about the environment and yet you buy water in a plastic bottle at lunchtime rather than refilling a reusable one before leaving home. Maybe you feel sad every time you rush past the old woman who sits alone in the park feeding the birds. Maybe you never open the emails you get from the human rights organization you signed up to with such enthusiasm. Or you bitch about a colleague rather than stand up for her.

Notice the moments and name them to yourself. Write them down so that you remember them. This isn't about making you feel bad. It's about becoming aware of the opportunities that exist every day that can help you to feel more powerful.

Think how great you'd feel if you decided – every day – to exercise one small choice that would increase the positive impact you have on the world around you. It doesn't even necessarily mean doing anything 'extra' – it can just involve doing something that you already do, but in a new way.

....

Acting

'Practise random kindness and senseless acts of beauty.'

ANNE HERBERT

Once we start becoming aware of the power we can exercise through our choices, a space opens up to begin making changes. Action Changes Things.

So commit to carrying out one deliberate act of kindness every day and see how differently you start to feel about your life.

It can be as simple as picking up a bit of litter or giving a compliment to a stranger on the bus. Perhaps it is making someone an unexpected cup of tea or paying for the unknown woman behind you in the queue for coffee. Small is beautiful. Often we feel that, unless we can do something big, there's no point in doing anything at all. This is not true. The more of us who hold up candles, the brighter our combined light will be.

Pick little things that fit into your life as it is now. If you're stuck for ideas you can look through the list you made in the previous exercise and pick just one of them. Or you might like to check out the website devoted to ideas for random acts of kindness recommended in the Resources section (p. 313).

Starting small is important. If you give yourself lofty or ambitious goals at this stage, you can set yourself up to fail or be burdened by yet another thing to add to your to-do list, and so creating an opening for your ego to rear its unhelpful head.

A HIDDEN PRICE TAG

Actions require energy, but *not* acting also carries a price. Often we carry a low level of guilt for the things we haven't done. These avoidances rattle around at the back of our awareness, weighing us down. When we start acting consciously, we release ourselves from guilt and become energized and empowered.

'Service is the rent we pay for being. It is the very purpose of life and not something you do in your spare time …'

MARIAN WRIGHT EDELMAN

This is not about showing how 'good' you can be — to yourself or to anyone else. It's about creating a new muscle group that will serve you as you walk forward on this spiritual path of activism and power.

ACTION LOG

When we act kindly it naturally boosts our self-esteem. Try keeping an action log of what you do to make a positive difference in the world.

Often we women minimize the good we do and compare it with the things we don't do. So notice and name your actions. Then, if you're feeling bad about yourself or powerless, you'll be able to see in black and white the power you have through the choices you make. You'll see you've done plenty to feel good about.

Try not telling anyone about your actions. Anonymity ensures we stay humble and prevents them from becoming ego-driven. Obviously with some actions (paying a compliment or signing a petition) you can't hide your identity, but be anonymous whenever possible and watch how great it feels to feed your soul rather than your pride.

> When I was about eight or nine, I offered to help an elderly woman carry her groceries down the road to her house. But afterwards I felt a huge amount of shame and for years I couldn't figure out why. Then I realized that the pride I had felt in myself was disproportionate to my action – and that even though I hadn't told anyone about it at the time, deep down I was embarrassed. But in retrospect, how cool that at that age it even occurred to me to do a good deed! Unfortunately, it may have been the last time until my twenties, and I don't doubt it was the shame that put me off doing it again.
>
> *GA*

MAKE YOURSELF HAPPY

Scientific research shows that a sure way to be happier is to be kind to others. A study at the University of California found that performing five random acts of kindness in a week increased happiness levels for up to a month.[40] In addition, various studies have shown that giving to others can increase well-being and longevity,[41] and inspire others to do the same.

Acts of kindness will change your default setting to one of affinity and compassion for others. That's not to say you'll always feel like being kind, especially if you're hurting. There'll be plenty of times when you'll feel like retaliating, complaining, ignoring or avoiding. You're human, after all! But acting kindly every day, no matter how mean you feel, will readjust your outlook, attitudes and responses.

With each act of kindness, you'll cut the cords that bind you to feeling disempowered and create new pathways and mental connections. And, of course, WE's magic multiplier will kick in. The more love and kindness you give, the more you'll start to receive. It's a win-win situation. You gain an increased sense of fulfilment, and the world gets more love.

As I've said before, I don't have the sunniest of dispositions. My natural state is grumpy and I have to work really hard at joviality. For most of my life people, even strangers, have said 'Smile!' because my resting face is depressed. When the winds are right or I've run out of things to complain about, or I've managed to force myself out of this status quo, I can come across as giddy and childish and endlessly silly ... until I'm not. But I'm telling you it takes work. And that work is usually climbing out of my head and my self-obsession and doing something for someone else – even if that something else is just being in a better mood. If I appear happy, it's because I'm choosing it! But funnily enough it pays off. When I do it for someone else, lo and behold I start to feel better, more in tune with those around me, and yes, even giddy.

GA

A workout for the soul

'With the disappearance of God the Ego moves forward to become the sole divinity.'

DOROTHEE SÖLLE

The full power of WE's principles are felt when we apply them all simultaneously. Kindness comes last because the preceding principles are entirely necessary to ensure that we don't use others' pain or drama to deflect attention away from our own.

Kindness is not self-abandonment or self-denial. It's a form of wholehearted giving that nourishes our soul. If we try to practise kindness without also practising self-care, meditation, affirmation and gratitude, we're at risk of people-pleasing, co-dependency or ego-tripping.

True kindness comes from a spiritually aligned place. It involves standing in our own shoes and affording others the same dignity. If you find yourself obsessing about another's suffering, gently remind yourself to step back into your own life. You do not need to play God or feel their feelings. Do what you can and then let go of the results. Remember the Serenity Prayer (p. 93).

No matter how huge your heart and how broad your shoulders, you can only give what you've actually got. Giving more than you have – whether in time, money or emotional resources – isn't giving, it's going into debt. When you're in debt in this way you slide out of alignment and onto the slippery slope that leads back to self-obsession and ego-driven actions and thoughts.

Practising kindness requires you to keep spiritually fit. When we're aligned with the greater good (or God or whatever you choose to call him/ her/it), we're able to work miracles in the world around us.

....

WHO'S IN CHARGE?

Check your motivation regularly to ensure you're acting from a place of genuine compassion rather than ego.

Ask yourself who is running your show. Is it the little girl who was starved of attention except when she was being especially good and helpful? Or is it the woman whose heart is moved by the pain of another? Has your ego and its need to be right climbed into the driving seat, or have you chosen not to tolerate abuses that you see around you? Look for tell-tale signs of ego and compulsivity – are you getting frantic? Is your life getting out of balance? Are you feeling important or indispensable?

When you're not sure, pause and return to centre. The more frantic you feel, the more time you need to set aside to meditate. Only when you detach from a situation will you gain clarity. If you return yourself to your still, centred core, the answers will be there waiting. Just make sure you create the space to hear them.

....

Giving

'If I can stop one heart from breaking, I shall not live in vain.'

EMILY DICKINSON

Often we feel too far away and too powerless to believe we can make a difference to another's suffering. But it's not true. Kindness isn't limited by geography, kinship or any other constraint.

Picture yourself in a street or park in your hometown.

Right in front of you a young girl falls face down into a small pond.

There's nobody else around. She's going to drown if you don't act. What do you do?[42]

You run and pull her out, of course. Wrap her in your coat or find her a blanket and look after her until her parents or guardian can come and get her. How about if you've got an expensive dress on that will get ruined? 'Who cares?' you'd say. 'She's drowning.' The answer is clear for all of us. Who cares about a dress when someone's life is at risk?

But what if the child were on the other side of the world? How does that affect your answer? Across the world one child dies every three seconds from preventable causes.[43] Do those children matter less? Of course not. But the way we live has encouraged us to think either there's nothing we can do or that it's not our problem.

Giving what we can is a solution that has been practised for centuries in many cultures, but which in our secular times many of us have lost touch with. It involves setting aside a percentage of our income – however small – to give to others who are in greater need.

It creates a shift within us that leads to a sense of freedom and empowerment. Most of us carry guilt for the suffering we know is happening around the world. Even if we think we don't care or it's not our responsibility, it's impossible not to be affected. We see it in the news and on our streets.

In the long term, global political solutions are the answer, but while we're waiting for our leaders to act, avoidable deaths are happening all around us.

Whether it's 10p, £10 or £10,000, setting aside a portion of your income will also stop you from feeling powerless and guilty. There is something you can do and you're doing it. If this isn't something you've done before, be prepared for internal objections to come flooding in. But giving what we can afford gives us a sense of agency, and it does so because it saves lives.

....

EXERCISE 3: Money Matters

....

This exercise is to help you empower yourself by getting honest about your spending. No matter how much or how little money we have, most people get stressed around finances. You may not have enough to meet your own needs or you may have plenty right now but still worry about what will happen in the future. Wherever you are on that spectrum, now is the time to empower yourself. So get curious.

Download a spending app or keep a small notebook in your purse. Without judging yourself, notice and name every penny you spend and record it. At the end of a month take a look at where your money went. Knowledge gives you the power to make conscious choices. Your spending patterns and priorities may already have shifted as you've been reading this book. Noticing and naming where your money goes will enable you to make new choices, so ... empower yourself.

....

LUCKIER THAN YOU THINK

If you have a refrigerator, a bed to sleep in and a roof over your head, you are richer than 75 per cent of the world's population. And if you are reading this book, you are luckier than the estimated three billion people in the world who can't read at all. Rather than comparing your life with those who have more, turn your focus in the other direction and acknowledge how fortunate you are.

....

We're often encouraged to be sceptical about giving – 'Charity does more harm than good, and doesn't it encourage dependency?' 'What about all the money that goes into administrative costs or is lost to corruption?' 'And what's the point anyway if my donation is only going to be a fraction of what's needed?' Except we wouldn't be, of course, if it was our daughter who was starving. Then we'd take every penny a stranger across the globe could afford to send.

....

THE LIFE YOU CAN SAVE

Some charities are a thousand times more effective than others. The same tools that are used to measure the efficacy of health treatments can be used to measure the effectiveness of charities. You can use an online calculator to check how much good a range of charities would do with what you donate. It's even possible to work out how many lives you can save over the course of your own life by giving a regular amount. Visit www.thelifeyoucansave.org in the US or www.givingwhatwecan.org in the UK.

....

WE encourages you to come out of denial. The choices you make affect others across the world. The money you spend on a coffee that you buy out of habit but don't actually enjoy could save the life of someone somewhere on the globe. Find whatever slack you can in your system and redirect it.

Once you start giving, you'll feel like a citizen of the world. It's another win-win – you'll be doing something to help another person who is in trouble, and in return you get to feel great. Start small and watch how your priorities start to shift. Before long you'll find yourself wanting to increase what you give and discovering that you can.

Joining

*'Just imagine your daughter was standing there. What would you do,
how would you fight?'*

ANURADHA KOIRALA

When you become an active member of your community, you create connections that bring healing both to yourself and to those around you. So while you're giving globally, try to find a way of acting locally. Many people are isolated, far from home and cut off from those they love. Local action dispels the alienation and loneliness that has become a familiar feature of modern living.

Most of us have a multitude of issues that we care about and it can be hard to know which to pick or where to start. Use your heart as your guide and the exercise that follows.

....

EXERCISE 4: Finding your cause

....

This exercise will help you identify your cause. Have your journal beside you to write down what you discover. Close your eyes and picture the world in which you live. Think about the suffering that exists – both locally and globally. Make a list of the issues that upset you the most – those which really move you. We're not looking here for the injustices that make you most angry or outraged (those are often signs that the ego is getting engaged), but the suffering that makes your heart feel as if it might break when you think about it.

If you're finding it hard to find any issues that you really connect with, look through a newspaper or watch the news. Which stories provoke a visceral response (not an intellectual one)? Your body will know what you cannot stomach. Try not to judge what you choose. There are no right or wrong answers. Your list doesn't need to be long or worthy.

This is not about your intellect; it's about your inner knowing. There is only what you know in your heart. You may care about children, nature or animals, trafficking or poverty. Maybe it's the thought of the homeless being cold and alone at Christmas or children in a refugee camp. Maybe it's animals being killed for their fur or female genital mutilation or the vulnerability of an asylum seeker far from those they hold dear.

Now examine your list and ask which one moves you the most. There may already be one that leaps out at you. If you're not sure, take it into your morning meditation. Look into your heart and ask which is the one that touches it the most deeply. Trust your first response. Once you've identified your biggest heartbreak, make a commitment. Agree with yourself to find a way of doing something locally about the issue you've chosen.

....

Even if your heartbreak is global, start local. Let the change you want to see begin with you right where you are. Maybe you find a dog rescue centre and volunteer on weekends, deliver meals to the elderly or start writing to a prisoner who has no one. If you're in a 12-step fellowship you can sponsor and do service. Or perhaps you'll find a local organization that works on the international issue you care most about.

'As we work to create light for others, we naturally light our own way.'

MARY ANNE RADMACHER

Spread your roots where you are planted. Becoming an active member of your community creates connections and a sense of belonging where you live, while bringing healing both to yourself and to the wider world of which you are a vital part. Even if you are already time restricted, trust that the space will emerge for your new commitment.

Remembering that small is beautiful. Do only what you can. You will find that as you do, your capacity grows and you will discover that you gain far more than you give.[44] It only takes a couple of minutes to get other mothers to sign a petition at the school gates or to make a phone call for a local charity or to drop some flowers at a sick neighbour's house.

....

PROGRESS, NOT PERFECTION

It's often easy to think there's no point in taking action, political or otherwise, unless we can do it perfectly. But baby steps are better than no steps at all. The global Meat-Free Monday campaign is a perfect example. If everyone went meat-free for just one meal a week in the US alone it would have the same environmental benefit as taking one and a half million cars off the roads and save 1.4 billion animals from being factory farmed. Plus, it would have a dramatic effect on world hunger, as the cereal needed to raise one cow could feed three people.[45]

....

I've often felt reluctant to take political action because I've felt so hypocritical. How can I campaign on climate change if I still fly and drive? How can I be against animal cruelty if I still wear leather? But then in the run-up to the 2009 climate change talks in Copenhagen I discovered that my flawed life could still be useful. Together with a group of other mothers and children we lobbied the government and held protests at parliament. Our message to MPs was loud and clear – we'll vote for the party that puts protection for the planet ahead of our individual rights to fly. We were able to show politicians and the media that the demands for action on climate change didn't just come from the environmentally pure, but also from those whose lifestyle would be adversely affected by the measures needed to tackle climate change.

JN

'Love costs all we are, and will ever be. Yet it is only love which sets us free.'

MAYA ANGELOU

The results are not up to you – it is your job only to plant the seeds by taking action. Once you start moving towards your higher purpose the universe always responds in kind.

Seek out others who are on this path and care about active change. Use WE's principles to start new conversations: in your neighbourhood, your local coffee shop, at the school gate – wherever you find yourself. Support each other. Set goals that relate to the issues that really matter to you, rather than the temporal and the material. If you stay open, you will always find sister-travellers to join you on your way.

Kindness gives us power in the face of suffering. It gives us the power to choose differently, act kindly, give what we can and join with others. When we do, we experience the magic and love that is generated when all our powerful *ME*s are joined together as *WE*.

Kindness in the wider world

'If you think you're too small to have an impact, try going to bed with a mosquito in the room.'

ANITA RODDICK

As a result of applying WE's spiritual principles to our lives, we come to see the extent to which we've been blown off course – by life itself, by our conditioning, by our choices – away from what we know really matters. This journey returns us to ourselves – our real values, our true nature.

This is a path of love, and kindness is the tool by which we give expression to it in the world.

Gratitude has taught us that we're lucky. Through an accident of birth we are lucky. Lucky to be here reading this book. Lucky that it is not our child who is begging on the corner or dying for want of a bowl of rice.

You may not be able on your own to topple an oppressive regime, change a polluting transportation system, or stop a much-needed women's refuge from closing, but when you stand together with others, with kindness in your heart, extraordinary things come to pass.

As you continue to practise kindness on a daily basis, you will see opportunities to effect bigger changes in your family, community and the world at large.

Your sensitivity to the suffering of others will increase. Kindness will push you into action. You won't be able to stand on the sidelines doing nothing because you now know that when you are spiritually aligned you are more powerful than you could ever have imagined.

Reflection

> *'Politics is about everything we do, from the moment we get up in the morning to the minute we go to bed at night. It's something everybody and anybody can be involved in.'*
>
> CAROLINE LUCAS

When I take action – no matter how small – I have the power to make the world a better place. Using kindness to align myself with the greater good gives me a sense of purpose and reminds me that I'm not alone. I'm part of a wonderful and growing movement of women who are walking into the light, guided by what we know to be right and true.

Action: Today I will choose to act kindly.

Affirmation: When I take action the world is a better place.

We started this journey searching. We knew there was a better, more fulfilling way of living. Now the principles have given us a direction and a focus for our lives.

Let's pause for a moment at the threshold of our new lives and allow that focus to zoom right out across our fragile earth to the 7.3 billion people we share our planet with.

Imagine how it would look if it were truly governed by spiritual principles.

How different things could be if, across the world, a desire to be fair rather than to have more became our primary motivation.

How would things change if compassion replaced judgement and if being kind became the new cool? If we all sought to put WE's spiritual principles at the centre of our lives.

Just as each of our individual lives has been blown off course by thinking that externals could heal internal pain, so many of our institutions and governments have been governed by doctrines that exacerbate rather than solve the challenges the world faces.

Suffering is an inevitable part of being human. But what about suffering that is avoidable, that is caused by inaction, neglect or greed?

We want to see the changes that have started within us translate into external shifts – not just for us, but for all those who suffer across the globe.

PART 3

The Manifesto

MANIFESTO

'Never believe that a few caring people can't change the world. For, indeed, that's all who ever have.'

MARGARET MEAD

This is not a manifesto in the traditional sense of the word. It's a rallying cry to commit to a new way of life – one that is based on spiritual principles.

It's a call to apply the tools we've now learned to every aspect of our lives – at home, at work, in the polling booth. To let them govern how we live, how we do business, how we raise our families, how we deal with our neighbours.

It's a call to a value-led existence – one that puts love at its centre. One that refuses to discriminate on the basis of race, class, creed or gender.

It's a call for love to become a way of life. To let it dictate your choices, your actions and your interactions.

To do the work that is required to heal your own emotional wounds so that you can be of service to another.

This manifesto will take commitment on your part. It will mean practising these principles on a daily basis. Like swimmers in deep water we have to keep moving in order to stay afloat. Any time we stop using them, we'll start to slip back into old patterns of criticism. competition and judgement. But if you continue walking this path and practising the principles in

287

your daily life, they will keep you resilient and focused, and strengthen your compassion and connection.

Practice is key. We are all practising. None of us gets to be perfect.

Perhaps you will want to work through the chapters again, maybe even with someone else to share what you've learned. At the very least, continue to meditate, write your gratitude list and take action to put kindness at the centre of your life.

This journey has no end – we'll be working on ourselves, our attitudes and our actions for the rest of our days – but if we walk forward together, one woman at a time, amazing things will come to pass both for us individually and for the world in which we live.

A WORLD IN
NEED OF LOVE

'Women of the world, united without any regard for national or racial dimensions, can become a most powerful force for international peace.'

CORETTA SCOTT KING

The challenges that the world faces are, in many ways, analogous to the challenges each one of us faces internally.

Fear and resentment cause the global equivalent of synthetic pain. Just think how different our world would look if the West's response to the tragedy of 9/11 had come from a place of concern and compassion rather than fear and judgement.

And how different would our world look if economic goals were focused on sustainability rather than harnessed to a model built on 'more' with its thirst for ever-increasing levels of consumption and debt?

The quick fixes we reach for when we're emotionally out of kilter are similar to the short-termism that drives much of today's politics. Just as many of us may battle with greed and pride, our governments, too, fail to end the arms trade for fear that someone else will get the profits or risk unpopularity at the polls by tackling the oil lobby.

Our collective preoccupation with the self has legitimized greed and prioritized individual advancement over the greater good. In place of the value systems that religions once provided for most of us – is a gaping spiritual void, which we've attempted to fill through the pursuit of material well-being. As a result, the richest have grown wealthier and the rest have been left behind.

....

A WORLD APART

In the US, the gulf between rich and poor is now wider than at any time since the 1920s – leaving the richest 0.1 per cent owning as much as the bottom 90 per cent. More than one in five American children now lives in poverty[46] – the highest rate in any developing nation.

Globally the wealthiest 62 individuals now own as much as the poorest half of the world's population.[47] Fuelling this extreme inequality is a global network of tax havens. As a result, poorer countries lose at least $170 billion a year – money that is desperately needed for vital services like healthcare and education.[48]

....

None of this is inevitable. It's about choices.

Our current system leaves us polarized. It's a binary system where some of us are winners and as a result all of us are losers. Where those of us with jobs often work insane hours and those of us who are out of work languish at the perimeter of society. Where the opportunities that the computer age promised for shorter working weeks and a fairer division of labour have been ignored in favour of a deregulated labour market, resulting in zero-hours contracts and round-the-clock working.

Where wealthy nations battle with rocketing scales of obesity and yet nearly 800 million people go to bed each night hungry.

....

HUNGER AT HOME

Hunger is not just a problem in the global South. In the UK, as a result of austerity policies, there's been a massive rise in the numbers turning to food banks to survive.[49] In the USA 48.1 million Americans now live in food-insecure households, with African Americans twice as likely to be food insecure as their white non-Hispanic counterparts.[50]

....

Those of us who are OK for now and have managed to achieve a degree of security find that it's increasingly accompanied by a nagging sense of unease. Deep down we know our current system isn't fair and that while we're winning someone else is losing. While our child rips open a mountain of presents on their birthday, elsewhere someone else's child has none. While we scrape edible but uneaten food into the bin, others are starving. Increasingly, we're unable to square the lie that we're not all connected, that our actions don't have an impact on each other.

If we made kindness the governing principle of our own lives, how much better could lives be across the globe and how much happier would we, as individuals, be?

Study after study shows that it's not how much we have absolutely that governs our levels of happiness, but the levels of equality, including income equality, within a community. On an international level, global inequality causes wars and mass migration. Domestically, it causes higher crime levels and societal divisions.

···

HAPPINESS VS WEALTH

Bhutan, a small land-locked kingdom nestled at the foot of the Himalayas, has pioneered another way of doing things. Instead of using Gross Domestic Product (GDP) as a measurement of success, it uses a Gross National Happiness index and its policies prioritize individual well-being and spiritual values over consumerism. Although it is one of the poorest nations on the planet, it regularly ranks in the top-ten happiest nations.

The United Nations is now investigating how Bhutan's model could be used across the globe.

···

'The voice of conscience is so delicate that it is easy to stifle it; but it is also so clear that it is impossible to mistake it.'

MADAME DE STAËL

Our current economic system has a twisted and at times grotesque set of values. All the money that changes hands to drill and sell oil counts as a positive, irrespective of the cost to the environment. And when there's an environmental disaster the money spent clearing it up gets counted as positive economic activity and added to the GDP as well.

We count as positive the money the arms trade adds to our balance of trade but fail to set against it the catastrophic human and financial cost of the wars that result. Across the world we now have cities in which children, asthmatics and the elderly can't breathe, but the cost of treating them isn't taken into account when factoring in the value to the economy of private cars – let alone the cost in terms of human suffering.

WE's Nine Principles provide a new way of calibrating what matters most to ourselves and our planet.

Equal means equal

'The world is awakening to a powerful truth: women and girls aren't the problem; they're the solution.'

CHRISTIANE NORTHRUP

As women, of course, we have additional battles.

Our fight for equality is far from won. And America now has a presidential team that threatens to turn the clock back still further.

The United Nations enshrines equal rights in its charter. But out of its 191 heads of state, only 12 are women.

In the UK Parliament, fewer than three out of ten MPs are female.[51] In the US there are more CEOs of leading companies named John than there are CEOs who are women. And less than 1 per cent of statewide elected executives are female and black.[52]

Across the globe, the work of women is consistently undervalued. Worldwide, when unpaid work such as housework and family care is included, women do 75 per cent of the work, receive 10 per cent of the pay and own 1 per cent of property.[53]

We are told business backs equality but the movement towards equal pay has stalled across Europe, leaving women's pay lagging behind men by roughly 26 per cent.[54] And in the States if you're a black woman the pay gap is 32.4 per cent, rising to a scandalous 44.1 per cent for Hispanic women.[55]

The US is alone among developed nations in not providing paid maternity or parental leave across all its states – the other two in the world are Papua New Guinea and Oman. That leaves nearly one in four American women returning to work within two weeks or less of having a baby. About half of those women were back to work in under a week.[56,57]

Caring professions like teaching and nursing, traditionally dominated by women, attract far lower salaries than careers that contribute far less but are dominated by men. And although Western economies would collapse without it, the work of caregivers isn't factored into GDP at all. In the UK, carers (mainly women) would cost the country £119 billion if it had to be paid for – that's three times the defence budget.[58] The Canadian government has estimated the value of unpaid caring to contribute over 30 per cent to the country's GDP. Imagine what would happen if we all went on strike!

....

TOGETHER WE CAN!

In 1975 Iceland's women went on strike, as 90 per cent of them walked out of their homes and jobs. The country ground to a halt. The following year, a law was passed that guaranteed equal pay. Five years after that, Iceland became the first country to elect a woman as president, and it now has the highest gender equality in the world. Despite its landmark legislation, in 2016, male pay still outstripped female pay by up to 18 per cent. So they went on strike again. At 2.38pm promptly, women left their places of work – giving themselves the time off for the 18 per cent of the day they weren't paid for.

....

'We are living in the modern age and we believe that nothing is impossible.'

MALALA YOUSAFZAI

In the West, men's contribution in the home is increasing, but women still do the bulk of household tasks – which amounts to an extra nine hours' work per week for women living in the developed world.[59]

Further afield, economic reform has similarly failed to deliver women what it promised. In China, capitalism has created greater gender inequality rather than less. While pay was roughly equal under communism, by 1988 women earned 87 per cent of men's pay and now they're down to 67 per cent.[60]

In India, growing economic prosperity has actually resulted in an increase in honour and dowry killings among the middle classes.[61]

Across Asia over the last three decades, 163 million female foetuses have been aborted or killed at birth on the grounds of their gender. That's more than the entire female population of the US, and the resulting spike in surplus males has resulted in an increase in trafficking and bride purchasing from poorer countries.[62]

Around the world 603 million women live in countries where domestic violence isn't considered to be a crime.[63] And a staggering 200 million women are estimated to have undergone female genital mutilation.[64]

In the UK two women are murdered by their partners each week. In the US, one woman is sexually assaulted every two minutes and yet rape convictions are falling. In the UK a woman who has reported being raped has only a 5.7 per cent chance of her attacker being convicted,[65] and in the US only 2 per cent of rapists spend more than a day in prison.[66] The vast majority of rapes are never reported.

While genuine equality eludes us, warring ideologies seek to contain and define us. One requires our bodies to be waxed, tucked and sliced, the other that we be hidden behind veils.

Our current way of living has catastrophically failed to provide freedom from exploitation and violence.

....

AN ALTERNATIVE APPROACH

Not all cultures prize youth and physical perfection in the same way as the West. For example, in Japan the aesthetic of *Wabi-sabi* places a higher value on age and imperfection than it does on youth. Wrinkles and signs of ageing are treasured as unique and precious and viewed as adding to a woman's beauty. How great would it be if we could choose a different attitude that saw our life experience as beautiful rather than something that made us increasingly culturally and sexually invisible?

....

Equality – a new paradigm

'We've begun to raise daughters more like sons ... but few have the courage to raise our sons more like our daughters.'

GLORIA STEINEM

As women we want equality, but we also want to live in a society that reflects our real values and the truth of who we really are.

We want 50–50, but we have to ask, 50–50 of what?

Too often we've found ourselves fighting for our fair share of systems and institutions that leave us obliged to choose between our career and our family. They were designed around a workforce who didn't give birth to children and weren't expected to nurture them. They don't work for us as women or for men, or for the generations that will come after us.

We don't want an economic system that puts profits ahead of people and limitless growth ahead of what's sustainable. That model fails to place any value on caring.

We don't want to lean in to win our share of systems that don't work for us.

We want a new model.

One based on the reality of who we are and what we need. One that gives us the opportunity to be real and messy and whole. That recognizes the value of our unpaid labour as well as conventional measures of financial gain. That enables us to be honest about who we are and to build systems that are fairer and meet all our needs – of whatever gender, creed or generation, and wherever we live in the world.

WE together

'You just need to be a flea against injustice. Enough committed fleas biting strategically can make even the biggest dog uncomfortable and transform even the biggest nation.'

MARIAN WRIGHT EDELMAN

Before walking this path many of us have felt powerless and insignificant. We've often been told there was nothing we could do to make a difference and we believed it. At some level it may have let us off the hook. But now we know – from our own personal journeys – that action really can change things. We're no longer prepared to tolerate the knowledge that others are suffering due to problems that have solutions.

Think again about what would happen if we really did each decide to subject government policies to the same spiritual test we're starting to apply to ourselves. If we collectively made kindness our guiding value in every aspect of our lives.

Our economic priorities would shift. Protecting the planet would be put ahead of maximizing short-term profits. Refugees wouldn't be left to drown at sea. Caring responsibilities and child rearing would be accorded their real worth and we'd share work more evenly so that we could all work to live rather than live to work.

'I wanted the world to get better and I knew that it couldn't get better if it was going to be ruled by men ... alone.'

NANCY ASTOR

The solutions that already exist to tackle poverty, inequality and the threat of runaway climate change would be implemented.

We'd elect wise, spiritually whole politicians with a mandate to end world hunger rather than perpetuate it. There is enough food to feed the world's starving. The problem isn't a lack of resources, it's a lack of will.

Blueprints exist for how it can happen – 193 countries have agreed to the United Nation's Global Goals, designed to end world hunger, inequality and climate change. But they won't be implemented unless we start speaking up and saying we're willing to have less so that others can have enough. And vitally, our voices will need to be heard above the hum of those whose vested interests our current systems reflect and serve.

Into action

'I am a dreamer and having a dream is sometimes challenging, but I never look at a situation as too difficult.'

SISTER ROSEMARY NYIRUMBE

Now that we've placed our lives on a spiritual foundation, we can take our values out into the world. We can take action to become fully congruent and to close the gap between what we believe and what we do.

If we ignore the obstacles our ego throws up and follow the nudging of our soul, we will each find our own path and our own way of being useful. The gentle revolution is already happening.

Across the world women are changing the paradigm.

A Pakistani schoolgirl won the Nobel Prize and is changing the face of education.

In Utah, a young mother's account of being poor in the US went viral and shifted attitudes about low wages.

In London, a mother's post on social media led to thousands marching for Syrian refugees.

In Iran, a student's hunger strike turned the world's attention to the continued oppression of women.

In Uganda, a nun turned her convent into a safe haven for trafficked women and girls.

Women all over the world are taking actions, big and small, and one by one creating change.

'As a woman, my country is the whole world.'

VIRGINIA WOOLF

Each of us has our own part to play. Nothing is asked of us that we don't already have to give. We all bring different qualities and different gifts. We are all needed. The Internet gives us ways of reaching each other and getting organized that have never existed before.

Every one of us has our own calling, dictated by our heart.

Some of us will lead, some of us will support. Some of us will march, some of us will make tea, some of us will sew banners, some of us will write research papers. Others of us will sit with someone who is lonely and feels broken as we have each felt in our own way.

But what we won't do is be indifferent to suffering. We won't tolerate discrimination and unfairness and we will no longer believe that our voices and our actions won't change anything, because together they can, they will and they already are.

THE NINE PRINCIPLES AT A GLANCE

The Nine Principles are a path of love – for ourselves and for the world. You might like to take a photo of or write out the following summary. Place the list somewhere prominent – on your computer desktop, by your bedside table, or in your purse – to remind you to allow the principles to guide you.

Principle 1: Honesty

Honesty is the guide that leads us home. It returns us to our true selves and enables us to live authentically, courageously and congruently.

Action: Today I will have the courage to be me, irrespective of what others think.

Affirmation: I am true to myself.

Principle 2: Acceptance

Acceptance gives us the ability to handle whatever life throws our way. It asks that we sit with what is – even when it's painful. In return it transforms our relationship with reality and enables us to find peace.

Action: Today I will embrace life as it is and feel whatever emotions need to be felt.

Affirmation: My feelings guide me home.

Principle 3: Courage

Courage is the principle that frees us from our past. It enables us to live fully in the present by shedding the stories and unresolved anger that keep us trapped. It puts us firmly on the path to whole-hearted, authentic living.

Action: I will take responsibility for feeling and releasing my anger safely.

Affirmation: Today I let go of being right so that I can be happy.

Principle 4: Trust

Trust is our antidote to fear. It aligns us with the flow of life – a magnificent energy that guides and directs us so that we live expansive, happy and fulfilling lives.

Action: When I feel fear I will ask myself what I would do if I weren't afraid and then do it.

Affirmation: Today I am safe and I am happy.

Principle 5: Humility

Humility allows us to be one of many, to know that we are wondrous and enough just as we are. When we practise humility, we have a strong sense of our own intrinsic worth that isn't dependent on anything we do, have or own.

Action: I treat every woman I meet as a friend.

Affirmation: My worth comes from within.

Principle 6: Peace

Peace resides in the stillness beneath the chatter of our thinking minds. In that state of serenity, we experience freedom from inner conflict and a sense of wholeness. We feel connected to the world in which we live and loneliness begins to evaporate.

Action: Today, if I feel overwhelmed I will pause and remind myself that underneath the surface, my true self resides.

Affirmation: Whatever else is happening, deep down I know I am absolutely OK.

Principle 7: Love

Love knows no bounds. It wants the best for everyone and doesn't discriminate or judge. Love is our authentic nature and is always present, but, like the sun, can be temporarily obscured.

Action: Today I will meet the gaze of all those I encounter with love.

Affirmation: I am love.

Principle 8: Joy

Joy feels like happiness, only better. It's generated from within and doesn't depend on what we have or haven't got – it's vital for our well-being and arises in the moment. Joy connects us with a sense of the divine.

Action: Today I will seek out joy and let it fill my heart.

Affirmation: I am resilient and filled with joy.

Principle 9: Kindness

Kindness is what love looks like when we take it out into the world. It pierces our hearts as keenly as any arrow, and in so doing it allows love to flow in and out. Through gentle, loving actions kindness transforms us into spiritual activists.

Action: Today I will choose to act kindly.

Affirmation: When I take action the world is a better place.

RESOURCES

*'Asking for help does not mean that we are weak or incompetent. It
usually indicates an advanced level of honesty and intelligence.'*

ANNE WILSON SCHAEF

Sometimes WE's journey awakens us to issues that go beyond the scope of
this book. Perhaps it's an addiction to something or someone, a trauma you
can't move beyond, a need for therapy, a new interest in women's
organizations or world issues, a desire to learn more about yoga, meditation,
or faith. Read more about these topics here, or visit our website
www.wewomeneverywhere.org.

Abuse

24-Hour National Domestic Violence Freephone Helpline (run in
    partnership between Women's Aid and Refuge), www.
    nationaldomesticviolencehelpline.org.uk, tel: 0808 2000 247
The NHS provides an informative page with many useful links at www.
    nhs.uk/Livewell/abuse/Pages/domestic-violence-help.aspx
The Samaritans, www.samaritans.org, tel: 116 123

Addictions

If you feel your life centres around a substance, person, relationship or pattern of behaviour that's making you unhappy and yet you can't seem to shake it, then the following fellowships may be useful:

Adult Children of Alcoholics (ACOA): www.adultchildrenofalcoholics. co.uk

AL Anonymous (Al-anon) (for families and friends of alcoholics): www.al-anonuk.org.uk

Alcoholics Anonymous (AA): www.alcoholics-anonymous.org.uk

Chemically Dependent Anonymous (CDA): www.cdawebsitedev.com

Co-dependents Anonymous (CoDA): www.coda-uk.org

Debtors Anonymous (DA): www.debtorsanonymous.org.uk

Emotions Anonymous (EA): www.emotionsanonymous.org

Food Addicts Anonymous (FAA): www.foodaddictsanonymous.org

Gamblers Anonymous (GA): www.gamblersanonymous.org.uk

Narcotics Anonymous (NA): www.ukna.org

Nicotine Anonymous (NA): www.nicotine-anonymous.org

Overeaters Anonymous (OA): www.oagb.org.uk

Sex Addicts Anonymous (SAA): www.saa-recovery.org

Sex and Love Addicts Anonymous (SLAA): www.slaauk.org

Underearners Anonymous (UA): www.underearnersanonymous.co.uk

These are anonymous, mutually supportive groups offering help for recovery from addictive, compulsive or mental-health patterns. They are free to attend and open to anyone who has a desire to change their relationship to a substance or behaviour.

Their sites are full of information, support and ways to connect online or via a meeting in your area.

Other useful resources

In the UK;

- AddAction: www.addaction.org.uk
- Mind: www.mind.org.uk/information-support/guides-to-support-and-services/addiction-and-dependency
- NHS: www.nhs.uk/livewell/addiction/Pages/addictionhome.aspx

In the US:

- National Institute on Drug Abuse (NIDA): www.drugabuse.gov
- www.helpguide.org will help you select treatment programmes
- National Institute on Alcohol Abuse and Alcoholism (NIAAA): www.niaaa.nih.gov

In Canada:

- www.canadiandrugrehabcentres.com offers a directory of treatment programmes
- www.ccsa.ca offers addiction information centres and helplines

In Australia:

- www.alcohol.gov.au offers drug and alcohol information services
- www.lifeline.org.au offers addiction information and helplines

Further reading

Alcoholics Anonymous, *Alcoholics Anonymous* (New York: Alcoholics Anonymous World Services, Inc., 2001).

Augustine Fellowship, *Sex and Love Addicts Anonymous* (Boston: Augustine Fellowship, 1986).

Carnes, P., *A Gentle Path Through the Twelve Principles* (Minnesota: Hazelden, 2012).

Co-dependents Anonymous, *Co-dependents Anonymous* (Dallas:

Co-dependent Anonymous, Inc., 1995).

Mellody, P., Miller, A. and Miller, K., *Facing Love Addiction* (New York: Harper San Francisco, 1992).

Trauma

'PTSD is a whole-body tragedy, an integral human event of enormous proportions with massive repercussions.'

SUSAN PEASE BANITT

In the aftermath of a traumatic event (a death, childhood neglect, sexual or physical abuse, disaster or war) it's natural to feel frightened, depressed, anxious, panicked and disconnected. But if these feelings don't fade with time and you feel stuck with thoughts and memories that won't go away, you may be suffering from post–traumatic stress disorder (PTSD). Here are some questions to ask yourself:

- Do you re-experience the event via repeated upsetting memories or dreams?
- Do you feel intense physical and/or emotional distress when exposed to things that remind you of the event?
- Do you try to avoid talking or thinking about it?
- Do you now have a more limited sense of your future options (for example, getting a job you love, getting married, having children or a normal lifespan)?
- Do you have problems sleeping or concentrating?
- Do you feel irrationally angry?
- Have you experienced changes in eating habits?
- More often than not do you feel sad, depressed, disinterested in life, worthless or guilty?

- Have you relied on drugs or alcohol in an attempt to alleviate your pain?

Sometimes we can have a similar response to persistent childhood events that may seem smaller but which can haunt our adult lives. This could be witnessing domestic violence or living with an addicted parent. Either way, you may feel you'll never get over what happened, but there are support systems and approaches that can help:

Therapy

Talking things over with a qualified therapist is the first thing you can do for yourself. There are different therapists with different approaches. Here are some that have worked for us:

- Counselling: Talking to a trained empathetic professional in a safe and private environment on a short-term basis.
- CBT (Cognitive Behavioural Therapy): Based on the idea that negative thoughts and feelings can trap you in a vicious cycle, affecting your mind, body and actions, CBT is a way to talk through your current issues by breaking overwhelming problems down into smaller parts and examining negative patterns to find practical ways to improve the way you feel.
- Psychotherapy: A deeper, more long-term look at your issues, searching for root causes.
- Psychoanalysis: An examination of early childhood experiences and the unconscious.
- Group therapy: A group that meets regularly to interact, support and heal.

Eye movement desensitization and reprocessing (EMDR)

A very practical, physical technique for dislodging memories that seem frozen.

Rewind technique

Working with a trained practitioner to replay disturbing memories as if on rewind or fast-forward modes until the scenes evoke no emotion.

Emotional Freedom Therapy (EFT, known as 'tapping')

Treatment involves tapping specific parts of the body while recalling the event and then experiencing and identifying the nature of the feelings that come up, verbalizing them and accepting or reframing them.

Body work

Exploring the many techniques that involve working with the whole body to shake trauma. These can include breath work, yoga nidra, Reiki and singing.

Finding the right therapist or practitioner

The Internet is a great resource, but there are many ways to find someone to help. Ask family and friends. Talk to your medical practitioner. Make a shortlist of potential therapists and call them to chat to see first if you connect over the phone. Research their background. Not all therapists are good, not all will be the right one for you. Don't just take the first option that becomes available to you, and assess your progress to make sure it really is working for you.

If you are working on a tight budget or even an extremely tight budget, it does not mean there is no hope for you to get professional help. There are plenty of therapists and counselling centres that work on a sliding scale and some that even do *pro bono* work. Talking to a therapist can be incredibly helpful when one has a complex past or just needs help getting through a tough period of life. It can become one of the most meaningful, rewarding and even life-changing relationships.

Women's organizations

'Feminism is an entire world view or gestalt, not just a laundry list of women's issues.'

CHARLOTTE BUNCH

There have been feminist campaigns, literature and heroines throughout recorded history, and during the mid-nineteenth century, mass-organized women's movements emerged in the US, the UK, Australia, New Zealand and Scandinavia. These nineteenth-century campaigning nations had certain things in common: Protestant culture, comparatively liberal political systems and early mass moral reform movements (against slavery and alcohol, for international peace) often organized by more marginal Christian groups that encouraged women's activity (Quakers, Unitarians).

The organizations they spawned were largely made up of middle-class women working closely with men (philosophers, radical liberal and socialist Members of Parliament). The first state to give some women the vote was New Zealand in 1893, followed by Australia in 1902 and the UK by 1918. In the US, all states complied by 1919.

Other countries took much longer and women are still unable to vote in Saudi Arabia and Vatican City to this day. The power to vote is only one step in our ongoing struggle for equal power, equal pay and equal rights.

If you want to get more involved, there are plenty of groups. These range from support groups to political movements to development associations, charities, museums, NGOs, online magazines and mentorship schemes. We've arranged them by country and what we outline overleaf are just highlights. Use the Internet or local networks to find more in your area, visit our website (www.wewomeneverywhere.org) to find more recommendations, or create your own group.

International

Nobel Women's Initiative: www.nobelwomensinitiative.org
UN Women: www.unwomen.org
Women's Refugee Commission: www.womensrefugeecommission.org
Women's WorldWide Web (W4): www.w4.org
Raging Grannies: www.raginggrannies.org

US

Big Sisters: www.bbbs.org
Equal Rights Advocates: www.equalrights.org
National Organization for Women: www.now.org
National Women's History Museum: www.nwhm.org
EMILY's List: www.emilyslist.org
Women for Women International: www.womenforwomen.org

UK

Women's Aid: www.womensaid.org.uk/
Women's Institute: www.thewi.org.uk
Southall Black Sisters: www.southallblacksisters.org.uk/
The Fawcett Society: www.fawcettsociety.org.uk
Mumsnet: www.mumsnet.com

Canada

National Council of Women of Canada: www.ncwc.ca
Girls Action Foundation: www.girlsactionfoundation.ca

Australia

Australian Women's Health Network: www.awhn.org.au
EMILY's List: www.emilyslist.org.au
National Council of Women of Australia: www.ncwa.org.au

World Issues

'There comes a time when humanity is called to shift to a new level of
consciousness ... that time is now.'

WANGARI MAATHAI

Our world is in trouble. It would have been impossible to mention all its myriad issues, but if while reading this book one or two struck a chord with you, here is a shortlist of just some of the many organizations and societies that you may want to get in contact with:

International

Amnesty International: www.amnesty.org/en/USA
GIVING What We Can: www.givingwhatwecan.org/trust
Global Fund for Women: www.globalfundforwomen.org
Greenpeace: www.greenpeace.org
HelpAge International: www.helpage.org
Human Rights Watch: www.hrw.org
International Planned Parenthood Federation (IPPF): www.ippf.org
Liberty: www.liberty-human-rights.org
Save the Children: www.savethechildren.net/
The Global Fund for Human Rights: www.globalhumanrights.org
The Life You Can Save: www.thelifeyoucansave.org
World Bank: www.worldbank.org
World Wildlife Fund (WWF): www.panda.org

US

American Civil Liberties (ACLU): www.aclu.org
Audubon Society: www.audubon.org
Earth Justice (formerly the Sierra Club Legal Defense Fund):
    www.earthjustice.org

Environmental Defense Fund (EDF): www.edf.org
National Association for Advancement of Colored People (NAACP):
    www.naacp.org
Natural Resources Defense Council (NRDC): www.nrdc.org
Poverty USA: www.povertyusa.org
Southern Poverty Law Center: www.splcenter.org
US Human Rights Network (USHR): www.ushrnetwork.org

Canada

Dalit Freedom Network Canada: www.dalitfreedom.ca
Food for the Hungry: www.fhcanada.org

UK

Child Poverty Action Group (CPAG): www.cpag.org.uk
Show Racism the Red Card: www.srtrc.org

Australia

Anti-poverty Week: www.antipovertyweek.org.au
Gecko: gecko.org.au
Get Up: www.getup.org.au
Grassroots and environmental groups directory: www.ecoshout.org.au

Giving

There are many valuable causes and charities wanting your support and donations – far too many to include in this book. For ideas on ways to ensure that you give to the most cost-effective charities, check out these two websites: www.thelifeyoucansave.org in the US or www.givingwhatwecan.org in the UK.

Acting

If you are looking for inspiration for daily acts of kindness then the following websites might be helpful:

Action for Happiness: www.actionforhappiness.org
Helping Network: www.helping.network
Love This City: www.lovethiscity.org
Random Acts of Kindness Foundation: www.randomactsofkindness.org

Menopause

British Menopause Society: www.thebms.org.uk
International Menopause Society: www.imsociety.org
North American Menopause Society: www.menopause.org

Yoga

'You cannot do yoga. Yoga is your natural state.'

SHARON GANNON

Yoga is a whole-body exercise with the power to improve physical, mental and emotional health. Flexibility increases, stress reduces, breath work teaches physical techniques to soothe worry and bring you back to a point of calm. It can help you to release the difficult emotions that get trapped in your body. The more you do, the more you learn to connect with what's happening right now. You'll find you sleep more deeply and feel generally better. For us it's led to a more balanced life and a way to access deep peace and harmony.

There are many types of yoga. What we outline below is just a start. Ask people you know, research online, try different options, see what works best for you. Cost-effective ways to practise include shopping around for studio offers. You can also learn by yourself at home, via a book or DVD or online video, although it's good to take a few lessons with a teacher at first. You may find initial 'taster' classes are free or many places offer low-cost classes: Yogability in Glasgow, UK, for example (www.yogability.org.uk).

Hatha

Gentle, often slower, focusing on the most traditional poses.

Iyengar

Focus on precision positions and alignments, with use of props (belts, blocks, bolsters) to ensure correct posture.

Ashtanga

Vigorous, quick moving, athletic. The whole class is one succession of moves flowing into another.

Mysore style

Ashtanga yoga taught one-to-one in a group setting where you set your own pace.

Vinyasa flow

Another fast-paced workout style with minimal talk from the teacher.

Bikram

Set poses (26 of them) done in special heated rooms: lots of sweating and flushing out of toxins.

Kirtain Chanting

A form of yoga that uses sound.

Kundalini

Designed to increase spinal energy. Classes involve breathing, chanting and meditation as well as physical exercises.

Yin

Quieter, seated poses held for up to ten minutes. A way to increase flexibility, release tension and learn the basics of meditation.

Restorative

Like Yin, but with less focus on flexibility and more on healing and relaxing.

Meditation

'Quiet the mind, and the soul will speak.'

MA JAYA SATI BHAGAVATI

All you need to meditate is a time and place to sit quietly by yourself – even five minutes in the bathroom is good. If you're looking for a more structured practice, below we list a few major traditions. You'll find plenty more online or by asking around.

In essence there are two types of meditation: structured and open. Structured meditation is built around a single thing for your mind to focus on while you meditate. This could be one word (often called a mantra), or a prayer or spiritual text. Open meditation simply invites you to sit (or lie, or stand) quietly, relax and observe what your body and mind are up to. The following may employ either approach:

Mindfulness

This Western, non-religious technique can employ breath awareness (focusing your attention on inhaling and exhaling) and body scanning
(focusing your attention on your physical body, starting from your toes and
heading up).

Zen (also known as Zazen)

This technique comes from Buddhism but can be useful to non-Buddhists.
The focus is on sitting still in one position, observing your breath and
mind. It sometimes involves ruminating on Buddhist teachings and is often
practised with a teacher.

Transcendental Meditation (TM)

Practitioners are given a mantra (a word or sound) by a teacher to focus on
during their meditation. You can also find mantras online.

Kundalini Yoga

This type of yoga can fuse with meditation to create an all-body practice,
tailored to help with specific issues (stress, anxiety, depression, addiction,
etc.), and is best done with a teacher.

Faith

> 'Religion is for people who are scared to go to hell. Spirituality is for people
> who have already been there.'
>
> BONNIE RAITT

Some of us find a faith through conventional religion; others through less
formal faith-based paths and even secular or atheist groups that remove
divinity but retain a sense of connection to an underlying truth.

Buddhism

More of a philosophy than a conventional religion, Buddhism focuses on personal spiritual development and uncovering deep truths about the nature of reality.

Christianity

Based on the teachings of Jesus, Christianity teaches that we should follow his life story, believe in his divinity, and emulate his self-sacrifice and service to humanity. It's the largest religion in the world, split into three major traditions: Orthodox, Catholic and Protestant.

Hinduism

A group of faiths based around many different Indian beliefs and scriptures, which may be the oldest religion in the world.

Islam

Islam means 'submission to the will of God'. Believers are called Muslims and follow the teachings of the Koran as revealed to the prophet Muhammad, who also venerated Abraham, Moses and Jesus as prophets. It has three major traditions: Sunni, Shi'ite and Sufism.

Judaism

One of the oldest monotheistic religions in the world. Jews believe they must follow a wide range of laws set for them by God governing almost every aspect of life.

Taoism

An ancient Chinese religious and philosophical tradition with worldwide popularity due to its manifestations in the Tao Ti Ching, Tai Chi, the I Ching and Qigong.

Unitarianism

An open, inclusive and tolerant approach to religion, developing out of Protestantism and incorporating teachings from many different faiths. Individuals are asked to create their own practice and answers.

Humanism

Religion without a god: an approach to life centred on human action and behaviour and looking to science rather than religion.

Paganism

Recognizes the rich diversity of spiritual traditions and is typically a poly-theistic or pantheistic, nature-worshipping religion.

Atheism

Lack, or an absence, of belief in deities.

Contemporary Female Spiritual Teachers

The Living Spiritual Teachers Project is an ongoing charitable project that provides biographical details of some of the most eminent spiritual teach-ers alive today. Here you can find biographical details, contact information, useful links, as well as a list of their publications: www.spiritualityandprac-tice.com

Starting WE communities

This is a *WE*, not a *me*, way of living. The more support you can gather around you, the easier you will find it to grow, heal and stay on the path. Look for others who are making the same journey or are keen to talk about the things that really matter. Gather them around you. Try working through the chapters in this book with others; share your experiences, your challenges and your insights. Together you will have support when you need it and have maximum impact when you take action. Find ways to become an active part of the movement away from *me* and towards *WE*. Here are some ideas. Come up with your own and let us know how you get on:

- Start a WE community by meeting in person regularly at a local school, church or community centre. Support each other in using the principles in your daily lives.
- Start a WE community online – break down the walls of geography by connecting with women across the globe.
- Start a fundraising drive or other action for one of your chosen charities and invite people in the WE community to donate or join you.
- Look online to find other members of the WE community who might want help or encouragement.
- Check out WE's website: wewomeneverywhere.org for ideas and inspiration.
- Look out for sister travellers in your community who might have health- or age-related issues that keep them housebound or could do with a visit over a cup of tea.
- Find creative and fun ways to take WE's simple manifesto of compassion out into the world.
- Wherever you spot suffering in the world, if you team up with others you'll find it easier to BE the love that you know is at your core.

Further reading

The wisdom in this book comes from many teachers, texts and sources. If you want to go deeper and further into the ideas behind WE's principles, these are some of the books we've found helpful along the way:

Principle 1 – Honesty

Brown, C., *The Gifts of Imperfection* (Center City, Minnesota: Hazelden, 2010).

Hay, L., *You Can Heal Your Life* (San Diego: Hay House, 1984).

Ferrucci, P., *What We May Be* (Los Angeles: J.P. Tarcher, 1982).

Lamott, A. and Lamott, S., *Some Assembly Required* (New York: Penguin Group, 2012).

Rosen, T., *Recovery 2.0* (London: Hay House, 2014).

Wolf, N., *The Beauty Myth* (London: Vintage, 1991).

Principle 2 – Acceptance

Fruehwirth, G., *Words for Silence* (London: SPCK, 2008).

Harris, T., *I'm OK – You're OK* (London: Pan Books Ltd, 1973).

Kipp, M., *Daily Love* (London: Hay House, 2014).

Kurtz, E. and Ketcham, K., *The Spirituality of Imperfection* (New York: Bantam Books, 1992).

Linn, D., *Four Acts of Personal Power* (London: Hay House, 2007).

Moore, T., *Care of the Soul* (London: Piatkus, 1992).

Sogyal, R., Gaffney, P. and Harvey, A., *The Tibetan Book of Living and Dying* (London: Rider, 2002).

Principle 3 – Courage

Bernstein, G., *May Cause Miracles* (London: Hay House, 2013).

Cantacuzino, M., *The Forgiveness Project* (London: Jessica Kingsley Publishers, 2015).

Myss, C., *Anatomy of the Spirit* (New York: Three Rivers Press, 1996).

Penny, L., *Unspeakable Things* (London: Bloomsbury, 2014).

Principle 4 – Trust

Carlson, R., *Don't Sweat the Small Stuff … and it's all small stuff* (London: Hodder Mobius, 2008).

Jeffers, S., *Feel the Fear and Do It Anyway* (London: Vermilion, 2007).

Lerner, R., *Living in the Comfort Zone* (Florida: Health Communications Inc., 1995).

Principle 5 – Humility

Bill, P. and Todd, W., *Drop the Rock* (Center City, Minnesota: Hazelden, 2005).

Epstein, M., *Going to Pieces Without Falling Apart* (New York: Broadway Books, 1998).

Peck, M., *Further Along the Road Less Travelled* (London: Simon & Schuster, 1993).

Silverton, S., *The Mindfulness Breakthrough* (London: Watkins, 2012).

Principle 6 – Peace

De Mello, A., *Sadhana, A Way to God* (New York: Doubleday, 1978).

Hawkins, D., *Transcending the Levels of Consciousness* (W. Sedona, AZ: Veritas Publishing, 2006).

Holden, M., *Boundless Love* (London: Rider, 2002).

Hyde, L. and Ladinsky, D., *The Gift* (New York: Vintage Books, 2007).

Idliby, R., Oliver, S. and Warner, P., *The Faith Club* (New York: Free Press, 2007).

Johnston, W., *The Cloud of Unknowing and the Book of Privy Counseling* (New York: Image Books, 1973).

Keating, T., *Intimacy with God* (New York: Crossroad, 1996).

Myss, C., *Entering the Castle* (London: Simon & Schuster, 2007).

Nhat Hanh, T., *Happiness* (Berkeley, CA: Parallax Press, 2009).

Nhat Hanh, T., *Peace is Every Step* (Bantam/AJP, 2013).

www.theforgivenessproject.com

Tolle, E., *The Power of Now* (London: Hodder & Stoughton, 2001).

Trans. Barks, C., *The Essential Rumi* (London: Penguin, 1999).

Principle 7 – Love

Augustine Fellowship, *Sex and Love Addicts Anonymous* (Boston: Augustine
    Fellowship, 1986).

Co-dependents Anonymous, *Co-dependents Anonymous* (Dallas:
    Co-dependents Anonymous, Inc., 1995).

Hendrix, H., *Getting the Love You Want* (London: Simon & Schuster, 2005).

Jackson, L., *The Light Between Us* (London: Century, 2015).

Mellody, P., Miller, A. and Miller, K., *Facing Love Addiction* (New York:
    Harper San Francisco, 1992).

Norwood, R., *Women Who Love Too Much* (London: Arrow Books, 1986).

Olds, S., *Stag's Leap* (London: Jonathan Cape, 2012).

Richo, D., *How To be an Adult in Relationships* (Boston: Shambhala, 2002).

Yalom, I., *Love's Executioner* (London: Penguin, 1991).

Principle 8 – Joy

Cameron, J., *The Artist's Way* (London: Pan, 1995).

Campbell, R., *Light is the New Black* (London: Hay House, 2015).

Csikszentmihalyi, M., *Flow: The Psychology of Happiness* (London: Rider,
    2002).

De Mello, A. and Galache, G., *Walking on Water* (Dublin: Columba Press,
    1998).

Donius, W., *Thought Revolution* (New York: Atria Books, 2014).

Ferrucci, P., *Inevitable Grace* (Los Angeles: J. P. Tarcher, 1990).

Huffington, A., *Thrive* (London: W. H. Allen, 2014).

Kingston, K., *Clear your Clutter with Feng Shui* (London: Piatkus, 1998).

Lamott, A., *Plan B* (New York: Riverhead Books, 2006).

Muzyka, Z., *Life by the Cup* (New York: Atria Books, 2015).

Olds, S., *One Secret Thing* (New York: Alfred A. Knopf, 2008).

Principle 9 – Kindness

Armstrong, K., *Twelve Steps to a Compassionate Life* (London: Bodley Head, 2011).

Harvey, A., *The Hope: A Guide to Sacred Activism* (London: Hay House, 2009).

Post, S., *The Secret Gifts of Helping* (San Francisco: Wiley, 2011).

Tolle, E., *A New Earth* (London: Michael Joseph, 2005).

Williamson, M., *A Return to Love* (New York: HarperCollins, 1996).

Williamson, M., *The Age of Miracles* (London: Hay House, 2008).

Part 3: The Manifesto

Adichie, C. N., *We Should All Be Feminists* (London: 4th Estate, 2014).

Benn, M., *What Should We Tell our Daughters?* (London: Hodder & Stoughton, 2014).

Campbell, B., *End of Equality* (London: Seagull Books, 2013).

Cobble, D., Gordon, L. and Henry, A., *Feminism Unfinished* (New York: Liveright Publishing Corp, 2015).

Hooks, B., *All About Love* (New York: Harper Perennial, 2001).

Klein, N., *This Changes Everything* (London: Penguin Group, 2014).

Neuwirth, J. and Steinem, G., *Equal Means Equal* (New York: The New Press, 2015).

Orenstein, P., *Girls & Sex* (New York: Harper, 2016).

Orr, J., *Marxism and Women's Liberation* (London: Bookmarks, 2015).

Sandberg, S. and Scovell, N., *Lean In* (London: WH Allen, 2014).

Walter, N., *Living Dolls* (London: Virago, 2011).

Wilkinson, R. and Pickett, K., *The Spirit Level* (London: Penguin Books, 2010).

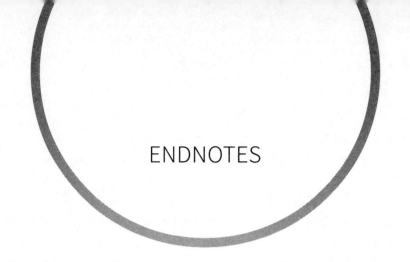

ENDNOTES

Why now?

1. Mary O'Hara, 'Osborne's budget cuts will cripple services for vulnerable BME women', *Guardian*, 16 March 2016: www.theguardian.com/public-leaders-network/2016/mar/16/budget-cuts-domestic-violence-services-bme
2. R. Wilkinson and K. Pickett, *The Spirit Level: Why Greater Equality Makes Societies Stronger* (Penguin Books, 2010).

Essential Practice 2: Gentleness

3. 'The Nocebo Effect: Negative Thoughts Can Harm Your Health': www.psychologytoday.com/blog/owning-pink/201308/the-nocebo-effect-negative-thoughts-can-harm-your-health
4. 'I do enough. I am enough,' from Susan Jeffers' book *Feel the Fear and Do It Anyway*.

Essential Practice 3: Responsibility

5. 'Moods & Hormones: Emotional health and well-being throughout the life cycle': www.womensinternational.com/connections/moods.html

Principle 1 – Honesty

6. Denis Campbell and Haroon Siddique, 'Mental illness soars in young women', *Guardian*, 29 September 2016.

7. Ibid.

8. 'Mice inherit specific memories, because epigenetics?': phenomena. nationalgeographic.com/2013/12/01/mice-inherit-specific-memories-because-epigenetics/

9. 'Licking rat pups: the genetics of nurture': sites.bu.edu/ombs/2010/11/11/licking-rat-pups-the-genetics-of-nurture

10. Thanks to Rokelle Lerner, Senior Clinical Advisor, Crossroads Antigua, for this: www.rokellelerner.com

Principle 2 – Acceptance

11. Exercise inspired by Julia Cameron's 'God Jar' in her *The Vein of Gold: A Journey to Your Creative Heart* (Putnam, 1997).

12. From Elisabeth Kübler-Ross and David Kessler, *On Grief and Grieving: Finding the Meaning of Grief Through the Five Stages of Loss* (Simon & Schuster, 2005).

13. Thanks to Eckhart Tolle for this idea.

Principle 4 – Trust

14. Sharon Horesh Bergquist, 'How stress affects your body': ed.ted.com/lessons/how-stress-affects-your-body-sharon-horesh-bergquist

15. Thanks to Jennifer's sister, Alison Nadel, for coming up with this acronym.

16. P. Lally, C. H. M. van Jaarsveld, H. W. W. and J. Wardle, 'How are habits formed: Modelling habit formation in the real world', *European Journal of Social Psychology*, vol. 40 (2010), pp. 998–1009, reported in the *Huffington Post*: www.huffingtonpost.com/james-clear/forming-new-habits_b_5104807.html

17. From Susan Jeffers' book *Feel the Fear and Do It Anyway: How to Turn Your Fear and Indecision into Confidence and Action* (Vermilion, 2007).

18. Ibid.

Principle 5 – Humility

19. Team Northrup, 'The power of positive thinking': www.teamnorthrup.com/2011/06/29/the-power-of-positive-thinking/
20. This list is one used by some 12-step fellowships.
21. Julie Borowski, '18 facts you need to know about US prisons' (23 February 2015): europe.newsweek.com/eighteen-facts-you-need-know-about-us-prisons-308860
22. Prison Reform Trust: Prison: the facts, summer 2014: fbclientprisoners.s3.amazonaws.com/Resources/Prison%20the%20facts%20May%202014.pdf
23. Ibid.
24. 'How many species are we losing?': www.panda.org/about_our_earth/biodiversity/biodiversity

Principle 6 – Peace

25. Paul Grossman et al., 'Mindfulness-based stress reduction and health benefits: A meta-analysis', *Journal of Psychosomatic Research*, vol. 57/1 (2004), pp. 35–43.
26. Michael D. Mrazek, Michael S. Franklin, Dawa Tarchin Phillips, Benjamin Baird and Jonathan W. Schooler, 'Mindfulness training improves working memory capacity and GRE performance while reducing mind wandering' (2012): pss.sagepub.com/content/early/2013/03/27/0956797612459659.short
27. Rachel Moss, 'How much time do we spend on our devices?' (10 September 2014): www.huffingtonpost.co.uk/2014/09/10/digital-detox-technology-addiction-facts_n_5795982.html
28. Thanks to Jack Kornfield for this analogy.
29. Neither of us can remember who first told us this story, but thank you to whoever it was and to whoever first told it!

Principle 7 – Love

30. Sex and Love Addicts Anonymous: www.slaa.uk.org, Love Addicts Anonymous: www.loveaddicts.org.

31. Dr Sharon Stills, 'Health benefits of masturbation': www.womenshealthnetwork.com/sexandfertility/health-benefits-of-masturbation.aspx

32. 'Domestic violence – the facts': www.refuge.org.uk/get-help-now/what-is-domestic-violence/domestic-violence-the-facts

33. According to the 2011 UN report 'Progress of the world's women: In pursuit of justice': www.theguardian.com/global-development/poverty-matters/2011/jul/06/un-women-legal-rights-data; progress.unwomen.org/en/2015

Principle 8 – Joy

34. Mihaly Csikszentmihalyi, *Finding Flow: The Psychology of Engagement with Everyday Life* (Basic Books, 1998).

Principle 9 – Kindness

35. Jen Green, *The Impact of Environmentalism: Food and Farming* (Raintree, 2013).

36. www.banthebottle.net

37. Paul Delaney, 'How long it takes for some everyday items to decompose' (14 February 2013): www.down2earthmaterials.ie/decompose/

38. Sarah Kaplan, 'By 2050, there will be more plastic than fish in the world's oceans, study says', *The Washington Post*, 20 January 2016.

39. Norm Schriever, 'Plastic water bottles causing flood of harm to our environment', www.huffingtonpost.com, 28 September 2013.

40. Sonja Lyubomirsky and Matthew D. Della Porta, 'Boosting Happiness, Buttressing Resilience: Results from Cognitive and Behavioural Interventions' (2008): sonjalyubomirsky.com/wp-content/themes/sonjalyubomirsky/papers/LDinpressb.pdf

41. Jason Marsh and Jill Suttie, 'Five ways giving is good for you' (13 December 2010): greatergood.berkeley.edu/article/item/5_ways_ giving_is_good_for_you

42. This metaphor comes from Peter Singer's short film, *The Life You Can Save in 3 Minutes* (2010): www.youtube.com/watch?v= onsIdBanynY

43. 'Every three seconds a child needlessly dies': www.savethechildren. org/site/c.8rKLIXMGIpI4E/b.7892381/k.F0A6/Every_3_Seconds_a_ Child_Needlessly_Dies.htm

44. Inspired by a lecture given by Andrew Harvey in the Open Center, New York City, in 2006.

45. Meat Free Monday: www.meatfreemondays.com/about

Part 3: The Manifesto

46. 'Hunger and poverty facts and statistics': www.feedingamerica.org/ media-centre/press-release/2016/01/02

47. '62 people own same as half world': www.oxfam.org/en/ pressroom/pressreleases/2015-01-19/richest-1-will-own- more-all-rest-2016

48. Oxfam poverty petition: act.oxfam.org/great-britain/cameron- inequality-petition-even-it-up

49. In 2008 26,000 Britons were fed by food banks. By 2012 that number had risen to 347,000: www.dailymail.co.uk/news/article-2517898/ Hunger-Britain-public-health-emergency-number-people-turning- food-banks-feed-families-soars.html

50. Feeding America, 'African American poverty': www.feedingamerica. org/hunger-in-america/impact-of-hunger/african-american- hunger/african-american-hunger-fact-sheet.html

51. www.5050parliament.co.uk

52. Amber Phillips, 'The sad state of black women in statewide political office' (5 December 2015): www.washingtonpost.com/news/the-fix/

wp/2015/12/05/the-sad-state-of-black-women-in-statewide-political-office/

53. Paid and unpaid labour report for the Sexual Assault Support Centre: www.sascwr.org/files/www/resources_pdfs/anti_oppression/ Economics.Paid_and_Unpaid_Labour.pdf

54. Beatrix Campbell, *End of Equality* (Seagull, 2014).

55. US Current Population Survey and the National Committee on Pay Equity; also Bureau of Labor Statistics: Weekly and Hourly Earnings Data from the Current Population Survey.

56. According to a 2012 survey conducted by the US Labor Department.

57. 'Family and medical leave in 2012: technical report': www.dol.gov/ asp/evaluation/fmla/fmla-2012-technical-report.pdf

58. David Brindle, 'Carers save the country 119bn a year', *Guardian*, 12 May 2011

59. Bryce Covert, 'Putting a price tag on unpaid housework' (30 May 2012): www.forbes.com/sites/brycecovert/2012/05/30/ putting-a-price-tag-on-unpaid-housework/#1ef1685a544f

60. Beatrix Campbell, 'Why we need a new women's revolution', *Guardian*, 25 May 2014. 57. Ibid.

61. Ibid.

62. Eleanor Clift, 'Asia's 163 million missing girls' (21 June 2011): www. thedailybeast.com/articles/2011/06/21/gender-selection-abortion-crisis-in-asia-india-u-s.html

63. UN Secretary-General's campaign UNiTE to End Violence Against Women.

64. According to a statistical report for the UN's International Day of Zero Tolerance for Female Genital Mutilation: www.unicef.org/media/ media_90033.html

65. Rape Crisis statistics: rapecrisis.org.uk/statistics.php

66. The Criminal Justice System: Statistics: rainn.org/get-information/ statistics/reporting-rates

ACKNOWLEDGEMENTS

This book owes its existence to many women. First among them is Claire Conrad, who was present from the moment *WE* was conceived and who has midwifed it into being.

Grateful thanks also to Lynn Nesbit and Rebecca Folland at Janklow & Nesbit, and Caroline Wood and all at Felicity Bryan. To our publishers on both sides of the Atlantic: at HarperCollins, Kate Elton, Carolyn Thorne, Polly Osborn, Isabel Hayman-Brown, Holly Kyte, Ellie Crisp and Dean Russell; at Atria, Judith Curr, who believed in it before it existed, Leslie Meredith and Jonathan Evans. And to Sandy Draper for her amazing editing of the early drafts.

Thanks also to: Mel Agace, Piper Anderson-Klotz, Helen Backhouse, Sam Bescelli, Alicja Brown, Saskia Burke, Jamie Byng, Sydney Davis, Denzyl Feigelson, Daisy Garnett, Elizabeth Gordon, Zoe Hunter Gordon, Oscar and Felix Griffiths, Reverend Bill Hague, Leon Hawthorne, Zara Hayes, Emma Hewitt, Jenny Howard and Gemma Knox at Sunshine, Susanna Kleeman, Dr Genevieve von Lob, Delphi Lythgoe, Sandra MacDonald, Professor Tessa McWatt, Peter Morgan, Deborah Nadel, Alison Nagle, Northeast Harbor Library, Paul Olsewski, Ciara Parks, Ruth Reid, Andrew Ruhemann, Arlo Nadel Ruhemann, Estralita Serano, Anne Shamash, Chloe Smith, Ardu Vakil, Felix Velarde, Sara Watkins at KW Interactive, Jack Wilson, Meghan Wilson and Theo Wilson.

And, of course, the women who've gone before us and those who will come after.

INDEX

ABOUT THE AUTHORS

Gillian Anderson

Gillian Anderson gained worldwide recognition in *The X-Files*, garnering awards and critical acclaim for her role as FBI Special Agent Dana Scully over the show's nine-year run. Some of her many screen credits include *The House of Mirth*, *The Last King of Scotland* and the acclaimed BBC dramas *Bleak House* and *Great Expectations*. She was nominated for an Olivier Award for her stage performance as Nora in *A Doll's House* and won the Best Actress *Evening Standard* Theatre Award for her portrayal of Blanche DuBois in *A Streetcar Named Desire*. Gillian stars in the BBC and Netflix's *The Fall* as DSI Stella Gibson, NBC's *Hannibal* as Dr Bedelia Du Maurier and Starz's *American Gods* as Media. She is an activist, speaking out regularly on issues ranging from feminism to climate change and human trafficking. Born in Chicago, she lives in London with her three children.

Jennifer Nadel

Jennifer Nadel trained as a barrister before becoming a writer, award-winning journalist and campaigner. She was one of the UK's most senior female television correspondents and has broadcast for the BBC, ITV and *Channel 4 News*. Her book on domestic violence was made into a BBC film and a Channel 4 documentary, and her report from Bosnia on the use of rape as a weapon of war was broadcast around the world. Her first novel, *Pretty Thing*, was published by Little, Brown in 2015. She is a trustee of the charity INQUEST and has a long history of activism. She stood as a candidate for the Green Party in the UK general election in 2015. A mother of three boys, she was born in Princeton, New Jersey, and is a dual US/UK national who lives in London.